Advance Praise for *Mexico Since 1980*

"Why has Mexico failed to grow its economy, break out of poverty, correct historic inequalities, and overcome political paralysis? Haber and his collaborators offer compelling answers to all these questions in this superb book. It is simply the best ever written on contemporary Mexican society, politics, and economy. Eminently readable, with a compelling story to tell, it also provides a clear and persuasive analysis of Mexico's problems and their potential solutions."

> – John H. Coatsworth, Dean, School of International and Public
>   Affairs, Columbia University

"*Mexico Since 1980* develops a new approach to understanding authoritarian regimes with wide applicability beyond Mexico to Latin America, Africa, and Asia. Despite economic liberalization, political reform, and the movement to multi-party democracy in the 1980s and 90s, Mexico has not grown. This book explains why. It argues that, while formal institutions (such as democracy) and elements of market policy (such as liberalization and trade openness) may change, nonetheless a range of informal institutions, practices, and policies remain. These include: weak rule of law, weak property rights, and a system of rents, privileges, and patronage, all of which greatly hamper reform. This book is a must-read for students and specialists in political economy, comparative politics, and economic development."

> – Barry R. Weingast Senior Fellow, Hoover Institution, and Ward
>   C. Krebs Family Professor, Department of Political Science,
>   Stanford University

"How are authoritarian regimes organized? How do they stay in power? Organize the economy? Read this book and you'll find out."

> – James Robinson, Harvard University

MEXICO SINCE 1980

This book addresses two questions that are crucial to understanding Mexico's current economic, political, and social challenges. Why did the opening up of the economy to foreign trade and investment not result in sustained economic growth? Why has electoral democracy not produced rule of law? The answers to those questions lie in the ways in which Mexico's long history of authoritarian rule shaped its judicial, taxation, and property-rights institutions. These institutions, the authors argue, cannot be reformed with the stroke of a pen. Moreover, they represent powerful constraints on the ability of the Mexican government to fund welfare-enhancing reforms, on the ability of firms and households to write contracts, and on the ability of citizens to enforce their basic rights.

Stephen Haber is Peter and Helen Bing Senior Fellow of the Hoover Institution and A. A. and Jeanne Welch Milligan Professor in the School of Humanities and Sciences at Stanford University. He is also Senior Fellow of the Stanford Center for International Development, Director of Stanford's Program in Social Science History, and a Research Economist of the National Bureau of Economic Research. He is the author of numerous books and articles on Mexican economic history and political economy.

Herbert S. Klein is Professor of History, Senior Fellow of the Hoover Institution, and Director of the Center for Latin American Studies at Stanford University. He is also the Gouverneur Morris Professor Emeritus at Columbia University. He is the author of numerous books and articles and is most recently the coauthor of *Brazil Since 1980*.

Noel Maurer is Associate Professor at the Harvard Business School in the Business, Government and the International Economy (BGIE) unit. Prior to joining the Harvard faculty, Maurer was Assistant Professor of Economics at the Instituto Tecnológico Autónomo de México. The author of several books and numerous articles on Mexican economic history, Maurer's primary interest is in how governments make credible commitments to protect property rights, with a particular focus on Latin America. His current research focuses on the question of whether foreign governments and international institutions can improve property rights systems inside sovereign countries.

Kevin J. Middlebrook is Reader in Latin American Politics at the Institute for the Study of the Americas, University of London. He is author of *The Paradox of Revolution: Labor, the State, and Authoritarianism in Mexico* (1995) and editor or coeditor of, among other works, *Confronting Development: Assessing Mexico's Economic and Social Policy Challenges* (2003) and *Dilemmas of Political Change in Mexico* (2004).

THE WORLD
Since 1980

This new series is designed to examine politics, economics, and social change in important countries and regions over the past two and a half decades. No prior background knowledge of a given country will be required by readers. The books are written by leading social scientists.

Volumes published

Brazil Since 1980; Francisco Vidal Luna and Herbert S. Klein
Israel Since 1980; Guy Ben-Porat, Yagil Levy, Shlomo Mizrahi,
    Ayre Naor, and Erez Tzfadia
The United States Since 1980; Dean Baker

Volumes in preparation

Britain Since 1980; Roger Middleton
China Since 1980; Ross Garnaut
France Since 1980; Timothy Smith
India Since 1980; Sumit Ganguly
Japan Since 1980; Thomas Cargill and Takayuki Sakamoto
Russia Since 1980; Steven Rosefielde and Stefan Hedlund

MEXICO
Since 1980

Stephen Haber
Stanford University

Herbert S. Klein
Stanford University

Noel Maurer
Harvard University

Kevin J. Middlebrook
University of London

CAMBRIDGE
UNIVERSITY PRESS

CAMBRIDGE UNIVERSITY PRESS

Cambridge, New York, Melbourne, Madrid, Cape Town, Singapore, São Paulo, Delhi

Cambridge University Press
32 Avenue of the Americas, New York, NY 10013-2473, USA

www.cambridge.org
Information on this title: www.cambridge.org/9780521608879

First published 2008

Printed in the United States of America

A catalog record for this publication is available from the British Library.

Library of Congress Cataloging in Publication Data

Mexico since 1980 / Stephen Haber, Herbert S. Klein, Noel Maurer, Kevin J. Middlebrook.
    p.   cm. – (The world since 1980)
Includes bibliographical references and index.
ISBN 978-0-521-84641-7 (hardback) – ISBN 978-0-521-60887-9 (pbk.)
1. Mexico – History – 1980–   2. Authoritarianism – Mexico – History – 20th century.
3. Democratization – Mexico – History – 20th century.   4. Mexico – History –
1970–1988.   I. Haber, Stephen H., 1957–
F1236.M482   2008
972.08′3–dc22   2007045631

ISBN 978-0-521-84641-7 hardback
ISBN 978-0-521-60887-9 paperback

Contents

List of Figures

Acknowledgments

This is a book aimed not just at specialists on Mexico but also at students who may be encountering Mexico for the first time. It is therefore fitting that a broad group of students helped shape this book in fundamental ways. Pamela Evers, Tucker Herbert, Victor Menaldo, Diane Raub, Hamilton Ulmer, and Nikki Velasco provided invaluable research assistance. An early draft of the book was then read by the students in a Stanford seminar on Mexico, and we thank those students for their comments: Andrew Barragan, Jacqueline Crespo, Joshua Harder, Jennifer Hernandez, Jessica Kinloch, Juan Mateos, Matthew McLaughlin, Melissa Morales, Araceli Ortiz, Juan Pasillas, Alejandro Quezada, Diane Raub, Sean Sandoloski, Nicole Saucedo, and Hamilton Ulmer. Finally, three Stanford graduate students, Victor Menaldo, Nikki Velasco, and Scott Wilson, read and commented on the entire manuscript multiple times. We cannot thank them enough for their helpful advice.

This book was also shaped by the very generous help that we received from a number of colleagues, who either commented on drafts of the manuscript or who provided us with valuable information on contemporary Mexico. We especially wish to thank Graciela Bensusán, Jeffrey Bortz, Vicente Corta, Gustavo del Ángel, Alberto Díaz-Cayeros, Joseph L. Klesner, Alan Knight, Sandra Kuntz Ficker, Fabrice Lehoucq, Moramay López Alonso, Luis Felipe López Calva, Horacio Mackinlay, Eric Magar, Tania Martinez Monroy, Juan Carlos Moreno-Brid, Douglass C. North, Raghuram Rajan, Víctor Rodríguez-Padilla, Luis Rubio, Tapen Sinha, Paul Sniderman, John Wallis, Barry Weingast, Jeffrey A. Weldon, and Eduardo Zepeda Miramontes. We also wish to acknowledge constructive suggestions from four anonymous Cambridge University Press reviewers.

This book would not have happened were it not for the generous financial support provided by the Hoover Institution on War, Revolution, and Peace. We especially thank Hoover's Director, John Raisian, and Hoover's Senior Associate Director, Richard Sousa, for creating an academic environment that encourages the free exchange of ideas.

Finally, we offer sincere thanks to Frank Smith, Publishing Director for Social Sciences at Cambridge University Press, for his patience and support of this project. Keller Kaufman–Fox did excellent work copyediting the manuscript, and Barbara Walthall ably coordinated final production of the book.

We remain, of course, responsible for any errors of fact or interpretation.

Abbreviations and Acronyms

ABM	Asociación de Banqueros de México/Mexican Bankers' Association
AC	Alianza Cívica/Civic Alliance
AFORE	Administrador de Fondos para el Retiro/Retirement Fund Administrator
AMDH	Academia Mexicana de Derechos Humanos/Mexican Academy of Human Rights
CANACINTRA	Cámara Nacional de la Industria de Transformación/National Chamber of Manufacturers
CCE	Consejo Coordinador Empresarial/Private Sector Coordinating Council
CD	Convergencia por la Democracia/Democratic Convergence
CFC	Comisión Federal de Competencia/Federal Competition Commission
CFE	Comisión Federal de Electricidad/Federal Electricity Commission
CMHN	Consejo Mexicano de Hombres de Negocios/Mexican Council of Businessmen
CNBV	Comisión Nacional Bancaria y de Valores/National Banking and Securities Commission
CNC	Confederación Nacional Campesina/National Peasants' Confederation
CNIE	Comisión Nacional de Inversiones Extranjeras/National Foreign Investment Commission

CONAGO	Conferencia Nacional de Gobernadores/National Governors' Conference
CONAMM	Conferencia Nacional de Municipios de México/National Conference of Mexican Municipalities
CONAPO	Consejo Nacional de Población/National Population Council
CONCAMIN	Confederación Nacional de Cámaras Industriales/National Confederation of Chambers of Industry
CONCANACO	Confederación de Cámaras Nacionales de Comercio/Confederation of National Chambers of Commerce
CONSAR	Comisión Nacional del Sistema de Ahorro para el Retiro/National Commission on Retirement Savings
COPARMEX	Confederación Patronal de la República Mexicana/Mexican Employers' Confederation
CROM	Confederación Regional Obrera Mexicana/Mexican Regional Labor Confederation
CTM	Confederación de Trabajadores de México/Mexican Workers' Confederation
EZLN	Ejército Zapatista de Liberación Nacional/Zapatista Army of National Liberation
FDI	Foreign direct investment
FDN	Frente Democrático Nacional/National Democratic Front
FICORCA	Fideicomiso para la Cobertura de Riesgos Cambiarios/Exchange-Rate Risk Hedge Fund
FOBAPROA	Fondo Bancario de Protección al Ahorro/Bank Savings Protection Fund
GATT	General Agreement on Tariffs and Trade
GDP	Gross domestic product
IFAI	Instituto Federal de Acceso a la Información Pública/Federal Institute for Access to Public Information
IFE	Instituto Federal Electoral/Federal Electoral Institute
IMF	International Monetary Fund

IMSS	Instituto Mexicano del Seguro Social/Mexican Social Security Institute
INEGI	Instituto Nacional de Estadística, Geografía e Informática/National Statistical Institute
INFONAVIT	Instituto del Fondo Nacional de la Vivienda para los Trabajadores/National Worker Housing Institute
IPAB	Instituto para la Protección del Ahorro Bancario/ Bank Savings Protection Institute
ISSSTE	Instituto de Seguridad y Servicios Sociales de los Trabajadores del Estado/Social Security Institute for State Workers
LFOPPE	Ley Federal de Organizaciones Políticas y Procesos Electorales/Federal Law on Political Organizations and Electoral Processes
MNCs	Multinational corporations
NAFIN	Nacional Financiera, S.A./National Credit Bank
NAFTA	North American Free Trade Agreement
NGOs	Nongovernmental organizations
OECD	Organisation for Economic Co-Operation and Development
OPEC	Organization of Petroleum Exporting Countries
PAN	Partido Acción Nacional/National Action Party
PANAL	Partido Nueva Alianza/New Alliance Party
PARM	Partido Auténtico de la Revolución Mexicana/ Authentic Party of the Mexican Revolution
PAS	Partido Alianza Social/Social Alliance Party
PASDC	Partido Alternativa Socialdemócrata y Campesina/Social Democratic and Peasant Alternative Party
PCM	Partido Comunista Mexicano/Mexican Communist Party
PDM	Partido Demócrata Mexicano/Mexican Democratic Party
PEMEX	Petróleos Mexicanos/Mexican Petroleum Company

PIDIREGAS	Programa de Infraestructura Productiva de Largo Plazo/Long–Term Productive Infrastructure Program
PMS	Partido Mexicano Socialista/Mexican Socialist Party
PMT	Partido Mexicano de los Trabajadores/Mexican Workers' Party
PNR	Partido Nacional Revolucionario/Revolutionary National Party
PPS	Partido Popular Socialista/Socialist Popular Party
PRD	Partido de la Revolución Democrática/Party of the Democratic Revolution
PRI	Partido Revolucionario Institucional/Institutional Revolutionary Party
PRM	Partido de la Revolución Mexicana/Party of the Mexican Revolution
PROCAMPO	Programa de Apoyos Directos al Campo/Direct-Support Program for the Farm Sector
PROCAPTE	Programa de Capitalización Temporal/Temporary Capitalization Program
PROCEDE	Programa de Certificación de Derechos Ejidales y Titulación de Solares Urbanos/Program for the Certification of Ejidal Rights and the Titling of Urban Plots
PROGRESA	Programa de Educación, Salud y Alimentación/ Program for Education, Health, and Nutrition
PRONASOL	Programa Nacional de Solidaridad/National Solidarity Program
PRT	Partido Revolucionario de los Trabajadores/ Revolutionary Workers' Party
PSD	Partido Social Demócrata/Social Democratic Party
PSN	Partido de la Sociedad Nacionalista/Nationalist Society Party
PST	Partido Socialista de los Trabajadores/Socialist Workers' Party
PSUM	Partido Socialista Unificado de México/Mexican Unified Socialist Party
PT	Partido del Trabajo/Labor Party

PVEM	Partido Verde Ecologista de México/Mexican Ecologist Green Party
SHF	Sociedad Hipotecaria Federal/Federal Mortgage Society
SOFOLES	Sociedades Financieras de Objecto Limitado/Limited-Objective Financial Societies
STPRM	Sindicato de Trabajadores Petroleros de la República Mexicana/Mexican Petroleum Workers' Union
TELMEX	Teléfonos de México/Mexican Telephone Company
TEPJF	Tribunal Electoral del Poder Judicial de la Federación/Electoral Tribunal of the Federal Judicial Branch
UDI	Unidad de inversión/investment unit
VAT	Value-added tax

1

The Second Mexican Revolution:
Economic, Political, and Social Change
Since 1980

This book is about a revolution – albeit an incomplete one. It had none
of the features that political analysts typically associate with revolutions:
no organized violence, no overturning of the social class structure, and
no defeated dictator fleeing into exile. Nevertheless, if by "revolution"
we mean a dramatic change in the institutions that organize economic,
political, and social life, then Mexico has undoubtedly been in the
midst of a revolution since the early 1980s.

In 1980, Mexico was largely closed to foreign trade and investment;
government-owned firms controlled a substantial portion of the economy. An "official" party, the Institutional Revolutionary Party (PRI),[1]
held a virtual monopoly on political power. Since its creation in 1929,
Mexico's government-supported party had won every presidential,
gubernatorial, and senatorial election. To maintain a façade of democracy, PRI-led administrations crafted a complex set of electoral rules
that allowed other parties, some of which were actually subsidized
by the government, to win seats in the federal Chamber of Deputies
(Mexico's lower house of congress). The PRI, however, always dominated this chamber by an overwhelming majority. The PRI used
its electoral dominance to maintain control over Mexico's regulatory
and legal systems: PRI-affiliated government officials named state and
federal judges and the directors of government-owned firms as well as
making appointments in the federal bureaucracy. So complete was the
political hegemony of the PRI that many of its opponents, as well as

---

[1] Many of the acronyms that appear in the text refer to an organization's Spanish-language
name. See the List of Acronyms for complete names and their English translation.

many foreign observers, accepted without question the way that the PRI framed the challenges and proposed solutions to Mexico's development problems: the assumption that "market failures" required active state intervention in economic affairs, the conviction that extensive restrictions on foreign trade and investment were necessary for economic development, and the belief that the successful defense of national sovereignty required that political power be concentrated in the federal executive and an "official" party.

Less than three decades later, Mexico is a multiparty democracy in which the PRI holds a minority of seats in the federal Congress. In fact, the country's two most recent presidents, Vicente Fox Quesada (2000–2006) and Felipe Calderón Hinojosa (2006–2012), have come from the opposition National Action Party (PAN). In addition, the Mexican economy is now open, and goods and capital move freely in and out of the country. The vast majority of state-owned firms have been privatized.

Mexico's political and economic transformations have not, however, been uniform or entirely successful. Mexico has become more democratic in terms of electoral competition and freedom of expression in the mass media, but the rule of law has not been consolidated. Indeed, in a number of states the governor still appoints the members of electoral tribunals and state court judges, who in turn often make rulings based on partisan grounds. Mexico's police forces remain notoriously corrupt. Property rights are vaguely defined and costly to enforce.

Although Mexico is now open to foreign trade and investment, and exports have boomed, these changes have not produced rapid, sustained economic growth. Whether we date Mexico's opening up to trade and investment from 1986, when Mexico joined the General Agreement on Tariffs and Trade, or 1994, when the North American Free Trade Agreement went into effect, the results are the same: Real (inflation-adjusted) per capita growth in Mexico between either date and 2005 averaged 1.3 percent per year – a slow rate by any comparative standard. It was 38 percent slower than the growth rate over the same period for comparable, middle-income developing countries (2.1 percent per year), 43 percent slower than the U.S. growth rate (2.3 percent per year), and 54 percent slower than Mexico's own growth rate from 1950 to 1980 (2.8 percent per year).[2] It was, moreover, slow

---

[2] Chapter Two develops these comparisons in more detail. See that discussion for the data sources for these calculations.

compared with the growth rate that would have been needed to provide employment for the roughly 1 million individuals who enter Mexico's labor market each year. More than half of these new workers do not find employment in Mexico; instead, they migrate to the United States.

In this book we examine the nature and causes of the momentous economic, political, and social transformations that Mexico has experienced since the early 1980s.[3] We particularly seek to understand why Mexico has had an incomplete "second revolution." Why did the opening up of the economy to foreign trade and investment not result in more rapid economic growth? Why has electoral democracy not produced rule of law? What are the principal challenges that Mexico must address to achieve such widely shared goals as sustained economic growth, effective democratic governance, and the rule of law?

Providing answers to questions such as these requires both facts and a conceptual framework that can organize those facts into a coherent explanation. In the pages that follow, we outline and contrast the political and economic logics of authoritarian and democratic regimes. Among other significant differences, authoritarian and democratic political institutions imply substantially different systems of property rights and taxation, and they produce as outcomes dramatically different levels of public investment and economic growth. In subsequent chapters we show how this framework helps make sense of Mexico's development experience both before and after its democratic opening, and we draw on this analytical approach to identify several of the most salient public policy challenges facing Mexico in the early twenty-first century.

The key point we wish to make is this: Some of the institutions that emerged during Mexico's prolonged period of authoritarian rule, such as those governing the certification of elections, can be swept away with the stroke of a pen; other institutional arrangements, however, are extremely difficult to reform and thus can persist well after a country has democratized. Pro-democracy forces struggled hard for many years to ensure free and fair elections, but the reforms enacted in 1996 that made the Federal Electoral Institute (IFE) fully autonomous

---

[3] We do not, however, pretend to offer a comprehensive account of the Mexican experience during this period. A number of important issues – ranging from significant changes in foreign policy (especially Mexico's relations with the United States) to the multiple problems posed by powerful drug-trafficking cartels to emerging environmental challenges – therefore remain outside the scope of our analysis.

and nonpartisan marked a clear break with decades of electoral manipulation and fraud. Yet other legacies of authoritarianism – including the weak rule of law, costly enforcement of property rights, and low taxation on capital – persist and continue to weigh heavily on Mexico. Reforming the legal and property-rights systems requires, at a minimum, reforming the tax system because honest judges and police forces and accurate property registers all come at considerable fiscal expense. Individuals and firms without substantial financial resources or political influence can only enforce contracts at very high costs, limiting economic growth and social mobility. Low taxation prevents the government from investing in physical infrastructure (roads, bridges, sewerage systems, and so forth), education, public health, and social insurance, which not only reduces the quality of life but also lowers the long-term rate of economic growth. Citizens find it difficult to secure their basic rights as long as they remain subject to extortion by corrupt police and venal public officials.

The Political Economy of Authoritarianism and Democracy

How political power is distributed marks the fundamental difference between authoritarian and democratic regimes. In authoritarian regimes, power is concentrated in the hands of a small elite group and is often exercised arbitrarily. Authoritarian rule may take many different forms, ranging from highly personalistic autocracies, to military juntas, to regimes dominated by either single or hegemonic parties.[4] In all these cases, however, governing elites typically combine repression, cooptation, and ideological justifications of their claim to rule to marginalize opponents and maintain tight political control.

Democratic regimes also vary significantly in their specific organizational arrangements and political practices (presidential versus parliamentary systems, for example). Yet all these regimes are based on the guarantee of clearly defined citizenship rights (including freedoms of expression and association, and especially protection against arbitrary state action), frequently scheduled and fairly conducted elections in which all citizens are free to participate (universal suffrage) in the selection of representatives who will exercise public authority, and ,

---

[4] On postrevolutionary authoritarian regimes and the Mexican case, see Middlebrook (1995), Chapter 1.

established procedures to ensure that citizens can, through the rule of law, hold elected officials accountable for their public actions. In a democracy, then, political power is dispersed among different branches and levels of government and its exercise is constrained both in law and in practice.

These contrasting regime characteristics have broad implications. To illustrate these differences more fully, this portion of our discussion highlights major themes from the emerging literature on property-rights regimes. We take this approach in part because the generation of wealth and its distribution are core concerns in capitalist democracies, as well as because economic issues such as investment and taxation have been so central to debates in Mexico about the country's development options. Our main purpose in adopting this particular analytical perspective, however, is to underscore the sharply contrasting internal logics of authoritarianism and democracy. In later chapters, we draw on this framework to illuminate the coalitional dynamics that have shaped major economic and social policy outcomes in Mexico since the late nineteenth century.

Whether under authoritarianism or democracy, individuals engaged in economic transactions and a wide range of other activities require an entity that can arbitrate contracts and enforce "property rights," broadly defined. In numerically small, geographically limited, and socially homogeneous societies, a variety of actors might perform this role satisfactorily. Once societies become large and heterogeneous, however, the only entity that can effectively arbitrate property rights is the government. This creates a dilemma: Any government powerful enough to define and adjudicate property rights is also strong enough to abrogate them for its own benefit. Unless the government can give the population credible reasons to believe that it will not act arbitrarily in its own short-run interest (for example, by seizing property or taxing away all of the income it produces), the population will not invest or engage in a wide range of other productive activities. If there is no investment, there will be limited economic activity, and hence there will be little for the government to tax. The result is a paradox: Unless institutions are created that limit the authority and discretion of government, the economy will not grow, and the government itself will have insufficient revenues to ensure its own political survival.[5]

---

[5] The problem of credible commitment is as old as government itself. Its first modern articulation can be found in James Madison's writings in the Federalist Papers. In the modern social science literature, the commitment problem reemerged in Schelling (1956, 1960). Schelling convincingly argued that a party that is unable to bind itself to a commitment is

Liberal Democracy as a Solution to the Commitment Problem

The most efficient solution to the problem of credible commitment is liberal democracy. A liberal democracy is composed of sets of mutually reinforcing institutions that constrain the government and safeguard citizens against the arbitrary abuse of state power. We tend to think of liberal democracies as being characterized first and foremost by electoral competition for public office, but elections are only one of a number of institutional arrangements that limit governmental actions and protect citizen rights. The reason is simple: Elections only occur periodically, after which politicians have opportunities to abuse their power.[6] At a bare minimum, preventing that abuse requires a number of other institutions, including a representative legislature, an independent judiciary, competitive political parties, a free press, and a professionalized civil service.

As we have noted, the exact configuration of political institutions varies from one liberal democracy to the next. Nevertheless, all democracies feature institutional arrangements that accomplish three goals. First, democracies have institutions that create "veto points" in the decision-making process, thereby limiting the discretion of any individual actor within the government. In the United States, for example, no single actor in the central government can create law. Instead, laws must be approved by two separate legislative bodies (the House of Representatives and the Senate), as well as by the president. Even then, they are subject to judicial review by the courts.

Second, liberal democracies have institutions that allow citizens, as well as actors within the government, to sanction public officials who exceed their authority. These sanctioning mechanisms include the ability of citizens to vote legislators and heads of government out of office, as well as such procedures as impeachment, recall initiatives, and the use of the judiciary to prosecute malfeasance in office.

Finally, democracies characteristically have institutional arrangements that generate incentives for different actors and bodies within

---

prevented from entering into an effective agreement with another party – and, therefore, is impelled to construct and/or adopt pre-commitment devices. North (1981, 1990) built on this problem in his neo-classical theory of the state. There now exists a broad literature on various problems related to credible commitment. For a sampling of relevant works, see North and Weingast (1989); Shepsle (1991); Weingast (1995, 1997); North, Summerhill, and Weingast (2000); Bates (2001); and Haber, Razo, and Maurer (2003).

[6] Persson, Roland, and Tabellini (1997).

the government to veto and sanction one another. Typically, these incentives stem from the existence of multiple political parties locked in competition with one another for power.

These core institutional features of liberal democracy have significant implications for the exercise of power. For instance, governments cannot act in an arbitrary manner against wealth holders. They may, of course, raise taxes or confiscate property in the public interest, but to do so they must navigate past multiple veto points in the decision-making process (for example, judicial appeals of laws that deprive citizens of their property without due legal process). These veto points may, of course, allow wealth holders to have influence beyond their numbers – especially if wealth holders can join a coalition that allows them to trade support of private property rights for their support of some other policy issue.[7]

Precisely because the government cannot act arbitrarily, wealth holders do not fear that the government will prey upon them by expropriating their property. They therefore deploy their wealth in visible assets (houses, farms, factories, and so forth) that generate economic transactions (buying and selling the output of those same farms and factories, for example) and produce streams of income (wages, rental and interest income, and profits).[8] All of these assets, transactions, and income streams can then be taxed by the government. The low probability of expropriation, and the larger tax base produced by the resulting expansion of economic activity, explain two important characteristics of liberal democracies: They generally have much larger economies and generate far larger tax revenues than other political systems.[9]

The same institutional arrangements that militate against the risk of expropriation or other arbitrary abuses of public authority also work against the creation of entitlement programs that benefit select, narrow constituencies. This is not to say that rent-seeking behavior[10] and

---

[7] Stasavage (2003).

[8] Goldsmith (1995), Leblang (1996), Henisz (2000), Keefer and Knack (2002), Keefer (2003).

[9] One implication of these features of liberal democracies is that they can mobilize far greater resources for military purposes than other political systems. As a result, they almost always triumph over other states in military conflicts. See Reiter and Stam (2002) and Schultz and Weingast (2003).

[10] Rent-seeking behavior consists of an economic or social actor's attempt to extract (typically financial) gains that are disproportionate to the investment or contribution made or that are based on unfair manipulation (often involving government action) of the economic environment. Thus, a company seeking protective tariffs is engaged in rent-seeking behavior

corruption are completely absent, or that there is absolute equality of citizens before the law in liberal democracies. It is to say, however, that democracies characteristically have institutions that are designed to sanction rent-seeking and corruption and that give actors within and without the government the incentive to levy those sanctions. In liberal democracies, moreover, property rights (broadly defined) tend to be enforced universally – for everyone, regardless of their ascriptive characteristics, political affiliation, or social standing. Indeed, popular entitlements such as education and retirement pensions typically expand over time as politicians seek voters' support.[11]

Authoritarian Rent-Seeking as a Solution to the Commitment Problem

What happens when a society is unable to create the institutions of liberal democracy? This situation creates a thorny problem both for the government and for those individuals who control a society's principal sources of wealth. The government depends on wealth holders to deploy their capital to generate economic activity that may be taxed, and wealth holders need the government to arbitrate contracts and enforce property rights. The problem is that there is nothing that prevents the government from behaving opportunistically – by seizing property or taxing away all of the income it produces – once wealth holders have invested their assets. The government cannot resolve this dilemma simply by promising to respect private property and contract rights because, if there are no sanctions for breaking promises, then no promise made by the government is credible.

One particularly common solution to the commitment problem in non-democratic political contexts is the creation of a rent-seeking coalition.[12] We focus on this solution because it was employed by both Porfirio Díaz, the dictator who ruled Mexico from 1876 until 1911, and the forces that claimed victory in the Mexican Revolution

---

insofar as it hopes to protect or increase its revenues without improving the quality of its products, raising its efficiency, or doing any of the things typically associated with profit-seeking behavior in competitive markets. Profit-seeking activities always carry an element of risk; rent-seekers characteristically attempt to insulate themselves against risking anything.

[11] Lake and Baum (2001).

[12] For a discussion of the various other solutions to the commitment problem, see Haber (2006).

(1910–1920) and monopolized political power until the electoral defeat of the PRI in the year 2000.[13]

Rent-seeking coalitions do not require formal institutions that limit the discretion and authority of public officials. Instead, the government coaxes wealth holders into deploying their capital by granting them special privileges designed to raise their rates of return high enough to compensate them for the risk that the government will expropriate their property. These special privileges include barriers to market entry that reduce competition, preferential treatment in the courts, and exemptions from taxation.

The whole point of these special privileges is to create an uneven playing field. Imagine, for example, two entrepreneurs: entrepreneur A, whose political connections allow him to win all legal cases brought against his firm; and entrepreneur B, who knows that he will lose all cases brought against him by entrepreneur A. Entrepreneur B is beaten even before he begins, and so he does not invest in the first place. Entrepreneur A can, therefore, charge higher prices than those that he would be able to charge if he faced competition from entrepreneur B. He thus earns "rents" (a rate of return on capital above that available without special privileges) from his political connections. Similar rents can be generated by establishing a tax that all firms must pay but then granting entrepreneur A an exemption from that tax or by requiring special licenses to operate a factory and then only granting that license to entrepreneur A.

What makes these arrangements credible? The wealth holders who have received special advantages know that the government has no real commitment to them; in fact, the monopoly rents they earn give the government an incentive to expropriate their enterprises. This means that unless the returns on capital available to them are astronomically high, some way needs to be found to align the incentives of the government with those of the select group of wealth holders. One such mechanism that investors can employ is to call on foreign states to threaten the government if it reduces their privileges. This approach only tends to work, however, when the investors are politically powerful citizens of those foreign states. A more common solution is for wealth holders to share some of the rents they earn from their special

---

[13] For two previous characterizations of Mexico's postrevolutionary governing coalition as a rent-seeking coalition, see Blum (1997), pp. 32, 38–9; Lawson (2002), p. 17.

privileges with individuals or organized groups whose support the government needs to remain in power. If the government then reneges on its agreement with wealth holders, the benefits flowing to individuals or groups that can sanction the government will also disappear, giving them an incentive to rebel or withdraw crucial support.

Political and economic systems dominated by rent-seeking coalitions can produce impressive rates of economic growth for sustained periods of time. Frequently, however, these systems contain the seeds of their own destruction. Over the long term, the very rent-seeking arrangements that underpin these systems come to weigh heavily on the economy. Resources are misallocated to industries in which the country has no real comparative advantage; monopolies and oligopolies develop in industries that should be characterized by near-perfect competition. Opportunities are denied to entrepreneurs who possess the required talent and skills but who lack political access or government protection. Moreover, the resources required to sustain the rent-seeking coalition must come from somewhere, usually everyone outside the coalition itself – which is to say, the vast majority of the population. What results is an uneven distribution of wealth and power, which on the one hand chokes off long-run economic development (by limiting the size and depth of markets) and on the other hand motivates groups outside the dominant coalition to rebel. The government can often stave off rebellions by forging an alliance with the organized groups that can rebel against it – but this move, paradoxically, can put the assets of the wealth holders at risk all over again. What is to keep the government and those groups from forming a coalition and jointly expropriating the wealth holders' assets? For all these reasons, then, authoritarian regimes dominated by rent-seeking coalitions are inherently vulnerable to internal conflicts. They are sometimes capable of producing high *rates* of economic growth over the short or medium term, but they generally cannot be sustained long enough to produce high *levels* of economic development.

By design, political and economic systems based on rent-seeking coalitions do not generate much tax revenue. They essentially have two economic sectors: a fast-growing sector that receives special privileges and is lightly taxed, and a slow-growing sector whose property rights are precarious and is subject (at least on paper) to heavy tax rates. The irony of this situation is obvious: The part of the economy that produces most of the output pays few taxes, whereas the other part of the economy produces so little that there is almost nothing to tax.

As a result, these regimes generally do not engage in many activities that benefit the population as a whole. What the government most needs is to generate benefits for two privileged constituencies: the select group of wealth holders that controls investment capital, and the organized groups whose support is essential if the government is to remain in power. Everyone else can, at least in principle, be ignored. As a consequence, the government typically allocates access to economic and social benefits on a selective basis, targeting education, health care, old-age pensions, and other "public" programs to the organized constituencies whose backing it needs to stay in power.

The same is true of property-rights enforcement or any of the other actions that promote the equal treatment of citizens under the law. Indeed, private wealth holders or other privileged groups that are politically powerful have strong incentives to prefer low levels of public investment in the institutions that protect universal rights. They can obtain all the protection they need through private deals with government officials. Moreover, in contexts in which institutional guarantees of rights are weak, they can use their political influence to prey upon other members of society.[14] For its part, the government has only weak incentives to spend its scarce tax revenues on rights-protecting institutions because financial resources devoted to strengthening the autonomy and transparency of the judiciary, reforming the police, and improving the accuracy of property registries is money that is not available to satisfy the demands of core constituencies capable of sanctioning the government (or not available to be stolen by corrupt public officials).

Understanding Mexico's Political Economy

From the late nineteenth century through the twentieth century, Mexico was governed by two different authoritarian regimes. The rent-seeking coalitions that underpinned these regimes differed in terms of their social composition and their degree of political institutionalization in such crucial areas as civil–military relations and the means of presidential succession. Both coalitions did, however, share one

---

[14] Sonin (2003).

central characteristic: They were based on the discretionary exercise of concentrated political power. Government officials were, therefore, able to allocate property rights and public policies selectively, principally to benefit core members of the ruling coalition. In both instances, moreover, the systemic uncertainties resulting from the limited accountability of government officials and the weak rule of law contributed to these regimes' eventual demise.

The first of these coalitions took shape under the dictatorial rule of Porfirio Díaz between 1876 and 1911 (a period known as the Porfiriato). During Díaz's reign, the institutions that aligned the incentives of the government with those of wealth holders were not complicated. In those parts of the economy that were dominated by foreign-owned firms – particularly mining and petroleum – wealth holders could call on their home governments to threaten Díaz. These threats were not military; rather, they involved threats to withdraw diplomatic recognition, withhold loans, or impose trade restrictions. In those parts of the economy that were dominated by domestic firms – especially banking and manufacturing – wealth holders transferred some of the rents that they earned from their special property rights to political entrepreneurs. These entrepreneurs, who included state governors (who controlled sizable militias), powerful cabinet ministers, and key members of the federal Chamber of Deputies and Senate, had the capacity to sanction Díaz by being able to depose him. The mechanisms that the select wealth holders used to transfer rents to political entrepreneurs were similarly uncomplicated: They appointed them to their corporate boards or loaned them money with no expectation of repayment. Firms with extremely lucrative concessions from the government often went one step further, appointing Porfirio Díaz's son to their boards, thereby allowing the Díaz family to share in the stream of rents generated by the concession.[15]

This union of political and economic power produced political stability and economic growth for more than three decades. The Díaz coalition, however, marginalized some parts of Mexico's elite and excluded (often through the use of physical force) broad sectors of the population from the benefits of economic expansion. The regime therefore sowed the seeds of its own collapse. Opposition forces eventually mobilized against Díaz and ousted him from the presidency in 1911.

---

[15] Haber, Razo, and Maurer (2003).

Years of armed struggle and political violence ensued. When the worst of the fighting had subsided, the victors negotiated a new constitution designed to establish democratic rule in Mexico. The Constitution of 1917 contained provisions recognizing both individual political rights (including the freedoms of expression and association) and collective social rights (including rights to land, a minimum wage, and free public education). It also divided authority among the executive, legislative, and judicial branches of government, and it established a federal system in which states and municipalities held significant rights.

The liberal-democratic project outlined in the Constitution was, however, stillborn. Revolutionary mobilization had brought to the fore political elites bent on the expansion and centralization of power. It also brought to the fore agrarian warlords who sought, in addition to political power for themselves, land for their followers. A similar dynamic emerged in the labor movement: Politically ambitious leaders sought improved working conditions for workers, in exchange for which they received the support of those workers. In short, armed force (or the threat of it), not skill at legislative compromise in a liberal constitutional order, was the real currency of power in Mexico during the 1920s.

This group of newly emergent elites spent much of the 1920s fighting among themselves. In 1929, after a decade of political assassinations, attempted coups d'état, and failed rebellions, they eventually united under the umbrella of an "official" government-supported party, the Revolutionary National Party (PNR). As we discuss in Chapter Two, over the course of the 1930s and 1940s, the PNR underwent a series of internal reorganizations that culminated in the formation of the PRI in 1946.

The centralization of political control meant, however, that no promise made by the government was credible because there were no sanctions for breaking promises. The absence of meaningful constraints on the government meant that it could (and sometimes did) expropriate property with impunity. Indeed, this threat was particularly real in postrevolutionary Mexico because the Constitution of 1917 was explicitly redistributionist: By giving the state the authority to reallocate property in the public interest, it in essence treated private property as a privilege rather than a right. There were, moreover, powerful currents in Mexican society – most particularly the peasant farmers who had fought in the revolution – demanding that the government make good on the Constitution's promises by expropriating landowners' properties and distributing land on a large scale. The constitutional provision declaring national ownership of surface, water, and subsoil rights also overtly challenged the existing property titles held by mining and petroleum companies.

Wealth holders in postrevolutionary Mexico therefore had few incentives to place their capital in productive investments. Unless they were willing to do so, however, there would be limited economic growth and therefore little economic activity for the government to tax. As Chapter Two of this book shows, in devising solutions to this dilemma, Mexico's postrevolutionary political leaders often followed the path charted by Porfirio Díaz: Government policies restricted market competition and thereby offered capitalists sufficiently high rates of return on their investments to compensate them for the risk of expropriation. In the banking sector, for example, postrevolutionary governments – working with many of the same individuals who had dominated Mexican finance during the Porfiriato – essentially allowed bankers themselves to draft major regulatory laws and severely restricted entry into the industry. Similarly, in the manufacturing industry the government shielded industrialists from foreign competition through a complex array of protective tariffs, quantitative restrictions on imports, and regulations that either excluded foreign investors from particular industries or required them to operate with majority Mexican partners. It also sheltered favored firms from domestic competition by establishing regulatory barriers to market entry and by granting them preferential access to subsidized credit from government-owned development banks.

Unlike workers and peasants, Mexico's economic elites were never integrated into the structures of Mexico's ruling party. What emerged in twentieth-century Mexico was a de facto alliance of convenience between the PRI and the country's most important capitalists. There were certainly periods of significant tension in this relationship, largely because the enforcement of property rights always remained at the whim of government officials. Yet from the 1940s through the 1970s this "alliance for profits" underpinned rapid industrialization and continuous economic expansion.

Some of the policies that benefited the national private sector wove a broader network of interlocking interests supporting the PRI-led regime. The same trade policies that safeguarded domestic firms from foreign competition increased job security in the protected domestic market, and the comfortable profit margins enjoyed by private-sector firms made them somewhat less resistant to demands for wage increases. Protectionist policies therefore received strong support from the organized labor movement, which, despite significant state controls on many forms of worker participation, became one of the regime's most loyal backers. Maintaining the support of the labor movement both bolstered the PRI's electoral fortunes and provided government policy makers with considerable room for maneuvering in their efforts to manage economic crises. Thus, what emerged in time was a durable coalition linking political entrepreneurs, industrialists, and organized industrial workers, all of whom shared in the rents generated by trade protection and thus all of whom had something to gain from the perpetuation of the regime.

This governing coalition delivered both long-term political stability (the last major armed rebellion against the government occurred in 1929) and several decades of uninterrupted economic growth. It nevertheless rested on shallow fiscal foundations. As part of the set of strategies designed to coax capital into production and to cement an informal alliance between the country's business class and the ruling political elite, PRI-led administrations taxed nonwage income (dividends, rents, and interest) at very low rates. For their part, business interests used threats of an investment boycott (and occasional episodes of actual capital flight) to protect their privileged tax status.

Government tax revenues therefore remained low (even by the standards of other Latin American countries), and, despite the PRI's revolutionary rhetoric and constitutional guarantees of broad social rights, the government lacked the fiscal wherewithal to provide universal access to the public goods required by a rapidly expanding population. The government did manage to fund social welfare programs for politically privileged constituencies (most particularly organized industrial workers and public-sector employees), but overall, Mexicans were no better off in terms of infant mortality, life expectancy, schooling, or literacy than the citizens of other Latin American countries who had neither experienced a revolution nor were governed by a "revolutionary" party. In fact, circa 1980, Mexico's principal social and demographic characteristics were those of a typical developing country, with high rates of population growth and rural–urban migration, chronic underemployment, and low levels of educational achievement.

During the 1970s the government's fiscal position came under strain. As the size of the labor constituencies that were a lynchpin of the regime expanded, as Mexico became increasingly urban, and as the costs of coopting potential opposition groups escalated, the costs of governing grew. It was simply not possible to keep the coalition that governed Mexico together with the meager tax resources at hand. The government responded by printing more money, by taxing a growing oil industry, and by leveraging oil revenues into a stream of loans that it contracted from foreign banking syndicates. This strategy, however, proved unsustainable. By 1982 the government found itself caught between the scissors of falling petroleum prices and rising international interest rates. President José López Portillo (1976–1982) sought to escape from this crisis by expropriating the wealth held by Mexico's banks in August 1982. In doing so, he attacked a group of private wealth holders on which the government had long lavished many privileges – and which the government had long counted on as a source of investment capital.

The 1982 debt crisis and the bank nationalization did not cause the PRI-led regime immediately to break down. The process by which the PRI eventually lost political control extended over a period of nearly two decades. It was driven forward, in no small part, by the failure of PRI governments to rekindle economic growth. President Miguel de la Madrid Hurtado's (1982–1988) initial response was to impose stringent economic stabilization and austerity measures. He also sought to liberalize the economy by eliminating subsidies and price controls, reducing barriers to imports, and closing or privatizing unprofitable government-owned companies. His successor, Carlos Salinas de Gortari (1988–1994), accelerated the process of market opening – privatizing the banks and other major public firms, liberalizing restrictions on foreign direct investment, and, most dramatically, negotiating the North American Free Trade Agreement (NAFTA) with Canada and the United States. The NAFTA in particular represented a bold effort by the government to regain the confidence of investors by making it more difficult for a future administration to revert to trade protectionism and by establishing mechanisms that firmly safeguarded the property rights of foreign investors.

The problem was that none of these policies was particularly successful at rekindling economic growth in a rapid and sustained fashion. The Mexican economy lurched and sputtered through the 1980s and 1990s. The employment gains that the government was hoping would be generated by opening up the economy to foreign trade and investment did not materialize. Thus, one of the PRI's core constituencies – organized labor – began to abandon the party in the 1980s.

For the private sector the bank nationalization epitomized the arbitrary abuse of concentrated power that characterized the PRI regime. As a result, a significant portion of Mexico's business class began to throw its support behind a center-right party that had existed at the margins of the Mexican electoral system since the 1940s, the PAN. Over the course of the 1980s the PAN's presence in state and municipal government grew considerably as it successfully capitalized on the economic and political discontent of the urban middle class and the business sector (see Chapter Five). When the PRI eventually lost the two-thirds majority in the federal Chamber of Deputies that allowed it to enact constitutional amendments at will, its leaders were forced to enlist the PAN's legislative support to adopt policies designed to spur economic growth. The PAN, in turn, used its increased political leverage to push forward a pro-democracy reform agenda.

The events of the 1980s also had a substantial impact on the political left. Even though leftist parties had been the principal beneficiaries of a liberalizing electoral reform enacted in 1977, their overall level of voter support remained quite modest until a serious split within the PRI produced a major realignment of political forces. In 1987–1988, nationalist elements within the ruling party who strongly opposed de la Madrid's privatization and market-opening policies bolted from the PRI and backed the presidential candidacy of Cuauhtémoc Cárdenas. Cárdenas's presidential bid failed, but the broad leftist alliance he had led subsequently founded the Party of the Democratic Revolution (PRD), the most electorally successful leftist party in Mexican history. Moreover, the blatant fraud required to ensure that PRI candidate Carlos Salinas prevailed in the 1988 presidential election marked an important turning point in the struggle for electoral transparency. In the wake of the 1988 elections, civil society groups mobilized extensively to promote free and fair elections, and the PRD itself became an important advocate for accelerated political opening.

As we note in Chapter Five, however, democratization in Mexico was certainly not inevitable. As prolonged economic stagnation during the 1980s sapped the PRI's traditional bases of electoral support, opposition parties on both the left and the right gradually gained strength. Yet the ruling party still benefited from government control over the mass media and government financing for its campaigns, and the de la Madrid and Salinas administrations both implemented regressive electoral reforms that safeguarded the PRI's congressional majority. Indeed, convincing victories in the 1991 midterm and the 1994 presidential elections suggested that the PRI might be able to retain its overall electoral dominance. It was only in the aftermath of major political crises in 1994 (including an armed uprising led by the Zapatista Army of National Liberation in the southern state of Chiapas, and the assassination of the PRI's presidential candidate) and a devastating financial crisis in 1994–1995 that opposition parties won institutional reforms offering them reasonable assurances that elections would henceforth be free and fair. In the wake of those electoral reforms, in 1997 the PRI finally lost its majority in the federal Chamber of Deputies and its control over the government of the Federal District (Mexico's equivalent of Washington, D.C.). In 2000, it lost its control of the presidency when the PAN's Vicente Fox Quesada was voted into office.

Economic and political developments after the early 1980s also had a marked impact on social welfare policy, the focus of Chapter Six. Over time, the pressures of competitive electoral politics, coupled with continuing resource constraints, led to important shifts in programs providing basic health care, housing, education, and retirement pensions. Because federal government tax revenues remained comparatively low, policy makers were in some cases compelled to choose between providing extensive welfare coverage to targeted constituencies (as the PRI had customarily done in the past) and offering modest benefits on a more general basis. Thus, the administration of Ernesto Zedillo Ponce de León (1994–2000) began to shift responsibility for welfare provision from the federal government to private firms, families, and individuals. This shift in approach accelerated under the administration of Vicente Fox. Similarly, these administrations implemented more selectively targeted programs designed to reduce extreme poverty in Mexico.

In sum, Mexico experienced truly momentous economic, political, and social changes after the early 1980s. Nevertheless, as we observed at the beginning of this chapter, this second Mexican revolution remains incomplete. Even though Mexico is open to flows of trade and investment and exports constitute a much larger share of national economic activity, the economy has not grown at a rate sufficient to meet the country's employment needs. Equally telling, as of 2005 average inflation-adjusted wages in the manufacturing sector remained well below their 1981 level. One reason for Mexico's laggard economic performance since the 1980s has been the continuing shortage of credit for businesses and households, a problem caused in part by property-rights institutions that developed under authoritarianism (see

Chapter Four). Similarly, despite importance advances since the 1990s in such areas as the proportion of the population covered by health insurance and in basic health care for children, the expanded availability of home mortgages, and higher levels of educational attainment, Mexico continues to be a highly unequal society and poverty remains endemic.

In politics, the 2000 and 2006 general elections amply confirmed the highly competitive character of Mexican party politics. Three major political parties contest power at the national level, and elections in most states and municipalities involve at least two-party competition. Mexico's president no longer has the power to make public policy virtually without constraint, and both the legislative and judicial branches of government act independently in an increasingly effective system of constitutional checks and balances. The authority exercised by party leaders, however, limits opportunities for more direct citizen participation, and Mexico's "no reelection" rules effectively limit the accountability of individual legislators to their constituents.

Mexico's electoral democratization has not automatically strengthened the rule of law. Although a more politically engaged civil society and intensified competition among mass communications media have dramatically intensified the public scrutiny of elected officials, it remains difficult to bring government officials to justice for either past or present corruption or abuses of power. In the absence of public certainty that justice will be served where the conduct of government officials is concerned, a deep-rooted culture of impunity persists.

With considerations such as these as background, the concluding chapter of this book examines several of the key challenges facing Mexico in the early twenty-first century. The successful transition to electoral democracy opens the way for the possible consolidation of a liberal-democratic political order in Mexico. In a number of areas, however, the country still labors under the lingering legacies of authoritarianism. The struggle to bring about a further deconcentration of political and economic power, guarantee citizenship rights, and enhance individual opportunities for social welfare will be slow and difficult. As one way of illuminating the difficulties involved, in Chapter Seven we analyze obstacles to establishing the effective rule of law, enforcing property rights universally, and securing the fiscal resources necessary to meet Mexico's development challenges.

2

Mexico Before 1982: The Political Economy of Authoritarian Rule

Mexico experienced major economic and political transformations during the 1980s and 1990s that ushered in an open economy and electoral democracy. These transformations are not understandable if viewed outside of the broader context of Mexico's history. Thus, a balanced assessment of both the importance and the limits of these changes requires an understanding of Mexico's political economy before 1982.

Twice in its history, Mexico was governed by authoritarian regimes based on rent-seeking coalitions. The first was the dictatorship of Porfirio Díaz (1876–1911, a period known as the Porfiriato); the second was the party-based authoritarian regime that took shape in the aftermath of Mexico's 1910–1920 revolution and held sway until the election of Vicente Fox Quesada in 2000. These two regimes differed greatly in their social bases, their degree of political institutionalization, and their resilience in the face of pressures for change. Yet these regimes also had some important things in common: They produced long periods of stable government, centralized political power in the presidency, and pursued protectionist economic policies. Both regimes also produced a highly unequal distribution of the benefits of economic growth – a direct result of the fact that they allocated public policies and property rights selectively, so as to benefit primarily the core members of the coalitions that supported them.

Mexico from Independence to the Revolution of 1910

Mexico achieved independence from Spain in 1821 but independence did not produce a stable political order. Political disagreements were often settled through violence. Indeed, in the 55 years from independence to 1876, Mexico had seventy-five presidents. One military strongman, Antonio López de Santa Anna, occupied the presidential palace on eleven different occasions. In the absence of a stable national government, Mexico's border states could secede almost at will. Texas seceded in 1836, and Yucatán left the Mexican federation in 1840, only to rejoin later of its own volition. The weakness of the Mexican state also made the country vulnerable to invasion – in 1846 by the United States (which took approximately half of Mexico's territory in the peace settlement) and then in 1862 by France (which ruled Mexico through a puppet, the Austrian Archduke Maximilian) until 1867.

In 1876 General Porfirio Díaz, a hero of the resistance to the French occupation, took power in a military coup d'état. Except for a brief interregnum between 1880 and 1884 when Díaz temporarily ceded formal authority to an ally, he retained the presidency until 1911. During his long reign, Díaz succeeded where his predecessors had failed to create political stability. He did this by rigging elections, repressing the opposition, and, most crucially, forging a coalition with Mexico's wealth holders by granting them special privileges that raised their incentives to invest their capital.

During the Porfiriato the Mexican economy grew rapidly. When Díaz came to power, Mexico had only five banks, a minuscule manufacturing sector, and a railroad system that consisted of some 400 miles of track. The economy was heavily dominated by agriculture, which used almost the same technologies it had employed since the sixteenth century. By the time Díaz was forced into exile in 1911, Mexico had a sizable banking system, a manufacturing sector that produced a broad range of consumer and intermediate goods in large-scale factories, and a 12,000-mile railroad system. Mexico had also become one of the world's leading metals producers, and it was emerging as a major petroleum exporter.

Much of Mexico's economic transformation under Díaz was the product of the special privileges granted to a coalition of large landowners, powerful politicians, bankers, and industrialists. For example, the industrialists who were close to Díaz not only received protective import tariffs, but they were also sheltered from domestic competition by regulatory and financial barriers to market entry. Bankers were similarly protected: Restrictions on bank chartering meant that there were rarely more than three banks competing in any market. Díaz also used his regulatory powers to transfer assets from groups that were weak and unorganized to individuals and groups who were politically well connected. This meant that large commercial farms expanded dramatically during the Porfiriato, at the expense of small farmers, who were made landless. Precisely because access to political power was a crucial part of business survival in Porfirian Mexico, influential politicians whose support was crucial to Díaz (including state governors, who controlled sizable militias) were able to share in the economic benefits generated by Díaz's policies. State governors, members of congress, and federal cabinet ministers frequently sat on corporate boards and received stock and director's fees from the firms whose interests they protected.[1]

The Revolution of 1910–1920

The Díaz regime sowed the seeds of its own collapse.[2] The same policies that encouraged the growth of large-scale commercial agriculture created a class of dispossessed small farmers who became radicalized and clamored for the return of their lands. Similarly, the growth of mining, railroads, and manufacturing produced a working class that began to organize and strike. The army and the rural police often brutally repressed these strikes; however, this response only served to fuel social and political discontent. Finally, the exclusive and selective nature of the Porfirian alliance with private economic interests gave rise to opposition to the Díaz regime from members of the economic elite who were outside the governing coalition. Foremost among these were the merchants, mine owners, and ranchers of Mexico's northern border states, who resented the fact that political power (and its attendant economic benefits) was concentrated in the hands of a small, Mexico City–based elite.

This broadening opposition crystallized in the 1910 presidential candidacy of Francisco I. Madero, a scion of a wealthy northern

---

[1] For a detailed analysis of the Porfirian regime, see Haber, Razo, and Maurer (2003); Razo (2003); Maurer (2002); Haber (1989); Beatty (2001); Márquez Colin (2002); and Gómez Galvarriato (1999).

[2] For discussions of the origins and course of the Mexican Revolution, see Knight (1986); Gilly (1994); Hart (1987); Womack, Jr. (1970); Katz (1981, 1998); and Haber, Razo, and Maurer (2003).

family with interests in ranching, mining, and manufacturing. When Díaz claimed victory in an election tainted by intimidation and fraud, Madero's supporters took up arms. The forces loyal to Madero never decisively defeated the federal army, but their successes on the battlefield convinced an elderly and demoralized Díaz to negotiate an exit. In May 1911, he resigned as president and sailed to exile in France.

The departure of Porfirio Díaz opened a two-decade-long period of military coups, rebellions, and civil war. Madero lasted only a little more than a year in power. His coalition dissolved as soon as the small farmers who had supported him began to demand that he make good on his promise to restore the lands taken from them during the Porfiriato. He could not accomplish land reform, however, without igniting resistance from the country's landed elite. He therefore reneged on his promise, which set off a series of armed revolts in various parts of the country. Madero charged the army, led by the same generals who had served Díaz, with putting down those movements – but they turned on him instead, overthrowing and murdering Madero in 1913. The leader of that counter-revolution, General Victoriano Huerta, was then overthrown by the same broad coalition that had deposed Díaz. In 1914, Huerta resigned the presidency and went into exile.

The forces aligned against Huerta were united only by their desire to drive him from power, and they quickly split into two camps that fought a vicious civil war lasting from 1914 to 1919. The "Constitutionalist" forces were led by Venustiano Carranza, a major landowner and former Porfirian politician. Carranza espoused liberal democracy but his military allies commanded troops who followed them principally on the basis of patronage and personal loyalty. To the extent that the Constitutionalists embraced any particular ideology, it was a commitment to nationalism – fueled by resentment over foreign investors' control of Mexico's mining and petroleum industries and three separate U.S. incursions into Mexican territory as the civil war raged.

The opposition to the Constitutionalists consisted of a loose combination of small farmers, organized into the Liberating Army of the South led by Emiliano Zapata, and miners, ranch workers, and villagers organized into the Division of the North led by Francisco "Pancho" Villa. These movements did not share a common political or economic agenda. The demand espoused by Zapata and his followers was socially and politically potent, but highly local: the return of lands taken from them by large landowners during the Porfiriato. Villa, in contrast, allowed pragmatic military considerations to guide his views on issues such as agrarian reform, labor law, and the taxation of foreign investment. In point of fact, even though his rhetoric echoed that of Zapata, he distributed almost no land.

Carranza's armies eventually defeated Villa and Zapata but only by forging alliances with groups that were committed to far-reaching social reforms, particularly industrial workers and small farmers. Some of the military commanders who fought under Carranza's banner embraced fairly progressive labor programs (including an 8-hour day and a minimum wage) to build their own local political organizations. Carranza even negotiated a pact with anarchist-inspired worker organizations mobilized into "Red Battalions." The Constitutionalists made similar alliances with radical peasants. Indeed, Carranza persuaded some of the agrarian groups allied with Zapata to switch sides by promising them land.

Precisely because Carranza had to ally himself with a wide variety of more radical groups, the 1916–1917 constitutional convention produced a document that was far more reformist than he initially envisioned. For example, Article 27 of the Constitution of 1917 altered land, water, and subsoil (mineral) property rights. Private ownership of these assets was no longer a right; rather, it was a privilege that the government could reallocate in the public interest. This declaration of the public ownership of these natural resources became the basis for an extensive agrarian reform and the nationalization of the petroleum industry in 1938. Similarly, Article 123 greatly expanded governmental oversight of worker–employer relations. Most fundamentally, it guaranteed the rights to organize and strike. It also introduced an 8-hour workday and a 6-day workweek, regulated the employment of women and children, established occupational health and safety standards, increased job security, and mandated a legal minimum wage, overtime pay, maternity leave, and profit sharing.[3]

Neither the signing of a new constitution nor the defeat and assassinations of Zapata and Villa ended political violence. In 1920 Carranza, who had served as president since 1917, was overthrown and assassinated by a coalition headed by his leading military commander, Álvaro Obregón. Obregón (who served as president from 1920 to 1924) and his hand-picked successor, Plutarco Elías Calles (who served as president from 1924 to 1928), faced major revolts led by their own generals

[3] Middlebrook (1995), Chapter 2.

and cabinet members in 1923, 1927, and 1929. Moreover, from 1926 to 1929 the Calles government fought a civil war against lay elements of the Catholic church, the Cristeros, who sought to overthrow Calles because of his attempt to implement anticlerical provisions of the 1917 Constitution.

To defeat these threats, Obregón and Calles recruited a diverse and unlikely set of allies. First, they sought to rally to their side Mexico's principal business groups. Obregón and Calles were compelled to do so because they needed a growing economy capable of generating the tax revenues required to, among other things, pay the army. As a consequence, they re-created the Porfirian system of special privileges for select wealth holders. Porfirian-era industrialists dominated the federal commission that determined import tariffs, and Porfirian-era bankers wrote the new banking laws.[4] Obregón and Calles did not undertake these initiatives simply to promote growth for growth's sake. Instead, they were trying to stay in power and to accomplish that goal they made a series of deals with manufacturers and bankers. The result was a system of selectively enforced property rights much like the one that had been fashioned during the Díaz regime.

Second, Obregón and Calles needed to muster farmers and workers into paramilitary units to face down rebellious army factions and the Cristeros. They therefore made selective land distributions designed to benefit the small farmers and their leaders who sided with the government at crucial moments. They also forged an alliance with the leading national labor organization, the Mexican Regional Labor Confederation (CROM). Not only did the CROM offer the mass political support needed to win elections but it also provided armed units that could guard railways and other installations, thereby freeing up regular troops to fight various rebel groups. In exchange, the government sided with the CROM in its disputes with employers and rival labor organizations. Cementing this alliance was the appointment of the CROM's leader, Luis N. Morones, as Minister of Industry, Commerce, and Labor in 1924. The fact that Morones was the only labor leader ever to hold this key cabinet position says much about the CROM's political importance to the postrevolutionary regime.[5]

Third, Obregón and Calles gradually consolidated their control over the armed forces by, among other measures, permitting military zone

---

[4] Haber, Razo, and Maurer (2003), Chapters 4, 5.
[5] Middlebrook (1995), Chapter 3.

commanders to amass large landholdings for themselves.[6] Obregón and Calles also participated in this land grab. Obregón became fabulously wealthy by cornering the chickpea market, Mexico's fastest growing agricultural export to the United States, and Calles and his family became major sugar growers and millers.

The Origins and Hegemony of Mexico's "Official" Party

Obregón and Calles planned to continue governing Mexico even after both had served their constitutionally mandated, single 4-year terms in office. Calles therefore engineered the reelection of Obregón by convincing Congress to amend the constitution to allow presidents a second, nonconsecutive term. He also lengthened the term in office to 6 years. Obregón then "won" the 1928 election by a landslide – the official tally recorded not a single vote for the opposition. The plan fell apart only when Obregón was assassinated by a Catholic militant shortly after the election.

Calles responded in three ways to the political crisis resulting from Obregón's assassination. First, under pressure from the United States, he made peace with the Cristeros by agreeing not to enforce the most harshly anticlerical provisions of the Constitution. This shift in policy not only contained the immediate threat posed by the Cristero rebels but it also reduced the political risks arising from an army discontented with fighting against the insurgency. Second, Calles avoided a costly factional struggle over the 1928 presidential succession by removing himself as a potential candidate. Instead, he installed a series of puppet presidents between 1928 and 1934 – an arrangement that allowed him to maintain overall political control without violating the constitutional prohibition against a president succeeding himself in office. Third, in 1929 he formed the Revolutionary National Party (PNR). This was not a political party in the usual sense of the word. For instance, it did not run slates of candidates embracing any particular party platform. Rather, it was a forum in which conflicts among generals, regional political bosses, and other powerful individuals could be brokered without violence. Party leaders determined beforehand what the electoral outcomes would be.

[6] For an analysis of military pacification during the 1920s, see Lieuwin (1968).

The PNR largely succeeded in containing violent factional conflict, but it was too narrowly based to incorporate the organized popular movements that had emerged since 1910. In 1934, Calles selected Lázaro Cárdenas as president, expecting him to be yet another political puppet. Cárdenas, however, outmaneuvered Calles and eventually forced him into exile in the United States. He also transformed the PNR into a mass party. The renamed Party of the Mexican Revolution (PRM), founded in 1938, was composed of labor, peasant, "popular," and military sectors, although the military sector was eliminated in 1940. In 1946 the party changed its name once again to become the Institutional Revolutionary Party (PRI).

The Political Hegemony of the PRI

Until the 1990s, the PRI held an effective monopoly on the exercise of political power. Indeed, the line between the party and the government blurred to the point that they were often viewed as one and the same. Over time, the blending of the party and the government gave rise to a cohesive political class that dominated Mexico's public life. Unlike the situation that prevailed during the Porfiriato, members of this political class were not drawn from the country's business elite. Instead, they tended to be urban middle class in origin, becoming part of the political elite through kinship ties or shared educational and occupational experiences.[7] Despite factional competition and conflicts over specific policy goals, this class was united for several decades under a broad nationalist program. Its members also largely agreed on certain norms of political action and economic goals, including regular rotation of personnel in elective and administrative offices and a sizable role for the public sector in the economy. The norm of rotation in office (underpinned by constitutional prohibitions on reelection of the president and on consecutive reelection of federal and state legislators, state governors, and mayors and municipal councillors) helped stabilize the system because upwardly mobile politicians stood a good chance of eventually occupying public office, with its attendant opportunities for personal enrichment.[8]

---

[7] For an analysis of Mexico's political elite, see Camp (1980).

[8] Middlebrook (1986), Magaloni (2006). On the importance of corruption in maintaining loyalty to the established political order, see Blum (1997) and Morris (1999).

Mexico never became a single-party state, as occurred in China and the former Soviet Union. Opposition parties such as the center-right National Action Party (PAN) continued to exist, and sometimes they even succeeded in winning office at the municipal level and in state and federal legislative elections. Nevertheless, by creating and sustaining a large, heterogeneous coalition and by grouping diverse constituencies (excepting only the business class) in party-linked organizations, the PRI held an unassailable position at the center of national political life. It reinforced its claim to rule by embracing nationalist themes and policies; indeed, PRI leaders often argued that continued political stability and the effective defense of Mexico's sovereignty depended on its retaining national political control.

It would be easy to argue that the PRI maintained its political dominance because government officials authorized or tolerated fraudulent electoral practices, and there is no doubt that they often did so. Indeed, there is abundant evidence that the party's control of the electoral system was born in violence and fraud. In the 1940 presidential election, for example, PRM activists (most of whom were mobilized from its labor wing, the Confederation of Mexican Workers, CTM) used deadly force to break up opposition rallies, attack the headquarters of the opposition candidate, and steal ballot boxes on election day, actions that resulted in the death of thirty people in Mexico City alone. The final count gave an implausible 94.6 percent of the vote to the "official" party's candidate, General Manuel Ávila Camacho.[9]

The selective use of political violence was in fact a crucial element in sustaining PRI rule. For example, the armed forces and the police were used to repress strikes by railroad workers and miners. The regime also deployed specially recruited thugs, as well as a special branch of the police "for the prevention of delinquency," against the leaders of student organizations, members of leftist parties, and other dissidents. Political protests in isolated rural areas often encountered particularly harsh responses from both government security forces and the "white guards" employed by landowners. Among the most spectacular (and politically consequential, in terms of its long-term impact) instances of state repression, in October 1968 the government ordered troops to fire on student demonstrators at Mexico City's Tlatelolco Plaza, killing or wounding several hundred of them.[10]

---

[9] Knight (1991), pp. 300–1.
[10] Aguayo Quezada (1998a).

Yet the PRI did not just rely on the coercive power of the state. It also developed a broad array of tools designed to win elections by overwhelming margins, thereby signaling to political entrepreneurs, both within the party and without, that resistance to the party was futile. They were better off staying inside the PRI than going outside of it.[11]

One of these tools was the ability to decide which opposition parties could legally run against it. The 1946 electoral law stipulated that political parties had to be legally registered, and it then created high barriers to registration. Parties had to have at least 30,000 members nationwide, with membership dispersed in groups of at least 1,000 across at least two-thirds of Mexico's thirty-two federal entities. These requirements were enforced by an electoral commission whose membership was made of up the Secretary of the Interior, two other cabinet members appointed by the president, one senator and one federal deputy (selected by their respective chambers, which the PRI dominated), and two representatives of national parties (who were chosen in common by the existing political parties). In short, the PRI directly controlled at least five of the seven seats on the electoral commission, in effect allowing it to decide which opposition parties were legal and which were not.[12]

The government also had tight control over the mass media. PRI politicians could determine what information was publicly available, how that information was framed, and thus the way in which the population thought about issues and envisioned alternatives to the policies and candidates on offer by the PRI. For instance, until 1993 Mexico had only one private television network, Televisa, which was allowed to maintain a lucrative broadcasting monopoly in exchange for reporting on PRI candidates in a favorable light and either ignoring the candidates of rival parties entirely or portraying them negatively. Indeed, one of the founding partners of Televisa was none other than former Mexican president Miguel Alemán (1946–1952), who realized in the 1950s that ownership of the newly emerging technology of television was going to be both economically lucrative and politically crucial.[13] PRI politicians also controlled the content of newspapers by bribing reporters and editors. In addition, the

---

[11] Magaloni (2006).

[12] Story (1986), p. 46.

[13] Lawson (2002), p. 28. Alemán deployed his political connections to obtain the necessary licenses, and his associates put up the capital.

government could cut off the supply of newsprint to publications
that strayed too far from the politically approved line, and it provided
newsprint to more compliant papers at subsidized prices. The government could do this because in 1935 it established a state-controlled
enterprise to distribute newsprint and then in 1938 expropriated the
country's only newsprint factory, thus creating a state-run newsprint
monopoly.[14]

The PRI as a Patronage Machine

The PRI's ability to win elections by overwhelming margins also
depended on the distribution of patronage to three large groups: small
farmers, organized urban and industrial workers, and unionized public
employees. This not only required the distribution of palpable, if
sometimes modest, benefits to rank-and-file members of these groups,
but it also involved giving peasant and labor leaders opportunities
for political and social mobility and personal enrichment. Patronage
resources were available to the ruling party because the state played
a strongly interventionist role – both directly (in the form of public-
sector firms) and indirectly (through the distribution of financial credit
and welfare benefits) – in economic and social affairs.

The system of patronage that linked millions of small farmers with
the PRI was rooted in the peculiar nature of Mexico's agrarian reform.
Under pressure from agrarian radicals, Carranza had relented on Article 27 of the Constitution of 1917, which created a legal basis for
a land reform. None of Mexico's first postrevolutionary presidents,
however, actually followed through on this commitment. Carranza,
Obregón, and Calles collectively redistributed only approximately 4
percent of Mexico's agricultural land, and much of what they did
distribute fell under the control of powerful revolutionary generals or
politicians – Obregón and Calles among them. In 1930, Calles, who
at the time ruled through a puppet president, declared the agrarian
reform a failure and called for an end to land redistribution.[15]

This situation changed radically under the presidency of Lázaro
Cárdenas (1934–1940), who sought to turn Calles's PNR into a mass
party. Cárdenas redistributed 45.4 million acres – almost 10 percent of
Mexico's total land area, benefiting some 723,000 families – during his

---

[14] Lawson (2002), p. 33.
[15] Markiewicz (1993), pp. 55, 59.

6-year term.[16] The land reform did not end with Cárdenas; successive administrations distributed an additional 78.1 million acres between 1940 and 1970, making the Mexican agrarian reform one of the most far-reaching in all Latin America.[17]

One significant feature of Mexico's land reform was that small farmers did not receive individual title to the land. Instead, they were typically granted use rights to a set of parcels within an *ejido*, a collective form of ownership. Neither the ejido as a corporate entity nor ejidatarios as individuals could legally sell or rent their land. The inalienability of ejidal land meant that the kind of land grab that had taken place during the Porfiriato could not be repeated. This characteristic of the reform increased social stability in the countryside; postrevolutionary Mexico was not subject to the extremely violent and widespread conflicts over land that characterized other Latin American countries (such as El Salvador or Colombia) during the twentieth century.

The inalienability of ejidal land also meant, however, that neither the ejido as a corporate entity nor ejidatarios as individuals could easily obtain financing from private credit markets because their land could not serve as collateral. Ejidatarios were, therefore, almost completely dependent on government development banks to finance the purchase of seeds, tools, and fertilizer.[18] Ejidos as corporate entities also had to rely on the government to finance large-scale infrastructure improvements, such as irrigation works and roads. Moreover, the property rights of the ejido were subject to discretionary government action: The government could expand the ejido by seizing and distributing additional private lands, or it could reallocate ejido lands for other projects that were deemed socially valuable – such as allowing former president Miguel Alemán (then serving as the minister of tourism) and his associates to convert the ejidos in and around Acapulco into private property, so they could construct swank hotels designed to attract the newly emerging jet set of the 1950s and 1960s.[19]

---

[16] Mackinlay (1991), Appendix 1.

[17] For a comparative examination of the dimensions and redistributive consequences of land reform in Bolivia, Cuba, Mexico, and Peru, see Eckstein (1982), pp. 347–86, especially table 11.4.

[18] Mackinlay and de la Fuente (1996), pp. 95–7.

[19] For examples of government officials' political manipulation of ejidos' property rights, see Purnell (1999), pp. 12–13, and Boyer (2003), p. 173. The very length of the administrative procedures required to approve land distributions constituted a form of government political influence over would-be peasant beneficiaries. See Warman (2001), pp. 59–60.

The ejido was an amazingly inefficient way to grow food. Precisely because ejidos were not private property, efficient ejidatarios could not expand their operations by purchasing neighboring parcels. They were also unable to put up their land as collateral to borrow from commercial banks to invest in land improvements, equipment, or seeds that would raise their productivity. At the same time, inefficient ejidatarios could not leave the land without losing their principal asset. Private farmers, for their part, often hesitated to make further investments because they feared expropriation of their property.[20] They also labored under a set of government price controls for agricultural products that were designed to appeal to urban constituents.[21] Thus, although agricultural productivity in Mexico doubled between 1948 and 1970, the rate of growth was much slower than in the rest of Latin America. After 1970, Mexico's agricultural productivity stopped improving altogether, the gap between Mexico and the rest of the hemisphere ballooned, and Mexico became a net importer of grain and other agricultural staples. By 1980 agricultural productivity in Mexico was less than half that of Chile, Colombia, or Venezuela, and less than a quarter of that of Argentina.[22]

Mexico's postrevolutionary agrarian institutions produced, then, a cruel paradox. The PRI maintained that the agrarian reform was the institutionalization of the 1910–1920 revolution, one of whose principal goals was to free Mexico's peasantry from poverty. Indeed, the PRI even appropriated the images of agrarian revolutionaries such as Emiliano Zapata and Pancho Villa, turning them into cultural icons through the party's influence over the mass media and control of the educational system. The truth of the matter was, however, quite different. In the first place, Zapata and Villa had nothing to do with the origins of the PRI. In point of fact, the victors of the revolution, Carranza and Obregón, had orchestrated their assassinations (Zapata in 1919 and Villa in 1923). Second, the very same patronage institutions that allowed the PRI to maintain political control in rural areas meant that agricultural productivity, and hence agricultural incomes, remained low. The vast majority of Mexican farmers – which is to say the vast majority of the Mexican population – were stunningly poor.

---

[20] Yates (1981), p. 175.
[21] Bazdresch and Levy (1991), pp. 231–2.
[22] Thorp (1998), Appendix Figure IV.3 and Appendix Table IV.1, pp. 327–9.

The ejido was, nevertheless, a very efficient way to mobilize votes for the PRI. All of the benefits that the government could bestow on an ejido – credit for its members, expansion of its boundaries, marketing of its output, irrigation systems and other infrastructure projects, schools, and access to public health facilities – could be withdrawn if ejidatarios failed to vote for the ruling party. This implicit threat, we emphasize, was not some distant theoretical abstraction. The local political bosses who typically dominated ejidal organizations made sure that ejidatarios voted the "right" way. These organizations, in turn, were members of the National Peasants' Confederation (CNC), which itself was a formal part of the PRI.

Controlling elections in cities was equally crucial – and much more difficult than in the countryside. Because urban society was more socially heterogeneous and mobile, voters could not be as easily manipulated by local political bosses. Moreover, urban demonstrations or uprisings could not be easily isolated and repressed, as was the case in rural areas. The PRI therefore needed to secure the loyalty of organized urban groups that would not only vote for the party in large numbers but that could also be mobilized for rallies and demonstrations, thereby signaling to the rest of the urban population that protest against PRI rule was futile. Two such constituencies that were already organized and whose interests could be linked with those of the PRI were public employees and industrial workers. In return for their loyalty to the PRI, successive administrations granted these two groups a host of benefits not available to other members of society.

Among the politically most important such arrangements were those protecting the position of both union leaders and rank-and-file members. From the 1930s onward, an array of legal, financial, and political subsidies bolstered the position of labor leaders who were linked to the "official" party.[23] For instance, the so-called separation exclusion clauses authorized by the 1931 federal labor law and generally included in collective work agreements required an employer to dismiss any worker who lost her or his union membership. Thus, if incumbent union leaders successfully manipulated internal union procedures to deprive political rivals of their union membership, the challengers lost their jobs. In addition, the leaders of "official" labor

---

[23] Middlebrook (1995), pp. 95–105.

organizations benefited from direct government financial support, forceful intervention by state authorities to defend them against serious challenges from rank-and-file union members or opposition labor or political groups, and preferential access to elective office (via candidacies allocated by the PRI) and government administrative positions. By fostering their dependence on government support, these institutional arrangements created a cohort of entrenched regime loyalists among the labor leadership, equivalent to the local political bosses who often dominated ejido organizations. In exchange for their security in office, "official" labor leaders maintained industrial-relations peace, reliably delivered union members' votes to the PRI, and provided the government with invaluable support in the management of periodic economic crises by accepting wage increases well below the rate of inflation.[24]

The linking of organized labor to the PRI through a formally constituted labor wing of the party, the CTM, and constitutional and legal provisions favorable to labor produced benefits for rank-and-file workers. Foremost among these was job security. Workers holding permanent positions were entitled to a constitutionally mandated separation indemnity consisting of 3 months' salary plus 20 days of pay per year of seniority, in addition to other benefits that might be provided by a particular company's labor contract (including, for example, provisions in some worker–employer contracts that gave preference in hiring to the children of current employees). This economic disincentive, combined with workers' capacity to resist unjust dismissal either through their union or through petitions filed with government conciliation and arbitration boards, made it difficult for firms to fire unionized employees. At the same time, high levels of trade protection helped secure many workers' jobs by shielding their employers from foreign competition. In industries covered by so-called contract-laws (including the textile, sugar, and rubber industries), the federal labor code safeguarded employment by establishing industry-wide wage scales and work rules, thereby setting essentially the same labor costs for all enterprises regulated by them. These industry-wide agreements thus protected incumbent firms – and their employees – from competition either from new entrants or from each other, thereby significantly reducing the likelihood that a company would fail and that workers would lose their jobs.

---

[24] Bortz (1988); Middlebrook (1995), pp. 288–91.

Unionized public employees and urban and industrial workers – a category that, even at the height of organized labor's power in Mexico, never represented more than one-sixth of the country's economically active population[25] – also won preferential access to social welfare programs that were not available to the rest of society, including retirement pensions and government-subsidized health care. Workers in the formal sector, where the unionized population was concentrated, were covered by the Mexican Social Security Institute (IMSS). At its founding in 1943, the IMSS provided benefits for only 355,000 employees. By 1950, the government had expanded its coverage to 1.1 million workers, but this still amounted to only 16 percent of the country's labor force.[26] In 1960, the government further extended social insurance coverage to all government employees. Their benefits (provided through the Social Security Institute for State Workers, ISSSTE) not only included pension plans and general health insurance, but also access to specialized hospitals and subsidized government-owned supermarkets.

PRI administrations also established housing programs to benefit their unionized constituencies. In 1972, the government created the National Worker Housing Institute (INFONAVIT), a federal agency that collected from private employers a levy equal to 5 percent of their wage bill and used those revenues to construct subsidized housing. Although this program was formally aimed at all urban formal-sector workers, in practice most of its benefits were captured by the CTM, the country's most politically influential labor organization and the PRI's official labor affiliate.[27] Indeed, some analysts believe that the government established INFONAVIT to reward the CTM for its support during the political crisis provoked by massive student demonstrations (and the government's harshly repressive response) in 1968.[28] CTM leaders derived multiple benefits from the program: They purchased land and sold it to INFONAVIT at inflated prices; they often owned or received kickbacks from the construction companies responsible for building housing; and they selectively distributed completed housing units to loyal supporters to strengthen their political position.[29]

---

[25] Middlebrook (1995), p. 114.

[26] INEGI (2000), table 4.3. See also Spalding (1980).

[27] By 1980, the federal government financed four-fifths of all formal-sector housing construction in Mexico, mostly through INFONAVIT. INEGI (2000), table 3.3.

[28] Story (1986), p. 88.

[29] Middlebrook (1995), p. 296.

Despite the gradual expansion over time of programs such as the IMSS, the majority of the Mexican population – including small farmers, ejidatarios, day laborers, and urban service-sector workers – was outside the system of social insurance. As late as 1980, only 44 percent of the population lived in a family covered by any social insurance program, and only 22 percent of this group (10 percent of the total population) enjoyed coverage under the more expansive programs available to public employees.[30]

Readers may wonder why the government did not provide universal access to social insurance. In particular, they may wonder why successive administrations did so little for rural Mexicans, who constituted the vast majority of the population and who tended to be desperately poor. The short answer is that they were not under strong political pressures to do so; the PRI could (and did) maintain political control in the countryside by, among other means, using its meager ejidal credit and marketing programs as a form of patronage. By a similar logic, the government allocated social insurance programs to the best-off urban and industrial workers because they were the organized groups most capable of collective action to support (or threaten) the regime.

This is not to say that the government did nothing for the general population. There were some types of social welfare programs, such as inoculation campaigns, whose benefits could not be directed principally to the PRI's core constituents; government agencies either inoculated everybody or they inoculated no one. In the 1940s and 1950s, for example, the government responded to infectious disease outbreaks by initiating a series of inoculation campaigns against tuberculosis, polio, diphtheria, and smallpox, and it also made substantial strides against malaria.[31] These campaigns produced concrete results. In 1930, 47 percent of all deaths were due to infectious diseases and parasites, but by 1980, only 14 percent of deaths were caused by these diseases.[32] Life expectancy at birth rose from 39 years in 1940 to 56 years in 1960, and to 67 years in 1980.[33] Infant mortality dropped from approximately 200 per 1,000 individuals in the 1920s to 130 in 1950, 90 in 1960, and slightly more than 50 by 1980. Despite these improvements, however, Mexico's public health achievements did not

---

[30] Calculated from data in INEGI (2000), tables 4.3 and 4.8.
[31] Pérez Astorga (1988), p. 311; de la Riva Rodríguez (1963), pp. 226–30.
[32] INEGI (2001a), p. 158.
[33] Oxford Latin American Economic History Database.

compare particularly well with those of other major Latin American countries that neither experienced a "social" revolution nor had a government that professed to embody a revolution. In 1980, for instance, life expectancy at birth was lower in Mexico than in other Latin American countries with a roughly similar per capita gross domestic product (GDP), such as Chile, Costa Rica, and Venezuela. The data on infant mortality and deaths from infectious disease show similar patterns.[34]

The Paradox of Low Taxation

A longer answer to the question posed previously is that even if the Mexican government had wanted to provide the entire population with social insurance, it lacked the fiscal capacity to do so. Until 1976, federal government revenues always represented less than 10 percent of the GDP, and until 1979 they were always less than 15 percent of the GDP. They finally topped 15 percent in the early 1980s, when revenues from oil exports skyrocketed.

Just how low Mexico's ratio of government revenues to GDP was can be seen in Figure 2.1, which compares Mexican government revenues as a percentage of GDP to averages for the rest of Latin America and for the other member states of the Organisation for Economic Co-operation and Development (OECD).[35] From 1950 to 1982, Mexico's ratio of government revenues to GDP was less than half that of the OECD average.[36] One might argue that this comparison is unfair because most OECD members are wealthy countries that can afford

---

[34] Oxford Latin American Economic History Database.

[35] The data only include revenues collected by the central government. We therefore do not include in this comparison countries in which there is substantial revenue collection at the state or provincial level. Hence, we drop the United States from calculations for the OECD countries, as well as Argentina and Brazil among the Latin American countries. Their deletion does not, however, affect the result. Central government tax collection in the United States and Brazil exceeded that of Mexico, whereas that of Argentina was comparable to Mexico. Data for the OECD countries are from the International Monetary Fund, International Financial Statistics Database (2006); data for Mexico are from the Oxford Latin American Economic History database (http://oxlad.qeh.ox.ac.uk/search.php).

[36] Mexico acceded to the OECD in May 1994. In 2007 the other OECD member states were Australia, Austria, Belgium, Canada, Czech Republic, Denmark, Finland, France, Germany, Greece, Hungary, Iceland, Ireland, Italy, Japan, Luxembourg, Netherlands, New Zealand, Norway, Poland, Portugal, Republic of Korea, Slovak Republic, Spain, Sweden, Switzerland, Turkey, United Kingdom, and the United States.

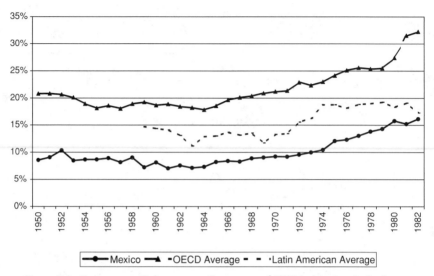

Figure 2.1: Government Revenues as a Percentage of GDP in Mexico, Latin America, and the OECD, 1950–1982. *Source:* International Monetary Fund, *International
Financial Statistics.*

to invest in the administrative capacity to collect taxes. The problem
with this argument is twofold. First, Mexico had a much lower ratio of
government revenues to GDP than other OECD countries at the same
per capita income level as Mexico; on average, Mexican revenues were
only 61 percent of those of Greece and 56 percent of those of Portugal.
Second, Mexico's ratio of government revenues to GDP was only 66
percent of that of the rest of Latin America. In point of fact, between
1950 and 1982 the Mexican government collected revenues at approximately the same ratio to GDP as the region's poorest countries, such as
Guatemala and Honduras.

Government revenues in Mexico were low mainly because capital
was, in effect, not taxed. Property taxes were set at such low levels as
to be virtually nonexistent, and taxes on financial wealth were similarly low. It was easy for sole proprietorships, partnerships, and corporations to evade taxation by exaggerating their expenses and shifting
costs among different segments of their business so as to reduce the
profits they reported. In principle, the government could have taxed
capital when corporate profits were distributed to shareholders as dividends. As a practical matter, however, there was no way to do so
because Mexico lacked a centralized registration of stock or bond
ownership; dividends were simply "paid to the bearer" of stock or

bond certificates. In a similar vein, almost no one reported income earned from property rental. In short, the vast majority of nonwage income (stock dividends, rental payments, and interest) was free from taxation.

The government was well aware of these characteristics of its tax system. A report prepared in 1961 by a distinguished group of economists, convened by the government to advise it on how to increase revenues, noted them, and commission members recommended that the government create a stock and bond registry so that it could tax corporate dividends and interest payments to individuals. They also advised the government to require banks and bond-issuing entities to withhold tax on interest they paid to individuals. Finally, they urged the government to close a particularly egregious loophole in the tax code: Wealthy individuals were allowed to fragment their total income into separate categories, which had lower tax rates than that which would have applied to their aggregate income.

Their recommendations were, however, ignored in the tax legislation subsequently adopted in 1964. Indeed, the Secretary of the Treasury went so far as to state publicly that taxes on the wealthy could not be increased without the acquiescence of those affected. In 1972 the government resurrected the same set of proposals to increase taxes on the wealthy, but they were again scuttled after a series of private consultations between the Secretary of the Treasury and leading industrialists.[37] Some of these initiatives, particularly the proposal to abolish anonymity in stockholding, were finally included in the federal tax code in 1985. Even then, the Mexican government continued to rely overwhelmingly on regressive taxes on salaried income and consumption (excise and value-added taxes).

Why would a "revolutionary" government that professed to represent the interests of peasants and workers leave capital untaxed? We would suggest that the answer lies in the lack of a credible commitment by PRI-led governments toward the property rights of Mexico's business class. The business class could not defend itself through the country's political institutions; the PRI controlled elections, Congress, and the courts. The business class was also unable to defend itself by shaping the views of the general population about the role of private enterprise; the PRI controlled the educational system and the mass

---

[37] Izquierdo (1995), pp. 69–81; Smith (1991), pp. 358, 368; Elizondo (2001), pp. 116–17, 131–8.

media. The only weapon the business class had at its disposal was the threat of capital flight or an investment boycott. This created, however, a problem for PRI-led administrations: The lack of a credible commitment toward private property meant that the government had to coax the business class into deploying its capital. One way to do this, which we will discuss later, was to limit competition. The other way to do it was intentionally to limit the taxation of capital.

Just because capital faced low rates of taxation did not mean, however, that Mexican firms were lightly taxed. Taxes came in the form of "rents" distributed to politicians, labor leaders, and the rank and file of labor unions. They included higher prices for intermediate and capital goods (caused by the tariffs that protected input-producing firms from foreign and domestic competition), the costs of dealing with the unwieldy import-permit process, the distribution of board seats and other sinecures to politicians or their family members, the need to maintain unproductive employees on the payroll, and, of course, an endless string of bribes, large and small, paid to political intermediaries and various government regulators, inspectors, and tax collectors.

Unlike tax payments, however, Mexico's unofficial rent payments did not generate public goods.[38] When firms pay taxes to governments in most OECD countries, the taxes raise their operating costs but those taxes are then spent on public goods. The benefits to private enterprises from public goods are obvious in the cases of spending on physical infrastructure (roads and bridges), law enforcement, public health, and education. Less obviously, but not less importantly, much government spending removes the burden of health care and pension benefits from individual firms and spreads them across the entire society. High levels of public goods explain in part why many OECD economies have been capable of achieving robust rates of economic growth despite high levels of taxation.[39]

The rents that Mexican firms paid to private parties did produce one important benefit for them: a modicum of protection against the possibility of expropriation or other arbitrary government actions. The political leaders who ultimately benefited from these payments had a stake in protecting the firms that paid them. This was significant because Mexico's business class did in fact have reason to fear expropriation. The assets of private bankers had, for example, been

<hr>

[38] Public goods are goods and services whose benefits are accessible to payers and nonpayers alike. They typically include such things as government-provided public health and education programs, national and domestic security, and a clean environment.

[39] Lindert (2004).

expropriated by Carranza in 1916 to obtain the resources needed to defeat Villa and Zapata.[40] Industrialists had been threatened with expropriation when they tried to curtail operations during the Great Depression of the 1930s. The Cárdenas administration had seized foreign-owned petroleum companies in 1938, and in that same year the government expropriated the country's largest paper mill so that it could fully control access to newsprint.[41] Commercial farmers, of course, had been subject to expropriation ever since the revolution, and they had seen many of their best lands taken over during the Cárdenas presidency.

How were private enterprises expected to generate sufficient profits to pay rents to political elites and remain in business? The government needed to find ways to raise rates of return high enough to compensate investors for the rent payments that they had to make. It did so in part by allowing private investors to write the regulations governing their own activities, by providing favored firms with subsidized production inputs, by crafting regulatory barriers to market entry that helped maintain oligopolies and monopolies, and by protecting domestic producers from foreign imports via tariffs and import permits.

These steps allowed the government to forge an alliance of convenience with Mexico's business class. This relationship often experienced significant tensions.[42] Nevertheless, this alliance – sardonically referred to by contemporaries as "the alliance for profits" (a play-on-words on John F. Kennedy's Alliance for Progress) – was not a theoretical abstraction. Mexico's business interests, although excluded from a formal role in the PRI, were closely linked to the state through a series of compulsory business associations and exercised considerable influence on public policies.[43]

---

[40] Haber, Razo, and Maurer (2003), Chapter 4.

[41] Haber, Razo, and Maurer (2003), Chapter 5.

[42] Vernon (1963).

[43] These organizations included the Mexican Employers' Confederation (COPARMEX), the Confederation of National Chambers of Commerce (CONCANACO), the National Confederation of Chambers of Industry (CONCAMIN), and the National Chamber of Manufacturers (CANACINTRA).

The 1936 Law on Chambers of Industry and of Commerce established the main institutional context for business political action. Until its reform in 1996, it served as one of the pillars of Mexico's system of interest representation and underpinned multiple agreements among government, labor, and the private sector. See, among other sources, Valdés Ugalde (1994) and Luna (2004). The panoply of major business organizations included groups not directly licensed by the state, such as the highly influential Private Sector Coordinating Council (CCE) and the Mexican Council of Businessmen (CMHN).

These very same steps, however, created a roadblock to long-run economic development: Low tax revenues guaranteed that public education would be underfunded relative to the levels of other countries. As late as 1980, education spending amounted to only 2.9 percent of Mexico's GDP, well below the levels found in Brazil, Chile, Costa Rica, and Venezuela. Low spending yielded low results. In 1940, for instance, 54 percent of Mexico's adult population was illiterate – a figure little different from Brazil or Venezuela (56 and 58 percent, respectively) and far lower than that of Chile, Colombia, or Costa Rica, countries that had not had "social" revolutions. One 1977 study concluded that two of every three adults in Mexico were either illiterate or very poorly educated. Fewer than 20 percent of preschool children attended kindergarten, and only 42 percent of all children completed primary school within 6 years.[44] As late as 1980, the Mexican government officially classified 18 percent of the adult population as illiterate, a proportion higher than every major Latin American country except Brazil.[45]

The steps that the government took to raise rates of return for industrialists constituted an implicit tax on consumers, small businesses, and the millions of small farmers who populated Mexico's countryside. Trade protection and oligopolies raised the prices these groups paid for manufactured products. The government tried to compensate urban workers for these higher costs by controlling the price of basic foodstuffs, but that only exacerbated the situation because those price controls were an additional implicit tax levied on farmers. The net result, then, was that the ultimate losers in Mexico's political economy were the same ejidatarios whom the PRI glorified in official party iconography.

The Politics of Trade Protection

PRI administrations built on a long-standing tradition of protective tariffs that went back to the 1890s, but they refined trade protection by progressively embracing a system of import permits that excluded foreign goods at any price. Until 1947, Mexico had protected domestic industry with a cascading tariff structure – that is, the tariff on

---

[44] Prawda (1988), p. 80; Pescador Osuna (1988), p. 156.
[45] Oxford Latin American Economic History Database (http://oxlad.qeh.ox.ac.uk/).

consumer goods was much higher than on imported raw materials and on imported machinery. The 1947 tariff act raised import tariffs slightly, pushing the rate on consumer goods to 50 percent, while keeping rates on raw materials and machinery at 5 percent and 10–15 percent, respectively.[46]

The permit system introduced in 1947 did more than limit the quantity of imported goods; it helped restrict domestic competition as well. In so doing, it made the government's commitment to job security for unionized industrial workers even more credible. Businesses could not apply for a permit until the imported goods had already arrived in customs. During the weeks that it took to process the permit, the importer had to bear an inventory cost equal to 8 to 10 percent of the value of the goods, in addition to paying the posted duties. Most crucially, the application could be turned down by Ministry of Industry and Commerce officials, who operated with tremendous discretion. The result was that unless a firm was politically connected at the outset, it was unlikely even to begin the process. Access to import permits therefore served as a barrier to market entry, limiting competition.[47]

Mexico's import permit system created incentives for the government continually to expand the range of goods subject to quantitative restrictions. When it was created in 1947, the system only applied to "luxury goods." Within a year, however, manufacturers of other consumer products began to pressure the government to expand the range of restricted goods, and the government granted those requests. As those consumer goods industries expanded, they imported ever-larger quantities of foreign-made intermediate inputs (products that become part of the final product in the manufacturing process, such as the steel used to make an automobile) and capital goods (the machinery and tools used to manufacture a product, such as the stamping machines used to fashion automobile body parts). As imports of those inputs soared, the balance of trade (the difference between the monetary value of exports and imports) went into deficit.[48]

The balance-of-trade problem could have been solved by increasing exports, but protectionism had a number of perverse consequences that frustrated attempts to promote export growth. First, Mexico's

---

[46] Reynolds (1970), p. 210.
[47] Reynolds (1970), pp. 221–2.
[48] Manne (1966).

industrialists had few incentives to pursue export markets; they were already earning enormous profits. It was not just that they did not have to compete with imported goods. Because Mexican industry tended to be highly oligopolistic, they did not have to compete very hard against other domestic producers.[49] In part, oligopolies were an outcome of a small domestic market that could only support a limited number of firms that used mechanized production technologies. In some economic activities, industry-wide labor contracts promoted oligopolies because new entrants could not out-compete industry incumbents on the basis of lower wages and more flexible work rules. The barriers to entry created by the import permit system also encouraged market concentration. Finally, differential access to finance – particularly the ability of existing firms to obtain financing from government-run development banks – played a role in restricting new entry.

Second, protectionism produced incentives for the government to increase export taxes, which put Mexican primary products at a competitive disadvantage in world markets. The whole point of protectionism was to raise the cost of imported goods to the point that the population chose not to purchase them. Once that happened, tax revenues from import tariffs collapsed, falling from 37 percent of revenues in 1941 to 10 percent by 1975. As a consequence, the government needed to find an alternative source of tax revenues. As we have already discussed, it chose not to increase taxes on income and wealth. It therefore compensated for the decline in import taxes by increasing taxes on exports, which doubled between 1940 and 1960.[50]

Finally, exchange-rate policies designed to subsidize the importation of capital goods for domestic industrialists placed exports at a big disadvantage. Between 1954 and 1976 the average price of goods and services sold in Mexico rose by a factor of 3:1, whereas prices in its major trading partner, the United States, increased by a factor of only 2:1.[51] To keep exports competitive, economic policy makers would have needed to devalue the peso. Instead, the government maintained a fixed exchange rate vis-à-vis the U.S. dollar. The appreciation of the peso vis-à-vis the dollar meant that the machinery, spare parts, and intermediate inputs that Mexican manufacturers imported from abroad were very inexpensive in peso terms. It also meant, however,

[49] Bulmer-Thomas (1994), p. 283; Hernández Laos (1985), p. 397.
[50] Reynolds (1970), pp. 217–18.
[51] Reynolds (1997), p. 1014.

that Mexican exports were very expensive in dollar terms, thereby reducing their competitiveness abroad.

Solving the balance-of-trade problem by increasing exports was thus not easily accomplished. Exports fell without stop from the early 1950s, when they averaged 10 percent of the GDP, to the early 1970s at which point the government abandoned its export-promotion programs.[52] By 1971, exports comprised less than 4 percent of the GDP. The only success that Mexico had in increasing exports occurred after the mid-1970s, when it was able to take advantage of high international petroleum prices and new oil discoveries in the Gulf of Mexico. Even that success, however, was a pyrrhic victory: Revenues produced by the jump in petroleum exports were eaten up by the need to import specialized drilling and pumping equipment to bring the oil to market. The balance of trade remained in deficit.[53]

Mexico could have compensated for a trade account that was continually in deficit by running a positive balance on the capital account (an account that tracks the movement of funds for investment and loans into and out of a country). That, however, would have required Mexico to be open to foreign direct investment (FDI). As we shall discuss in detail later, there were strong political pressures on the government to do precisely the opposite. As a result, government restrictions severely limited the ability of foreign firms to do business in Mexico.

Unable to increase exports, and unable to run a surplus on the capital account, the Mexican government chose to close the trade imbalance by expanding the system of protection. If, as a consequence of the growth of consumer goods industries, imports of intermediate and capital goods were causing a trade imbalance, why not use the permit system to encourage the growth of intermediate and capital goods industries in Mexico? The proportion of imports covered by the permit system grew from 28 percent in 1956 to 65 percent in 1965, and to 74 percent in 1974.[54] The expanded permit system was remarkably effective at reducing imports of intermediate and capital goods, whether measured as a percentage of all imports, of GDP, or of total manufacturing production before the late 1970s oil boom. Imports

---

[52] The in-bond manufacturing (*maquiladora*) program established along the Mexico–U.S. border in 1965 was the exception. See Bulmer-Thomas (1994), p. 328.

[53] These are the authors' calculations based on data presented in Cárdenas (2000), tables A-4 and A-8-a. Mexico began to expand its petroleum production in 1973 but it was still a net importer of oil until 1977. See ibid, p. 324.

[54] Ten Kate et al. (1979), p. 94; Cárdenas (2000), p. 187.

of intermediate goods as a proportion of total Mexican production of intermediate goods dropped from 24.5 percent in 1950 to 17.3 percent in 1960 and 10.6 percent in 1969. Imports of capital goods as a share of domestic capital goods production fell from 55.1 percent in 1950 to 44.3 percent in 1960 and 29.3 percent in 1969.[55]

Foreign Direct Investment and "Mexicanization"

The response of foreign firms to Mexico's restrictive trade policies was to seek the benefits of protection for themselves by establishing local production facilities. This shift began in the 1920s with the arrival in Mexico of the Ford Motor Company, Palmolive, and several other multinational corporations (MNCs). By the 1950s the process was in full swing. Virtually all of the growth in U.S. FDI in Mexico between 1950 and 1959 occurred in the manufacturing sector, so that by 1959 some 47 percent of all U.S. direct investment in Mexico was in manufacturing. As a result, in 1959 U.S. investors held claims on 8 percent of total Mexican manufacturing investment.[56]

Multinational enterprises were not constituents of the PRI, but the domestically owned manufacturing firms that competed against them were. Thus, it was not long before the national private sector brought to bear political pressures to regulate and limit FDI. These pressures grew significantly during the 1960s as MNCs began to take over existing Mexican firms as one of their principal strategies for expansion.[57] The fact that demands to regulate foreign investment were completely consistent with the PRI's self-portrayal as a revolutionary party that safeguarded Mexican sovereignty made the government's moves to protect domestic capitalists politically compelling.

As early as 1944, the administration of President Manuel Ávila Camacho (1940–1946) adopted a law requiring that all companies operating in Mexico be majority owned by Mexicans. The law was never fully enforced, but it constituted a lever that the government could use whenever it sought to extract concessions from foreign firms operating in "strategic" industries.[58] For example, in 1958 President Adolfo López Mateos (1958–1964) declared that the production of

---

[55] Graham (1982), pp. 23, 25.
[56] Reynolds (1970), pp. 190–1.
[57] Whiting (1992), Chapter 4.
[58] Evans and Gereffi (1982), p. 143.

government–owned commercial bank, the Banco de México, which lent most of its funds to private bankers and powerful politicians.[66]

As soon as postrevolutionary governments began to consolidate their power, they began to take back some of the policy-making authority initially delegated to private bankers. In 1932, the government converted the Banco de México into a central bank. A further reform in 1936 required commercial banks to maintain cash reserves in the Banco de México, which is to say that banks had to lend part of their deposit base to the government. That same law also transferred many bank supervisory functions from the banker-influenced National Banking Commission to the Banco de México. In a further set of reforms enacted in 1941, the government forced commercial banks to divest their investment banking operations into separate corporations.[67]

Mexico's bankers did not roll over and play dead when the government began to reshape banking policies to its own ends. They had considerable influence in the Banco de México and the Ministry of Finance because prominent bankers moved back and forth between the private sector and the government, often serving as directors of the Banco de México or in high positions in the ministry. In point of fact, the annual meeting of the Mexican Bankers' Association was always opened by the finance minister and the director of the central bank, and sometimes by Mexico's president. The social organ of the bankers' association, the Bankers' Club, actually had its offices inside one of the buildings of the Banco de México.[68]

Private bankers were able to use their influence to serve their own ends. As a legal matter, Mexico possessed at least three different types of banks between 1941 and 1982: commercial banks, which handled most retail banking operations and made short-term loans to business enterprises; investment banks (*financieras*), which made long-term loans to businesses and often held equity positions in those firms; and government-run development banks (the first of which had been founded in the 1930s), which made long-term loans to business enterprises, collateralized by shares in those firms. As Figure 2.3 demonstrates, as early as the 1940s government development banks were as important as a source of credit as the commercial banks, with other

[66] Maurer (2002).

[67] Del Ángel–Mobarak (2002, 2005).

[68] Del Ángel–Mobarak (2002).

basic petrochemicals was strategic and compelled foreign producers to sell their operations to the state-owned Mexican Petroleum Company (PEMEX). The following year, López Mateos decreed that the maximum level of foreign participation in the production of secondary petrochemicals (products derived from basic petrochemicals or manufactured from crude petroleum and natural gas) should not exceed 40 percent.[59]

The campaign to "Mexicanize" the economy expanded in the 1960s and 1970s. In 1961 the government decreed that foreign mining companies had to sell majority stakes to Mexican investors.[60] In 1962 López Mateos moved to limit foreign ownership in the automobile parts industry to 40 percent.[61] In 1966 President Gustavo Díaz Ordaz (1964–1970) ordered that the banking industry had to be domestically owned. In 1967, he limited foreign ownership in the sulfur industry to 34 percent. Three years later, Díaz Ordaz declared his intention to Mexicanize the steel, cement, glass, fertilizer, paper, and aluminum industries.[62]

In 1973, President Luis Echeverría (1970–1976) transformed the ad hoc nature of the Mexicanization campaign – in which foreign ownership limits were set on an industry-by-industry basis – into a blanket policy. New foreign investments had to be 51 percent Mexican-owned and under Mexican control unless there were already more restrictive foreign-ownership limits established for that industry.[63] A parallel measure restricted foreign firms' use of patents and trademarks. Echeverría also tried to promote Mexicanization by raising taxes on foreign enterprises, limiting tax deductions for the depreciation of physical assets and advertising expenses while increasing the gross mercantile revenue tax. As a result, by 1972 foreign companies faced tax obligations equal to 46 percent of gross revenues.[64]

How much did these policies affect the growth of FDI in Mexico? Foreign investors had a number of weapons that they could deploy to protect themselves from Mexico's new laws. Firms could mitigate somewhat the effect of government tax increases by claiming inflated production costs and shifting expenses among different parts of their

[59] Evans and Gereffi (1982), p. 133.

[60] Bernstein (1964).

[61] Izquierdo (1995), p. 117.

[62] Izquierdo (1995), pp. 112, 119.

[63] Evans and Gereffi (1982), p. 144; Whiting (1992), Chapter 4.

[64] Evans and Gereffi (1982), p. 151.

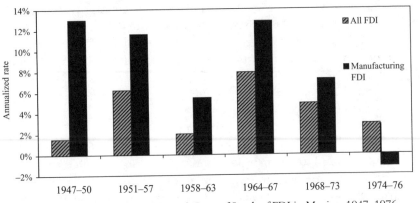

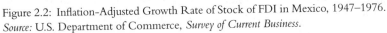

Figure 2.2: Inflation-Adjusted Growth Rate of Stock of FDI in Mexico, 1947–1976.
Source: U.S. Department of Commerce, *Survey of Current Business.*

business so as to reduce the profits they reported. Limits on foreign ownership could be avoided by recruiting "straw man" Mexican partners, who nominally owned 51 percent of the stock but exercised no actual managerial control. Alternatively, multinational enterprises could create elaborate ownership arrangements involving multiple holding companies. Nevertheless, the evidence suggests that the Mexicanization drive took its toll on FDI. As Figure 2.2 shows, the rate of growth in the stock of FDI began a monotonic decline in the late 1960s. By the mid-1970s, the rate of growth of FDI in the manufacturing sector had become negative. Foreigners had begun to liquidate their investments in Mexican manufacturing.

Politics and Banking

PRI-led governments also forged an alliance of convenience with Mexico's bankers. This alliance was always much more tenuous than the one established with domestic manufacturers. The alliance between the government and manufacturers was bolstered by organized industrial workers, whose own interests helped align the government's incentives with those of industrialists: If the government withdrew trade protection and thereby undermined workers' employment security, the PRI would risk losing this crucial base of political support. No such mechanism existed, however, to underpin the alliance between the government and private bankers. When the

government was desperate for funds, there was little to keep it from preying upon the banking system. In fact, as we shall show, when the government began to face serious budgetary constraints in the mid-1970s, one of its first steps was to undermine the private banking system.

The alliance between the government and bankers went back to the mid-1920s. During the Mexican Revolution, various political factions, including the victorious Constitutionalists, preyed on the banks established during the Porfiriato to finance their military campaigns — so much so that by the time the armed phase of the revolution had ended there was virtually no banking system to speak of. The lack of a functioning financial system, however, threatened the survival of the Obregón and Calles administrations, which needed sources of revenue beyond those they could obtain from taxation. Moreover, other important economic actors whose support was politically crucial to Obregón and Calles, most particularly manufacturers, clamored for the creation of a banking system that they could use to finance their operations.[65]

The problem was that bankers did not view the government as a credible partner. There was nothing to keep the government from raiding bank assets again. Indeed, the bankers knew that the government did not have to confiscate assets outright to expropriate them. It had a number of tools available with which to accomplish a de facto expropriation, including loan defaults, tax increases, inflationary monetary policies coupled with interest rate ceilings, negative real (inflation-adjusted) interest rates on required reserves, and directed credit programs that forced banks to lend to politically favored firms.

The government therefore had to work with the bankers to craft a series of institutions designed to raise the rate of return on banking high enough to compensate them for the risk of expropriation. These institutional arrangements were laid down in 1925 at a convention that the government organized with the country's private bankers. The banking law that emerged from this convention was essentially written by the bankers themselves. Not surprisingly, the law they created severely limited competition by keeping foreign banks out of retail banking and by giving the National Banking Commission, on which they had strong representation, the right to regulate the number of charters granted to new banks. The law also created a

[65] Haber, Razo, and Maurer (2003), Chapter 4.

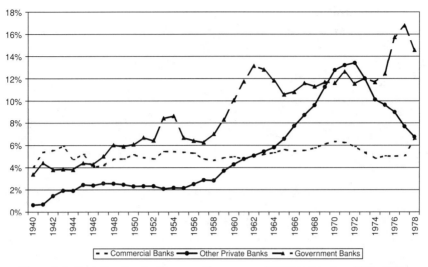

Figure 2.3: Bank Lending by Type as a Percentage of GDP in Mexico, 1940–1978.
Source: Del Ángel-Mobarak (2002).

private financial entities (of which investment banks were the most important) accounting for only a small fraction of total credit. By the 1950s, commercial banks' participation in the credit market had begun to stagnate, with other private banks and government development banks providing progressively larger amounts of financing. By the early 1970s, investment banks were the most important source of credit, followed by development banks, with commercial banks a distant third.

Regardless of who owned them, all three types of banks worked together to finance Mexico's largest industrial and commercial enterprises. Indeed, Mexico's industrial conglomerates typically owned both a commercial bank and an investment bank, and the portfolios of these banks tended to be composed of shares held in the enterprises that were part of the conglomerates.[69] These commercial and investment banks were, in essence, the treasury divisions of the conglomerates; they had little relationship to the impersonal credit intermediaries of economic theory. As a result, in 1974 the Mexican government gave up the legal fiction that commercial and investment banks were independent of one another, allowing them to merge into enterprises that were called multi-banks.

[69] Del Ángel-Mobarak (2002, 2005).

The policy justification for government-owned development banks was that they existed to compensate for an inadequate private banking system. Like many of the government's interventions in other areas of the economy, there was a lack of fit between the rhetoric in which the government's economic intervention was couched and its actual design and implementation. In this case, the rhetoric was about the need to rectify a market failure. The facts suggest, however, that government-owned banks served as a mechanism to subsidize the private banks and the industrial conglomerates that were associated with them.

One of the functions of Mexico's government development banks was to serve as second-tier lenders, repurchasing loans made by commercial banks through special programs designed to channel credit to sectors the government deemed economically important.[70] These directed-credit programs represented a government guarantee to private banks because all of the default risk was born by the development bank, while the private bank earned income from originating and servicing the loan. Moreover, many of the firms that received these loans were not small and mid-sized enterprises. They were large manufacturers and commercial enterprises, often with unionized workforces, that had the political clout to arrange to be designated as a strategic industry. This meant that industrial and commercial conglomerates could fund risky enterprises through the development banks rather than from the private banks that were under their control. It was not private bank depositors and shareholders who bore the risk; rather, it was the taxpayers who subsidized the development banks.

Development banks also made direct loans to private manufacturers, further subsidizing large industrial firms as well as the private banks that owned them. The largest and oldest development bank in Mexico, Nacional Financiera (NAFIN), obtained its capital by selling government-backed bonds and then made long-term loans to manufacturers that were collateralized by blocks of shares issued by those firms. NAFIN was supposed to provide credit to small and mid-sized manufacturing companies, which were often unable to obtain financing from commercial and investment banks. As a practical matter, however, NAFIN allocated most of its credit to the very same industrial conglomerates that received financing from private banks. The political pressure to lend to large firms, whose owners were politically

---

[70] Del Ángel-Mobarak (2002).

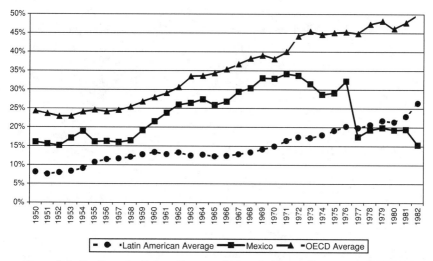

Figure 2.4: Credit to the Private Sector and Households as a Percentage of GDP in Mexico, Latin America, and the OECD, 1950–1982. *Source:* International Monetary Fund, *International Financial Statistics.*

well connected and which often had large, unionized, and electorally significant workforces, simply outweighed whatever original mandate NAFIN may have had.[71]

NAFIN typically took a minority shareholder position in companies to which it extended credit. If the firm performed well, NAFIN's stake would, over time, become purely nominal. If, however, a firm performed poorly, NAFIN would often lend additional funds and enlarge its equity stake. Many of these enterprises were large employers, whose unionized workforces were politically important to the PRI. This meant that the government came to use NAFIN as a mechanism to bail out manufacturers that were not economically viable. Worse, the policy of bailouts encouraged moral hazard: Knowing that they would be bailed out, manufacturers undertook activities of doubtful profitability. In part for this reason, the number of government-owned firms mushroomed over time. In 1970 there were eighty-five state-owned firms. By 1976 there were 740. In 1982 there were 1,155, including sugar refiners, steel mills, airlines, and hotels.[72]

This set of arrangements between the government and private banks produced a large and rapidly growing banking system. As Figure 2.4

[71] Cárdenas (2000), p. 190.
[72] Valdés Ugalde (1994), table 9.2; Cárdenas (2000), p. 195; Smith (1991), p. 371.

indicates, the amount of private credit in Mexico grew from 16 percent of the GDP in 1950 to 34 percent in 1971. This meant that the ratio of private credit to GDP in Mexico was approximately twice the average for Latin America. It also meant that from 1950 to the early 1970s, the rate of growth of private credit in Mexico was faster than that in the OECD countries.

The Economic Impact of Mexico's "Alliance for Profits"

The arrangements between the government and Mexico's private bankers would, however, soon be undermined. The alliance would end in hyperinflation, a foreign debt crisis, the expropriation of the banks, and an economic collapse that would, in time, also erode the PRI's monopoly on power. Before we consider the factors leading to the breakdown of this system, it is worthwhile taking stock of its accomplishments.

The alliance of convenience between successive PRI administrations and the private sector succeeded in coaxing capital into production. Trade protection, domestic barriers to market entry, the creation of bank-centered industrial conglomerates, and subsidized government credit produced rapid industrialization and a substantial increase in GDP per capita. Between 1940 and 1980 the volume of output in the manufacturing sector grew at a rate of more than 10 percent per year.[73] By 1980, there was virtually no major consumer item that was not domestically manufactured in Mexico, including durable consumer goods such as automobiles and household appliances. Mexican manufacturers also produced a broad range of intermediate goods, such as steel and petrochemicals. They had even moved into the production of a number of items whose engineering or scientific requirements make them difficult to manufacture, such as pharmaceutical products, seamless steel pipes, and special-application glassware.

One outcome of the rapid expansion of industry was that labor productivity in the aggregate grew by 165 percent over the period from 1950 to 1982 (see Figure 2.5). This increase in GDP per worker was the result of two factors: Workers moved from low-productivity agricultural activities into higher-productivity manufacturing activities, and workers in manufacturing had progressively larger amounts

[73] INEGI (1994), p. 609.

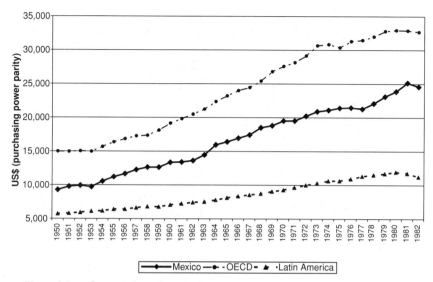

Figure 2.5: Inflation-Adjusted GDP per Worker in Mexico, Latin America, and the OECD, 1950–1982. *Source:* Heston, Summers, and Aten (2002).

of capital with which to work. The residual gains in productivity (that is, the share of productivity growth that cannot be accounted for by sectoral shifts in the distribution of the labor force or by increases in capital) were quite trivial.[74]

Whether Mexico's productivity growth from 1950 to 1982 should be characterized as "fast" or "slow" depends on with what it is compared. Compared with the rest of Latin America, Mexico's productivity performance was admirable. As Figure 2.5 demonstrates, there was a sizable productivity gap between Mexico and the rest of Latin America in 1950 and that gap widened over the course of the next three decades. The problem with using the rest of Latin America as the standard of comparison, however, is that during this period all of the other countries in the region embraced the same distortionary policies that Mexico did – protective tariffs and import permits, financial policies that directed credit to favored economic activities and compelled banks to hold government bonds paying below-market interest rates, tight restrictions on FDI, and overvalued exchange rates. Indeed, some Latin American countries went even further, creating multiple exchange rates, government-run marketing boards, and restrictions on

[74] Reynolds (1970), p. 166.

profit repatriation by foreign-owned companies. Comparing Mexico with these countries tells us little, then, about whether Mexico's policies helped or hindered productivity growth.

Figure 2.5 therefore also compares average inflation-adjusted output per worker in Mexico with other members of the OECD. By this standard of comparison, Mexico's post–World War II "economic miracle" does not look particularly miraculous. There was approximately a 30-percentage point gap in average productivity levels between Mexico and other OECD countries during the 1950s. The ratio of Mexican to OECD productivity levels then held fairly constant through the 1960s and most of the 1970s. The only break in this pattern occurred in the years from 1978 to 1982, when Mexican productivity grew faster than the OECD average because of the (very short-term) impact of oil revenues and massive foreign borrowing.

Some readers might object to this comparison, arguing that the OECD includes a number of wealthy countries (the United States, Great Britain, France, and others) that were different from Mexico on so many dimensions that comparisons among them do not have analytical meaning. These readers might argue that a more meaningful exercise would be to compare Mexico with members of the OECD that had similar levels of GDP per worker in 1950 and that, broadly speaking, were similar to Mexico in terms of the structure of their economies and their underlying political and social characteristics.

We therefore draw a comparison between Mexico and Spain, Greece, and Portugal in Figure 2.6. All three of these countries broadly resembled Mexico in the 1950s in that they had authoritarian governments, agrarian economies, and low levels of educational attainment and human capital formation. In point of fact, all three were substantially poorer than Mexico in 1950. In the 1950s, Spain's average output per worker hovered stubbornly at approximately 90 percent of the Mexican level. Within 2 years of Francisco Franco's decision in 1960 to liberalize trade, however, Spain opened up a sizable lead on Mexico. That gap then grew over the next two decades; Spain's average labor productivity advantage over Mexico was 19 percent in the 1960s and 47 percent in the 1970s. The data for Greece tell a similar story. In the 1950s, Greece's output per worker was only 75 percent that of Mexico's. Greece's productivity levels then closed on those of Mexico in the 1960s and overtook Mexico (by 30 percent) in the 1970s. Even in Portugal – which remained protectionist until 1974, when long-time dictator Antonio Salazar was finally overthrown – average

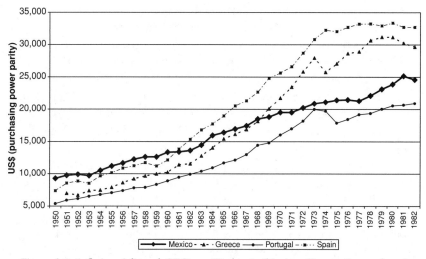

Figure 2.6: Inflation-Adjusted GDP per Worker in Mexico, Greece, Portugal, and Spain, 1950–1982. *Source:* Heston, Summers, and Aten (2002).

GDP per worker grew faster than in Mexico. In the 1950s, average output per worker in Portugal was 63 percent of that in Mexico. By the 1960s, the average productivity gap had shrunk to 74 percent, and by the 1970s Portugal's GDP per worker averaged 89 percent of that of Mexico's.

A balanced assessment of the evidence therefore suggests that Mexico's distortionary policies did promote rapid industrialization. As a result, productivity grew, raising living standards. For example, GDP per capita (in constant 1980 U.S. dollars) rose from $546 in 1950 to $908 in 1960, $1,574 in 1970, and to $2,904 in 1980.[75] Welfare gains of this magnitude were certainly not trivial accomplishments. They did not, however, constitute an economic miracle. When all was said and done, Mexico remained a rather poor country.

The Beginning of the End: Deficits, Inflation, Bank Expropriation, and the Debt Crisis

Mexico's established political and economic order had a fundamental weakness: It was based on a regime of low taxation but it inevitably

[75] Urquidi (2003), table 15.2.

required higher levels of government spending. To coax the private sector to invest, successive administrations had acceded to a situation in which capital was taxed at very low rates (or not at all). At the same time, however, industrialization and urbanization produced growing numbers of unionized manufacturing workers and public-sector employees who demanded social welfare programs. Moreover, rapid urbanization set in motion by policies designed to industrialize the country increased the need for physical infrastructure, such as subways, sewerage systems, water works, and roads. Finally, government credit policies designed to hasten industrialization also generated the need for continual subsidies for the many money-losing enterprises that the government came to own.

The lack of balance between the government's spending requirements and its taxation policies only became obvious over time. During the 1950s, the Mexican government had a balanced budget; in fact, the fiscal deficit was typically on the order of 0.1 percent of GDP. In the 1960s, however, it began to spend at a rate that outpaced growth in its revenues. It would have been prudent for the government either to increase tax rates or to improve the efficiency of tax collection (or both), but it chose not to adopt such measures as the taxation of corporate dividends. As a result, deficits began to escalate, averaging 1.9 percent of GDP across the decade. The situation worsened appreciably during the 1970s (the fiscal deficit averaged 6.6 percent of GDP), largely because President Luis Echeverría aggressively expanded the number of state-owned enterprises to maintain full employment and increased the funding of social welfare programs designed to maintain the loyalty of the industrial and public sector workers who were a core part of the governing coalition. By 1981, as a consequence of even more lavish government spending during the heady years of Mexico's oil boom, the deficit was a staggering 14 percent of GDP.[76]

Unwilling to bear the political costs of raising taxes or cutting expenditures, the government embraced three ad hoc tactics to finance its deficit. The first was to expand the money supply, which had the

---

[76] Economists generally consider government deficits in the range of 3–5 percent of GDP to be a serious problem. The resulting size of the budget deficit sharply contradicted López Portillo's expressed view that the most pressing economic problem facing Mexico after the 1979 spike in international oil prices was "the management of abundance." See Bazdresch and Levy (1991), p. 249.

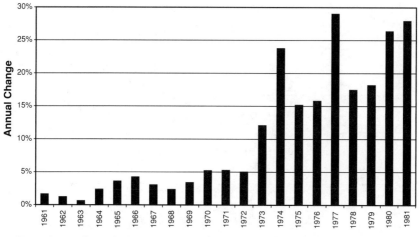

Figure 2.7: Inflation in Mexico, 1961–1981. *Source:* INEGI (2000), table 4.3.

predictable effect of raising the rate of inflation. As Figure 2.7 indicates, the average annual rate of inflation in Mexico accelerated from 2.7 percent in the 1960s to 16.8 percent during the 1970s. By 1981, the annual rate of increase in consumer prices reached 27.9 percent.

The government's second strategy to fund the growing deficit was to force private banks to lend it the deposits they held by having the Banco de México raise banks' reserve requirements. These reserves had to be held in government bonds paying below-market interest rates, producing a phenomenon known as "financial repression."[77] The consequences of this strategy are illustrated in Figure 2.8. Bank reserve ratios (the ratio of reserves to total assets) had trended downward throughout the 1950s and 1960s, with reserves representing 11 percent of assets in 1971. The following year they began to grow substantially, reaching 33 percent in 1975 and 43 percent in 1978. The ratio of reserves to assets then leveled off until the bank nationalization of 1982. Inasmuch as the Banco de México held a large proportion of private banks' deposits (in the form of their forced investment in government bonds), earning interest rates lower than those available on alternative investments, the banks responded by offering interest rates on deposits that were lower than the prevailing rate of inflation. As a result, depositors began to withdraw their money from the banking

[77] Izquierdo (1995), p. 95.

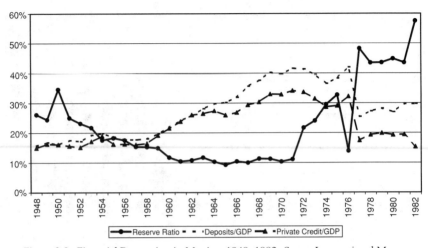

Figure 2.8: Financial Repression in Mexico, 1948–1982. *Source:* International Monetary Fund, *International Financial Statistics. Note:* See accompanying text for a definition of "financial repression."

system. Indeed, the ratio of bank deposits to GDP declined by more than 40 percent in the late 1970s.

The combination of falling deposits and increased lending to the government (through higher reserve requirements) had a predictable effect: The supply of bank credit for private purposes declined dramatically. Total private claims on the banking system (including development banks and private banks) had amounted to 34 percent of GDP in 1971. By 1977, however, that ratio had fallen by half (to only 17 percent), where it leveled off before falling again in 1982 when the government expropriated the private banks (see Figure 2.8). At this point, Mexico's level of financial development was low compared with either OECD countries or other Latin American countries.

The government's third strategy was to borrow money from abroad. Fortunately for the Mexican government, at the same time that its demand for foreign loans was increasing, the supply of capital in foreign banks was growing. The sharp rise in international oil prices that the Organization of Petroleum Exporting Countries (OPEC) induced after 1973 transferred financial resources from petroleum-importing nations to the oil-exporting countries of the Persian Gulf. These countries sought investment returns on their new-found wealth, and so they deposited a sizable proportion of their oil receipts in the European affiliates of U.S. banks. Major international banks, in turn,

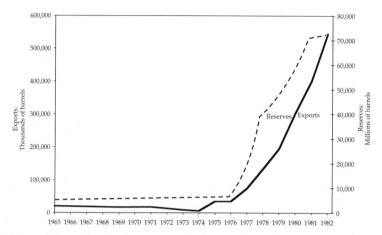

Figure 2.9: Mexican Oil Exports and Reserves, 1965–1982. *Source:* Exports: For 1959–1973, Meyer and Morales (1990), table 19; for 1974–1982, PEMEX, *Anuario estadístico, 1985*, p. 116. Reserves: Wright and Czelusta (2003), table 1.

needed to find profitable ways of investing these funds.[78] In short, U.S. banks had a large supply of available funds, and Mexico had a high demand for foreign bank loans.

From the perspective of international bankers, Mexico looked like a particularly good candidate for foreign loans. In the mid-1970s, Mexico's state-owned oil company, PEMEX, had discovered large oil and natural gas deposits in the states of Campeche, Chiapas, and Tabasco, and it needed investment capital to develop them. As Figure 2.9 shows, Mexican petroleum output skyrocketed. Foreign bankers assumed, therefore, that Mexico would easily be able to repay its loans from the future stream of oil revenues that those loans would help finance.[79]

From the Mexican government's point of view, foreign borrowing was an attractive option because U.S. private banks were prepared to make loans at interest rates not much higher than the prevailing rate of inflation. Indeed, the inflation-adjusted interest rate on U.S.-dollar denominated commercial bank loans to Latin American countries averaged only 0.3 percent during the 1974–1978 period, and it actually turned negative in 1979 as inflation in the United States rose.[80] As a result, the Mexican government borrowed massively, and the public

[78] Massad (1986), pp. 172–7; Thorp (1998), p. 207.

[79] Meyer and Morales (1990), p. 174.

[80] Morgan Guaranty Trust Company, *World Financial Markets*, various issues.

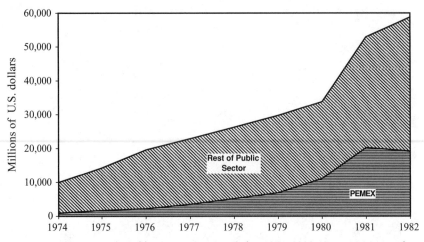

Figure 2.10: Mexico's Public-Sector Foreign Debt, 1974–1982. *Source:* Meyer and Morales (1990), table 39.

sector debt grew from roughly US$10 billion in 1974 to $30 billion in 1980, and to $60 billion in 1982 (see Figure 2.10). A substantial proportion of Mexico's borrowings was used to finance the expansion of the petroleum industry. Between 1974 and 1981, some 45 percent of Mexico's total foreign borrowing went to PEMEX, which used the money to construct and operate offshore drilling platforms, build onshore processing facilities, enlarge its refineries, engage in further exploration, and purchase capital goods and technical expertise from abroad.[81] The rest was used to cover the Mexican government's expanding budget deficit.

Neither foreign banks nor the Mexican government monitored very closely the amount that Mexico was borrowing. The formation of international banking syndicates and the introduction of variable interest rates in international commercial lending reduced the risks U.S. banks faced when making loans to Mexico (and other Latin American countries) in the 1970s. Syndication meant that the risk associated with foreign loans was spread among various banks, reducing the incentive for any particular bank to monitor precisely how the Mexican government and its agencies were using their credit. Variable interest rates protected lending banks from increases in the U.S. rate of inflation.[82] Remarkable as it sounds, even the Mexican government

[81] Meyer and Morales (1990), Chapter 7.
[82] Bulmer-Thomas (1994), p. 361.

did not monitor exactly how much was being borrowed or on what terms. There was neither centralized institutional control over foreign borrowing nor any easy way to gather the relevant information about the size of the country's growing debt. State-owned companies and government agencies borrowed with few restrictions and little knowledge of the overall condition of the country's finances.[83]

Both the Mexican government's borrowing strategy and foreign banks' lending strategy were vulnerable to changes in international oil prices, the volume of Mexico's petroleum reserves, and movements in interest rates. All of these factors, unfortunately, moved against Mexico. In 1981, international petroleum prices fell by 10 percent. Although this was only a minor drop in the context of the price run-up that had occurred between 1973 and 1981, the decline caused foreign investors to begin to doubt optimistic projections that Mexico's oil revenues – and, with them, the country's capacity to sustain its borrowing on international capital markets – would continue to rise indefinitely. At the same time, PEMEX stopped finding new petroleum reserves (see Figure 2.9), a development that led analysts to wonder whether, if oil prices fell further, Mexico would be able to earn the hard currency revenues required to repay its U.S. dollar-denominated loans. Finally, the U.S. Federal Reserve Board began to raise interest rates in an attempt to curb domestic inflation. Because Mexico's dollar-denominated commercial bank loans were made at variable interest rates, rising interest rates substantially increased the burden of its foreign debt.

Mexico entered a debt spiral. To meet rising interest payments on the country's long-term foreign debt, the government resorted to short-term borrowing. From 1980 to 1981, Mexico's short-term debt rose from US$1.5 billion to $10.8 billion.[84]

Throughout 1982 Mexico made a heroic attempt to avoid default on its foreign debt obligations but these efforts ultimately proved counterproductive. The first line of defense was the government's decision to devalue the peso on February 18, 1982, which cut the exchange rate from 27 pesos per U.S. dollar to 47 pesos per dollar. The government took this step to curtail the flight of dollars out of Mexico. Unfortunately, the devaluation also meant that Mexico's GDP, measured in U.S. dollars, dropped 42 percent on the day of the devaluation. The

---

[83] Thorp (1998), p. 207.
[84] Cárdenas (1996), pp. 113–14.

dollar value of its debts remained unchanged, however, so the debt burden effectively increased.

The government also sought more credit from commercial banks, which loaned an additional US$2.5 billion to Mexico between February and August 1982. When the banks refused to extend still more credit, the government imposed multiple exchange rates on August 5, 1982 to conserve its foreign-exchange reserves. Importers of "unnecessary" goods were forced to use an exchange rate twice as high as that for debt repayments. Government officials hoped that, in response, Mexicans would import less, thereby making more dollars available to the central bank.

When this policy proved insufficient, the government confiscated all U.S. dollar-denominated deposits in the banking system, converting them to pesos at an official exchange rate that was approximately one-third below the prevailing market rate. In addition, the government imposed capital controls to prevent people from taking their savings out of the country. The controls did not work very well because Mexico's long borders were simply too permeable.

Unable to gain effective control over its citizens' dollar reserves, the government announced on August 20, 1982 that it was unable to repay the roughly US$10 billion in short-term debt that would fall due a few days later.[85] Desperate to prevent the Mexican private sector from using the banking system to spirit dollars out of the country, President José López Portillo (1976–1982) expropriated the country's private banks on September 1, 1982.[86]

The debt default and the bank expropriation together sent the Mexican economy into a tailspin. By the end of 1982, real (inflation-adjusted) GDP began to fall, the rate of unemployment doubled from 4 percent to 8 percent, and gross new investment fell by 27.8 percent in inflation-adjusted terms.[87] The situation did not improve any in 1983. Real GDP per capita fell by 5.4 percent that year, and gross new investment declined by a further 30.6 percent.[88]

The Mexican economy limped along for the next several years, the government simultaneously trying to fight an inflation rate that sometimes exceeded 100 percent, growing unemployment, and the national private sector's fundamental lack of confidence in the PRI.

---

[85] Cárdenas (1996), pp. 114–15; Del Ángel-Mobarak (2005).

[86] Del Ángel-Mobarak, Bazdresch, and Suárez Dávila (2005).

[87] Cárdenas (1996), p. 116; Heston, Summers, and Aten (2002).

[88] Heston, Summers, and Aten (2002).

The government ultimately came up with a solution to these problems: open the country to foreign trade and investment. As we shall see in Chapters Three and Four, this solution produced only limited economic success. Moreover, as the discussion in Chapter Five shows, this solution ultimately undermined the very sources of support that had allowed the PRI to dominate electoral politics. The economic and political changes set in motion by the 1982 debt crisis were, then, momentous indeed.

3

The Causes and Consequences
of Free Trade

The Institutional Revolutionary Party (PRI) was fortunate that the presidential election held in July 1982 took place before the government announced a debt moratorium in August and nationalized private banks in September. For several decades the party had sought to legitimate its monopoly on power on the basis of Mexico's record of sustained economic growth and rising living standards for urban and industrial workers and other key constituencies. Those claims to legitimacy were, however, now difficult to sustain. The value of the peso had collapsed. In 1981 the peso–U.S. dollar exchange rate was 26:1; by 1983 it was 144:1, and by 1985 it was 372:1. Inflation skyrocketed. Investment contracted, with the ratio of gross fixed capital formation to gross domestic product (GDP) falling from 27 percent in 1980 to 18 percent in 1983 (see Figure 3.1). The wages of Mexican workers went into a free fall. Hourly wages in the manufacturing sector, adjusted for inflation, fell by 26 percent from 1981 to 1983 – and then kept falling. By 1986 they were only 51 percent of their 1981 level (see Figure 3.2).

The government needed to find ways of protecting the interests of its principal constituencies or the party risked losing its hold on power. The immediate challenge was to rekindle growth, which required that the government devise some means of inducing investment. The problem was that the expropriation of private banks had seriously undermined the alliance of convenience that had been forged between Mexico's political elite and its business class. José María Basagoiti, then the head of the Mexican Employers' Confederation (COPARMEX), summarized private-sector attitudes when he stated that after the bank nationalization, "Anything could happen in

66

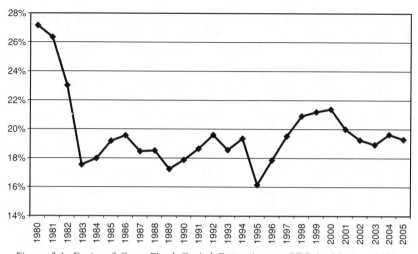

Figure 3.1: Ratio of Gross Fixed Capital Formation to GDP in Mexico, 1980–2005. *Source:* International Monetary Fund, International Financial Statistics Database (2006).

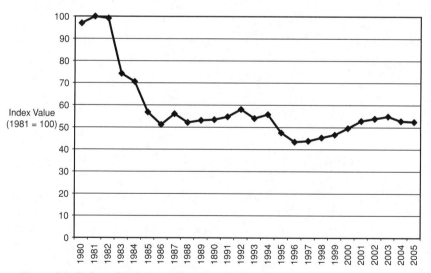

Figure 3.2: Index of Inflation-Adjusted Manufacturing Wages in Mexico, 1980–2005. *Source:* For 1980–2003, International Labor Office (1995, 1997, 2002, 2005); for 2004 and 2005, Banco de México (2005). Nominal values were deflated with the consumer price index available in International Monetary Fund, *International Financial Statistics* (2006).

Mexico."[1] The former head of the Confederation of National Chambers of Commerce (CONCANACO) went even further, arguing that businesspeople should stop supporting state interventionism, which had previously benefited them, because they could no longer constrain the state.[2] In a 1985 survey of 200 Mexican businessmen, 96 percent of respondents called the decision to expropriate the banks "extremely important" in terms of reducing their confidence in the government, and the remaining respondents called the decision "very important" in this regard.[3] Not surprisingly, then, many entrepreneurs began to switch their political loyalties from the PRI to the more conservative National Action Party (PAN), which had long championed private property interests.[4]

What inducements could the government offer to encourage either domestic or foreign investors to deploy their capital in a country where there was a palpable risk of expropriation? This was not an easy problem to solve. As we shall discuss in detail, PRI administrations struggled with it throughout the 1980s and 1990s – and they never fully resolved it. Indeed, in the view of important segments of the business community, a credible commitment by the government not to prey upon the private sector only emerged in 2000, when the National Action Party's Vicente Fox finally ousted the PRI from the presidency.

The Free-Trade Gamble

Circa 1983 there were two facts that gave the government some hope that it could regain the confidence of the private sector. The first was that Mexico shared a 2,000-mile border with the largest economy in the world. This meant not only that the country could access the U.S. market but also that it was geopolitically important to the United States. The second was that the peso, which had been devalued twice in 1982, was significantly undervalued. The shoddy products that the Mexican public had been forced to buy for years because of

---

[1] Hernández Rodríguez (1988), p. 260. See Valdés Ugalde (1994) for an assessment of national business organizations' different responses to the 1982 bank expropriation.

[2] Hernández Rodríguez (1988), p. 258.

[3] Maxfield (1989), pp. 227–9.

[4] Arriola (1988), p. 31; Maxfield (1989), p. 232; Camp (1989), pp. 136–8; Mizrahi (1995), pp. 83–5; Loaeza (1999), pp. 12, 17, 23; Bizberg (2003), pp. 164–5.

trade protectionism could not be sold abroad at any price but higher-quality goods would be competitive as a result of the undervalued peso. What was required, however, was a willingness on the part of national and foreign capitalists to invest in new plants that would make those products. No one would invest in export-oriented industries if the peso was in danger of becoming overvalued again, and entrepreneurs would not be likely to invest if the government continued to finance unprofitable state-owned firms by expanding the money supply and thereby raising the rate of inflation.

Although President Miguel de la Madrid Hurtado (1982–1988) initiated Mexico's shift toward more market-oriented economic policies, he began his term in office with constitutional reforms that reinforced the government's economic rectorship. Among other things, these reforms emphasized the importance of state-led economic planning and reserved "strategic" economic sectors (petroleum and basic petrochemicals, telecommunications, electrical power generation, nuclear energy, railroads, and banking) for exclusive public control.[5]

Yet de la Madrid soon adopted two other policies that the private sector found more appealing.[6] First, to signal a commitment to macroeconomic stability, his administration began to cut government budget deficits. The government accomplished this by imposing stringent controls on wage increases (which lagged severely behind the rate of inflation), reducing or eliminating many subsidies and price supports, and closing or privatizing hundreds of money-losing public enterprises. There were 1,155 state-owned firms, public trusts, and decentralized agencies at the beginning of the de la Madrid administration; there were just 412 by its end.[7]

Second, breaking sharply with protectionist policies dating back to the Porfiriato, the de la Madrid administration moved to liberalize trade. In 1983 the government reduced the number of manufactured products subject to import quotas from 100 percent to 83.6 percent, and by the end of 1985 less than half of all manufactured goods were still subject to import permits (see Figure 3.3). In 1986 Mexico acceded to the General Agreement on Tariffs and Trade (GATT), which committed it to even steeper reductions in trade protection.[8]

---

[5] Valdéz Ugalde (1994), pp. 223–4; Camacho Solís (2006), p. 194.

[6] See Middlebrook and Zepeda (2003), pp. 10–16, for a discussion of the political conditions that made possible Mexico's abrupt shift in economic policy.

[7] Valdés Ugalde (1994), p. 226.

[8] Cárdenas (1996), p. 137; Tornell and Esquivel (1995), p. 5.

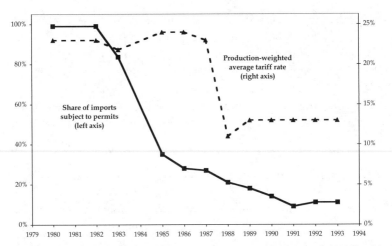

Figure 3.3: Trade Protection in Mexico, 1979–1994. *Source:* Tornell (1995), table 1: Cárdenas (1996).

This step was especially significant because de la Madrid's predecessor, President José López Portillo (1976–1982), had considered and then rejected GATT membership in 1980.

The de la Madrid administration was gambling. If the plan to open the economy to foreign trade proved successful, the country would build new, export-oriented industries faster than its old, highly protected industries collapsed. If the plan failed, however, and the old industries collapsed faster than the new ones grew, then the PRI would have a lot of unemployed and politically disaffected industrial workers to contend with in the 1988 presidential election.

The gamble that the de la Madrid administration took on trade liberalization was highly unusual. Most countries faced with a massive balance-of-payments crisis try to conserve foreign-exchange reserves by raising trade barriers to reduce imports as much as possible. For example, when Brazil encountered balance-of-payments difficulties in 1980, the Brazilian government established a "negative list" of products whose importation was banned. It expanded the negative list in 1982 and created an import-control program, under which companies had to have all imports approved by the Department of Foreign Trade. The Brazilian government did not begin to liberalize trade until 1990 – 10 years after the balance-of-payments crisis. Moreover, when it did finally liberalize trade, it did so in a gradual manner, reducing tariffs slowly and retaining a panoply of nontariff trade barriers, including differential excise taxes and restrictive product regulations.[9]

Other Latin American victims of the 1982 debt crisis reacted similarly to Brazil. Argentina and Peru enacted trade restrictions and retained them until 1989 and 1990, respectively. Even the government of General Augusto Pinochet in Chile, which had embraced free-trade policies in the 1970s, raised trade barriers when confronted by the 1982 debt crisis. It hiked the uniform tariff from 10 percent to 20 percent in 1983, and then to 35 percent in 1984. Only after the balance-of-trade crisis had passed did the government gradually reduce tariffs back to their 1982 level.[10]

The gamble that the de la Madrid administration took on trade liberalization did not pay off. As proponents of free trade imagined, some industries died whereas others grew. Cigarette, textile, footwear, and electrical machinery manufacturers all went into decline, whereas the production of motor vehicles, engines and automobile parts, glass, cement, and chemicals expanded.[11] Opening more markets to foreign trade did not, however, produce the boom in investment, trade, and economic growth for which the government had hoped. To begin with, the opening of the economy had only a modest effect on exports. The massive peso devaluations of 1982 and 1983 did make Mexican exports more competitive in international markets, pushing up the ratio of exports to GDP from 10 percent in 1981 to 19 percent in 1983. Yet de la Madrid's subsequent trade reforms, including Mexico's accession to the GATT in 1986, do not appear to have had a further incremental effect. By 1988, when he left office, the ratio of exports to GDP had not advanced appreciably beyond its 1983 level (see Figure 3.4).

The fundamental shortcoming of de la Madrid's gamble on trade liberalization and macroeconomic stabilization was that it did not address domestic and international investors' lack of confidence in the PRI. De la Madrid's decision to join the GATT was not a guarantee that future presidential administrations would not overvalue the exchange rate, revert to protectionism, or confiscate assets to fund government deficits. Thus, the hoped-for boom in investment did not materialize. As Figure 3.1 shows, the ratio of gross fixed capital

[9] Averbug (1999), p. 11.
[10] Bergoeing et al. (2001), p. 10.
[11] Tornell and Esquivel (1995), figure 8.

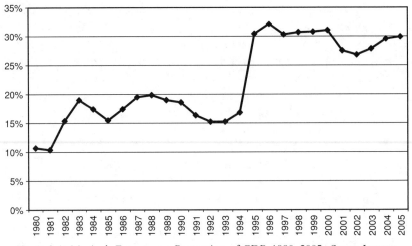

Figure 3.4: Mexico's Exports as a Proportion of GDP, 1980–2005. *Source:* International Monetary Fund, *International Financial Statistics* (2006).

formation to GDP barely budged between 1983 and 1988. At the end of de la Madrid's term, the investment ratio was only 19 percent, compared with 27 percent in 1980. Inflation-adjusted GDP per capita continued its downward slide, falling until 1988, when it was 13 percent below its 1981 level (see Figure 3.5).

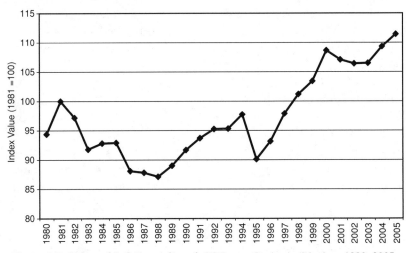

Figure 3.5: Index of Inflation-Adjusted GDP per Capita in Mexico, 1980–2005. *Source:* International Monetary Fund, *International Financial Statistics* (2006).

The continued decline in real (inflation-adjusted) wages and the overall deterioration of economic conditions meant that the PRI faced an increasingly discontented electorate. The de la Madrid administration was compelled, for example, to recognize several opposition party victories (mainly by the National Action Party) in municipal elections in 1983. In 1987, as the debate about national economic strategy intensified, the PRI suffered one of the most significant schisms in its history, leading to the formation the center-left National Democratic Front (FDN) that backed Cuauhtémoc Cárdenas as a candidate in the 1988 presidential election. Some analysts believe that Cárdenas actually won the election, but the government's firm control over the electoral process allowed the PRI's candidate, Carlos Salinas de Gortari, to prevail in the official vote tally – albeit by a narrow margin in an election that was widely regarded as fraudulent.

The economic and political reality of Mexico in the late 1980s – economic stagnation and widespread discontent with the PRI – compelled the Salinas de Gortari administration (1988–1994) to go beyond the steps that de la Madrid had taken to reignite growth and restore confidence in the government. One of his first actions was to renegotiate Mexico's foreign debt. Unless debt payments could be reduced, investors would be reluctant to deploy their capital because the government would still have an incentive to default on its debts or confiscate private assets to cover debt payments.[12] The Salinas administration therefore undertook protracted negotiations with the United States, which resulted in a 1990 agreement converting Mexico's commercial bank debt into "Brady bonds" (named after U.S. Treasury Secretary Nicholas Brady). The U.S. government guaranteed the interest on the bonds, whose US$5.4 billion in collateral was financed by new borrowing from the World Bank, the International Monetary Fund, and the Export-Import Bank of Japan. Under the terms of the agreement, Mexico's total foreign debt increased in nominal value, but annual debt payments declined to a much more manageable level.[13]

Salinas's second major initiative was to liberalize restrictions on foreign investment. Legislation adopted in 1989 allowed the National Foreign Investment Commission (CNIE) to waive any foreign direct investment (FDI) restrictions that it considered contrary to the "public

---

[12] In 1986 approximately 70 percent of federal government expenditures had been devoted to servicing Mexico's foreign debt; Salinas de Gortari (2002), pp. 937–8.

[13] Orme (1996), pp. 30–1.

interest." The reforms authorized the CNIE to permit foreigners to own up to 100 percent of manufacturing businesses located outside Mexico's major cities, as well as to purchase shares (albeit without voting rights) in Mexican firms.[14] In 1991, the Salinas administration removed most of these remaining limitations on foreign investment, except in the energy and banking sectors.[15]

The third step in Salinas's campaign to attract more foreign investment was to accelerate the privatization of state-owned enterprises. Under Salinas, the government auctioned the banks that it had expropriated in 1982, as well as state-owned steel plants, airlines, and the telephone monopoly.[16] These sales generated approximately US$23 billion in revenues. By using these funds to pay down the domestic public debt, the government substantially reduced its interest payments and was able to achieve a federal budget surplus by 1992.[17]

Nevertheless, not even these steps attracted the hoped-for wave of investment. The ratio of gross fixed capital formation to GDP was exactly the same in 1993 as it had been in 1988: 19 percent (see Figure 3.1). Foreign investors, in particular, remained gun-shy of Mexico. As Figure 3.6 demonstrates, the flow of FDI into the country grew compared to the early 1980s, but given that the level in the early 1980s was close to zero, this was not much of an accomplishment. In point of fact, the average annual amount of FDI entering Mexico during the first 3 years of the Salinas administration was not significantly higher than the level attained during the last 3 years of the de la Madrid administration. In the minds of potential foreign investors, Mexico was still tarred by its history of property seizures, "Mexicanization" laws that transferred foreign assets to Mexican owners, and protectionism.[18]

In an even bolder effort to repair the credibility of the Mexican government, Salinas proposed a free-trade agreement with the United States. Because a treaty with the United States would be economically and politically costly for the Mexican government to revoke, Mexican businessmen could be assured that their investments in export-oriented industries would not suffer from a reversion to protectionism. Furthermore, the North American Free Trade Agreement (NAFTA)

---

[14] Clarkson (2002), p. 237.
[15] Pill (2002), p. 2; Salinas de Gortari (2002), pp. 416–19.
[16] Pastor and Wise (2002), p. 183.
[17] Pill (2002), pp. 12–13.
[18] Orme (1996), p. 32.

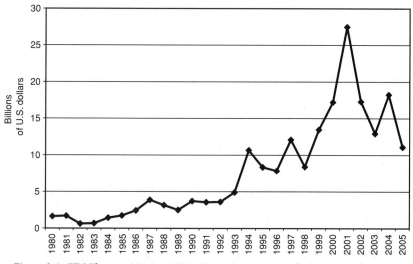

Figure 3.6: FDI Flows to Mexico, 1980–2005. *Source:* Secretaría de Economía (www. inegi.gob.mx).

went beyond tariff issues to ensure the protection of foreign investment – a move that would bolster the confidence of foreign investors that the Mexican government would not undermine their property rights.

The notion that the NAFTA was not principally about trade may sound odd, until one recalls that Mexico had already reduced tariffs and quotas in the 1980s and early 1990s. In 1993, the year before the NAFTA took effect, only 11 percent of imports were still covered by the permit system, and Mexico's average tariff was only 13 percent (see Figure 3.3). With the exception of steel, textiles, and a few minor agricultural products, U.S. tariffs on the goods Mexico produced were, on average, even lower – only 3.5 percent ad valorem before the NAFTA. The small impact that additional trade liberalization under the NAFTA would have on the Mexican economy was known to both the Mexican and the U.S. governments at the time that they were negotiating the treaty. Studies estimating the impact of lowering U.S. tariffs from 4 percent to zero, and lowering Mexican tariffs from 20 percent to zero, all concluded that there would be only very small, one-time gains (on the order of 3 percent of Mexico's GDP) from the NAFTA's trade liberalization provisions.[19]

[19] Tornell, Westermann, and Martínez (2004).

What the NAFTA did do, however, was to establish mechanisms protecting the property rights of foreign investors. As part of the NAFTA, Mexico agreed to give U.S. and Canadian companies the same treatment offered to Mexican firms. Mexico could no longer require U.S.-owned manufacturing plants to purchase a share of production inputs from Mexican sources or to export a greater value of goods than they imported,[20] and Mexico could no longer prevent Canadian and U.S. firms from repatriating profits. Finally, Mexico committed itself not to expropriate foreign firms. Article 1110(1) of the treaty is quite explicit on this point:

> No Party may directly or indirectly nationalize or expropriate an investment of another Party ... or take a measure tantamount to nationalization or expropriation ... except: (a) for a public purpose; (b) on a nondiscriminatory basis; (c) in accordance with due process of law ... and (d) in payment of compensation.

Article 1139 extended this guarantee against expropriation to all "property, tangible or intangible, acquired in the expectation or used for the purpose of economic benefit or other business purpose."[21]

The NAFTA also created international institutions with the authority to sanction any signatory government that violates its terms. Investors who believe that the Canadian, Mexican, or U.S. government has violated the terms of the NAFTA may demand compensation and have their case judged by a NAFTA tribunal. The actions of state and local governments are specifically covered by the agreement, although it is the federal government of each signatory country that is responsible for paying compensation. In addition, private parties can go before a NAFTA tribunal to appeal judicial decisions should national courts make rulings that they consider to be against national or international law. The decisions of NAFTA tribunals can be appealed to national courts but only in the country where the case is brought. This means that Mexico cannot use its court system to overturn summarily the decisions of a NAFTA tribunal. If it did so, thereby violating the provisions of the NAFTA, the other signatory governments could impose trade sanctions.[22]

By accepting such stringent protections of foreign investors' property rights, the Salinas administration sought to stimulate significantly

---

[20] Orme (1996), p. 130.
[21] Condon and Sinha (2003), p. 129.
[22] Condon and Sinha (2003), pp. 127–8.

increased flows of foreign capital to Mexico. The assumption was that foreign-financed enterprises would raise Mexican productivity both directly (by creating more efficient enterprises) and indirectly (by forcing Mexican companies to compete with them). Both U.S. and Mexican policy makers expected a massive inflow of FDI that would cause the Mexican economy to grow at quite rapid rates.

The Economic Effects of the NAFTA

In the short run, the NAFTA[23] did generate an increased flow of FDI to Mexico. In fact, foreign investment in Mexico leaped in the very quarter that the U.S. Congress ratified the agreement, and during the first year after it went into effect (1994) FDI flows, particularly from the United States, more than doubled (see Figure 3.6). The agreement's longer-term effects on investment patterns have, however, been rather modest. Much to the surprise of both Mexican and U.S. policy makers, FDI flows to Mexico grew until 2001 and then began trending downward – to the point that the amount of new FDI in 2005 was no higher than it had been in 1994 (see Figure 3.6).

The upshot is that FDI accounts for only a fraction of total new investment in Mexico. The exact ratio of FDI to new investment varies depending on how one chooses to measure the two components but all measures produce broadly similar qualitative results. In Figure 3.7 we calculate the ratio of FDI (as measured by the Mexican government) to gross fixed capital formation (as reported by the Mexican government to the International Monetary Fund). We note that this measurement method tends to overestimate the relative importance of FDI because gross fixed capital formation includes only investments in new plant, equipment, and structures, whereas the FDI flows reported by the Mexican government cover all investments (including the purchase of preexisting plant and equipment, as well as investments in nonphysical

---

[23] Although this discussion focuses only on the NAFTA's economic impact on Mexico, the agreement also marked a significant departure in Mexican foreign policy. Mexico subsequently negotiated bilateral trade and investment agreements with a broad range of countries as part of its efforts to open markets for its exports and attract productive investment. See Vega and de la Mora (2003), pp. 170–1, 183–8. The NAFTA also had broad importance for the conduct of Mexico–United States relations (see Domínguez and Fernández de Castro 2001), although it certainly did not eliminate bilateral tensions over such topics as migration, drug trafficking, border security, or even trade issues.

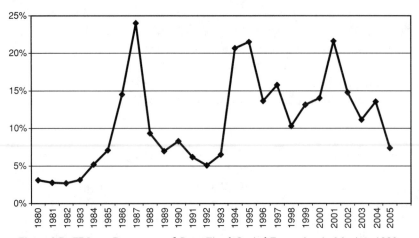

Figure 3.7: FDI as a Percentage of Gross Fixed Capital Formation in Mexico, 1980–2005. *Source:* Data on FDI are from the Secretaría de Economía (www.inegi.gob.mx); data on gross fixed capital formation are from the International Monetary Fund, *International Financial Statistics* (2006).

capital, such as firms that provide financial services).[24] Even with the upward bias that these category definitions create in our estimates, the data indicate that, on average, FDI accounted for only 15 percent of total new investment in Mexico between 1994 and 2005. The data also show the same tendency as our measure of FDI in absolute amounts (Figure 3.6): The trend from 2001 to 2005 was strongly downward. In fact, FDI as a proportion of gross fixed capital formation in 2005 was lower than in any year since the signing of the NAFTA.

Because the rate of new investment has been low, the Mexican economy has grown much more slowly than the government (and the public) expected at the time that the NAFTA was signed. Between 1994 and 2005, Mexico's inflation-adjusted GDP per capita grew at an average rate of only 1.3 percent per year. Any statement about 1.3 percent per year being "fast" or "slow" implies a counterfactual (that is, a comparison) to a hypothetical Mexico that could have grown at a different rate. By definition, this "counterfactual Mexico" does not exist. We must therefore draw a set of comparisons, explain why those

---

[24] The United Nations Commission on Trade and Development (UNCTAD) compiles a series on FDI as a percentage of gross fixed capital formation that excludes nonfixed investments. That series, published in the *World Investment Report*, shows slightly lower ratios than the ones we produce here. The drawback to that series is that it only covers the years from 1991 to 2004.

comparisons represent the potential rate of growth of the Mexican economy, and then measure Mexico's actual growth against those comparisons.

One simple counterfactual is to compare Mexico after the NAFTA with Mexico during the period before the NAFTA but after it joined the GATT. In this comparison, we assume that Mexico would have continued to grow at the same rate after 1994 as it grew between 1986 and 1993. This exercise, however, finds no difference between the post-GATT (1986–1993) and post-NAFTA (1994–2005) growth rates. Between 1986 and 1993 Mexico grew at an average of 1.3 percent per year – the same rate as from 1994 to 2005. The implication is that the NAFTA had no discernible marginal effect on Mexican growth rates.

A second easy comparison is to Mexico's rate of growth before the 1982 debt crisis, the period between 1950 and 1980. One reason to pose this counterfactual is that Mexican public officials suggested that Mexico could achieve growth rates of this magnitude once the NAFTA went into effect. By this standard, Mexico's post-NAFTA performance looks quite anemic: Real GDP per capita grew by an average of 2.8 percent per year from 1950 to 1980 – more than twice its post-NAFTA rate.

A third, somewhat more complicated, counterfactual is to imagine a Mexico that grew fast enough to create jobs for all new entrants into the labor force. Specifying this comparison requires the estimation of an econometric model that measures how job creation responds to the growth rate of GDP. We do not estimate such a model here. Nevertheless, one way to get a rough approximation of how fast the Mexican economy would need to grow to accommodate all new labor force entrants is to calculate the ratio of new jobs created in Mexico to actual GDP growth and then use that ratio to estimate the rate of GDP growth necessary to create jobs for all new labor force entrants – that is, those who find jobs in Mexico and those who emigrate instead to the United States. The Mexican labor force grows by approximately 1 million workers per year. In Figure 3.8 we use the U.S. census to estimate average annual net Mexican migration to the United States during the 1990s: 514,000 workers per year. These findings suggest that the Mexican economy generates roughly half the number of jobs required to accommodate new labor force entrants and that Mexico under the NAFTA has grown at approximately half the rate necessary to absorb all new entrants into the labor force. We note that this

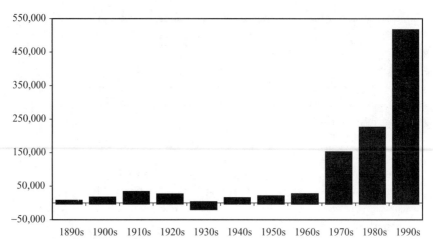

Figure 3.8: Estimated Annual Net Migration from Mexico to the United States, 1890s to 1990s. *Source:* Authors' calculations based on data in United States Bureau of the Census (2000).

counterfactual and the historical 1950–1980 counterfactual produce results that are broadly consistent with one another. We also note that Figure 3.8 explains why they produce similar results: When the Mexican economy was growing at an average of 2.8 percent per year, Mexicans emigrating (permanently) to the United States did so in trivial numbers.

A fourth comparison is Mexico's post–NAFTA growth rate relative to that of the United States. In this counterfactual, full mobility of capital should have produced a Mexico that grew at least as fast as its NAFTA partner. Here again, Mexico's actual growth rate was dramatically different from the counterfactual: U.S. per capita GDP grew by an average of 2.3 percent per year from 1994 to 2005, 77 percent faster than in Mexico.

A final counterfactual is to compare Mexico's growth rate with that of other middle-income developing countries that liberalized their economies during the 1980s and 1990s. If the NAFTA conferred a large advantage on Mexico, above and beyond that obtained from joining the GATT, then we should observe that Mexico's economy outgrew others that were similar to it in 1994 but which did not have the benefit of a NAFTA-like agreement with the United States. The results of this exercise suggest that post–NAFTA Mexico

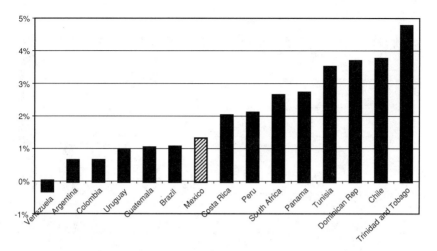

Figure 3.9: Compound Annual Growth Rates of Inflation-Adjusted GDP per Capita in Selected Middle-Income Liberalizing Economies, 1994–2005. *Source:* Wacziarg and Welch (2003), table 1; International Monetary Fund, *International Financial Statistics* (2006).

underperformed other middle-income liberalizing economies (see Figure 3.9).[25] The average annual rate of GDP per capita growth of the fourteen other middle-income liberalizers was 2.1 percent over the 1994–2005 period, compared with 1.3 percent in Mexico. In fact, as Figure 3.9 shows, eight of the fourteen other liberalizing economies grew very fast compared with Mexico (with average growth rates ranging from 2.0 to 4.7 percent per year), whereas the countries with lower average annual growth rates tended to cluster at or near Mexico's growth rate. Of the fourteen countries, only three grew significantly more slowly than Mexico: Venezuela, Argentina, and Colombia.

None of this is to argue that Mexico should not have opened up to foreign trade and investment. If our standard of assessment is the Mexican economy from the onset of the debt crisis in 1982 until the time

[25] Starting with a set of liberalized economies from a dataset developed by Wacziarg and Welch (2003), we restrict the comparison to those economies that were roughly similar to Mexico, which we define as those countries whose U.S. dollar-denominated GDP per capita was no higher or lower than 50 percent of Mexico's in 1994. (The countries are Argentina, Brazil, Chile, Colombia, Costa Rica, the Dominican Republic, Guatemala, Panama, Peru, South Africa, Trinidad and Tobago, Tunisia, Uruguay, and Venezuela.) We then compute growth rates in inflation-adjusted domestic currency units, noting that we obtain similar qualitative results when we do the estimations in purchasing power parity-adjusted U.S. dollars.

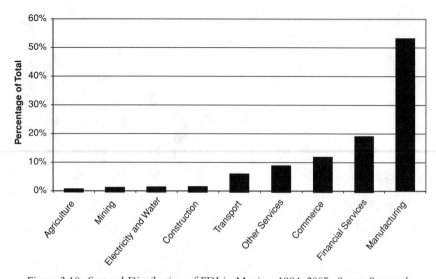

Figure 3.10: Sectoral Distribution of FDI in Mexico, 1994–2005. *Source:* Secretaría de Economía (www.inegi.gob.mx).

that Mexico joined the GATT in 1986, there is no doubt that economic liberalization was positive for the country: Inflation-adjusted GDP per capita *shrank* by an average of 2.3 percent *per year* between 1982 and 1986. There is, then, every reason to think that Mexico would be substantially poorer today had it not liberalized its trade policies in the 1980s and its foreign investment policies in the 1990s. That said, neither joining the GATT nor signing the NAFTA were panaceas for Mexico's diverse economic ills.

The NAFTA and Mexico's Manufacturing Sector

Although the NAFTA has had only a modest effect on Mexico's overall economic performance, it has had a significant impact in some specific sectors. The evidence strongly indicates, for example, that closer integration with the U.S. and Canadian economies has had a positive effect on Mexico's manufacturing sector. Some sense of the NAFTA's disproportionate impact on manufacturing can be gleaned from Figure 3.10, which shows that between 1994 and 2005 the manufacturing sector accounted for 53 percent of all FDI flowing into Mexico. Construction, electrical power generation, and mining accounted for only 1 percent each, whereas foreign investment in agriculture was virtually zero. FDI in transportation, other services (mostly the

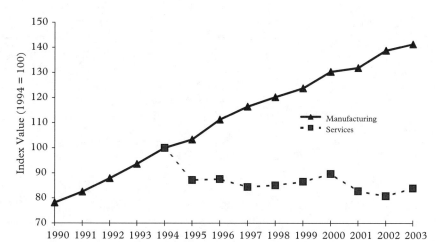

Figure 3.11: Productivity in Mexico in Manufacturing and Services, 1990–2003. *Source:* Banco de México (2005).

tourism industry), and commerce was also low: 6, 8, and 11 percent, respectively. The balance of FDI flows during the 1994–2005 period (19 percent) represented the purchase of Mexico's banks by foreign banks.[26]

As one would expect, FDI in manufacturing has contributed to rapidly rising productivity. As Figure 3.11 indicates, manufacturing productivity increased by 41 percent between 1994 and 2003. During the same period, productivity in the service sector – which employs the largest proportion of the labor force, but which has received little FDI – actually fell. Aggregate productivity growth in the sector was on average just 1 percent per year between 1994 and 2003.

Rising productivity has fostered wage growth in the manufacturing sector. Figure 3.2 tracks annual changes in real (inflation-adjusted) manufacturing wages from 1980 to 2005. The data indicate that real manufacturing wages fell by 49 percent between 1981 and 1986. Wages began to recover thereafter but they fell back again as a result of the 1994–1995 financial crisis. As a consequence, inflation-adjusted manufacturing wages in 1996 were only 43 percent of their 1981 level. From that point onward, the expansion of export manufacturing produced a 20-percent increase in real wages by 2005. This growth was considerable but it was not enough to reverse more than a decade

[26] Secretaría de Economía (www.inegi.gob.mx).

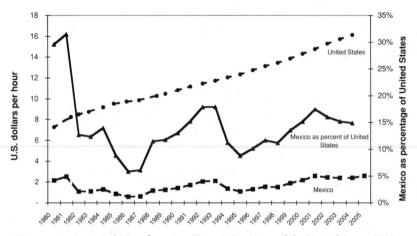

Figure 3.12: Nominal Manufacturing Wages in Mexico and the United States, 1980–2005. *Source:* For 1980–2003, International Labor Office (1995, 1997, 2002, 2005); for 2004–2005, Banco de México (2005).

of wage erosion before the NAFTA. Thus, manufacturing wages in 2005 were still only 53 percent of their 1981 level.

One consequence of the long-term erosion of real wages in Mexico has been a growing gap between the compensation received by Mexican and U.S. workers. As a first-order estimate of this phenomenon, Figure 3.12 presents data on hourly wage rates (in current U.S. dollars) in manufacturing in both countries and on the ratio of Mexican to U.S. wages. In dollar terms, wages in Mexico's manufacturing sector collapsed during the 1980s, falling from $2.52 per hour in 1981 to 57 cents per hour in 1986. By 1993 they had regained virtually all of the lost ground, but in 1995 they again fell sharply as a result of the country's financial crisis. Dollar-denominated wages in Mexican manufacturing industries slowly recovered after 1995, so that by 2005 they were back at their 1981 level. Over the 1980–2005 period, however, nominal U.S. manufacturing wages grew at a steady pace. Over time, therefore, the gap between compensation levels in the United States and Mexico increased. In 1981, dollar-denominated manufacturing wages in Mexico were 30 percent of U.S. manufacturing wages; in 2005, Mexican wages were only 15 percent of U.S. wages. This gap has been an important stimulus both for labor-intensive U.S. manufacturing industries to relocate to Mexico and for Mexican workers to migrate to the United States in search of more highly paid employment.

The NAFTA and Mexican Agriculture

The NAFTA's effects on Mexican agriculture, a sector that employs one-fifth of the country's working population,[27] have been decidedly more mixed. There are three groups that have clearly benefited from reductions in tariffs and quotas on agricultural products: fruit and vegetable farmers in Mexico's Northwest, livestock producers, and urban consumers. Now that fruit and vegetable growers can export their produce to the United States, farmers in the northwestern state of Sinaloa have been able to earn higher incomes because their proximity to markets in California and Arizona means that transportation costs do not drive a large wedge between the prices paid by consumers and the prices received at the farm gate. Livestock producers and urban consumers have gained because grain imports under the NAFTA have induced a decline in the price of yellow corn, which is fed to cattle and hogs.

The gains to urban consumers have, however, imposed substantial costs on Mexico's corn farmers, who must now compete with more efficient (and subsidized) U.S. producers. The affected population is large, comprising some 35–40 percent of the rural workforce and approximately 10 percent of the employed population nationwide.[28] Despite low rural wages, Mexican corn farmers pay input costs approximately one-third higher than those faced by their U.S. competitors. Some sense of why lower wages in Mexico do not translate into lower agricultural production costs can be discerned from the following facts: Most corn-producing plots in Mexico are less than 12 acres, only 9 percent of farmers have access to irrigation, and only 35 percent of Mexican farmers use tractors.[29] Moreover, Mexico's corn farmers face high transportation costs, which produce a substantial difference between the price that farmers receive and the price that urban consumers pay. For example, it costs three times more to ship corn to Mexico City from Sinaloa by land than to ship it from New Orleans via the port of Veracruz.[30] These factors, in conjunction with a Mexican government decision to accelerate corn purchases from the United States well in excess of the quotas that had been agreed in the NAFTA, explain why U.S. corn exports to Mexico almost tripled between 1994

[27] De Grammont (2003), table 10.10.
[28] INEGI (2001b); de Grammont (2003), p. 356.
[29] Zahniser and Coyle (2004), p. 5.
[30] *The Economist*, 28 November 2002.

and 2003. They are likely to grow even more once the last remaining restrictions on corn imports are removed (as mandated by the NAFTA) in 2009.[31]

During the 1990s, the Mexican government implemented several measures designed to improve the competitiveness of Mexico's peasant farmers. To increase the incentives for private investment in agriculture, in 1992 the Salinas administration amended Article 27 of the Constitution to permit, with the agreement of the local community, the sale, sharecropping, or rental of communally held (*ejido*) lands. The implementing legislation for this reform, the Program for the Certification of Ejidal Rights and the Titling of Urban Plots (PROCEDE), delineated and certified ejido properties, thus facilitating the creation of ejido land markets and expanding rural producers' potential access to credit by allowing them to use the right to cultivate their land as collateral.[32] In addition, the government moved to support small farmers through the Direct-Support Program for the Farm Sector (PROCAMPO). As of 2004–2005, PROCAMPO paid farmers with plots smaller than 12 acres US$41 per acre, whereas all other farmers received $34 per acre.[33]

These initiatives have not, however, achieved their main goals. Relatively few ejido members have titled their lands, and most land transactions remain informal and unregistered – perhaps in part because lands titled under PROCEDE are subject to property taxes. Banks and other private creditors have been very reluctant to extend financing to ejido farmers with PROCEDE titles because the law does not allow such land to be seized in the event of nonpayment; only the right to till the land can be legally embargoed by creditors.[34] As a result, agricultural productivity has not improved.

The economic pressures on small farmers, coupled with the growing manufacturing wage gap between Mexico and the United States, have produced a dramatic increase in migration to the United States since the 1990s.[35] Mexican workers have, of course, been migrating to the United States since at least the 1890s, and between 1942 and

---

[31] De Grammont (2003), p. 357; Zahniser and Coyle (2004), p. 3.

[32] Giugale, Lafourcade, and Nguyen (2001), p. 332.

[33] Zahniser and Coyle (2004), p. 7.

[34] Mackinlay and de la Fuente (1996), pp. 105–10; Giugale, Lafourcade, and Nguyen (2001), p. 333.

[35] See de Grammont (2003), pp. 369, 377 for a discussion of the economic and social conditions in rural areas that stimulate out-migration.

1964 the Bracero Program legally authorized Mexican farm workers to work temporarily in the United States. Until the 1970s, however, the number of new emigrants was balanced by an almost equal number of migrant workers returning to Mexico. Indeed, the data portrayed in Figure 3.8 (which uses changes in the total Mexican-born population between U.S. censuses to estimate net Mexican migration to the United States) indicate that this total was on the order of 25,000 persons per year from the 1890s through the 1960s. The data then indicate a fivefold increase in net immigration in the 1970s, which became nearly a tenfold increase during the prolonged economic crisis of the 1980s. Mexico's policy of trade liberalization did not reverse this flow; rather, trade liberalization was accompanied by a rapid acceleration of net migration to the United States. Our estimates for the 1990s place the flow at more than 500,000 persons per year.[36] More detailed estimates made by Mexican demographers suggest that a significant proportion of Mexico's rate of natural population increase (0.3 percentage points) was lost to emigration, reducing the annual population growth rate from 1.7 percent to 1.4 percent.[37] As a result, the Mexican-born population of the United States has risen precipitously – from 4.3 million people in 1990 to 9 million in the year 2000, and to 10.6 million in 2004.[38]

Explaining the NAFTA's Limited Impact on Growth in Mexico

Why has FDI clustered in Mexico's manufacturing sector, and why has foreign investment in manufacturing not served as a more powerful engine of growth for the rest of the economy? There are myriad issues here but three considerations are paramount. First, Mexico changed its policies regarding foreign trade and investment but it did not fully liberalize its economy. Incomplete liberalization raises the cost of doing

---

[36] Beginning in the early 1990s, the U.S. government devoted substantially more resources to enforcing border controls and deterring illegal immigration, a policy that encouraged a higher proportion of undocumented immigrants to remain permanently in the United States.

[37] Consejo Nacional de Población (2001b), Chapter 2, p. 12.

[38] U.S. Bureau of the Census (2003), table 42, p. 43; Verduzco (2003), p. 25; Schmidley and Robinson (2003), table A2; Deardorff and Blumerman (2001), table 2; Passel (2005), p. 37.

business in Mexico. Second, the tax system that evolved under decades of authoritarian rule largely remains in place. The result is a serious shortfall of public investment in such areas as education and infrastructure, which in turn has meant that Mexico has had to compete against other developing economies solely on the basis of low wages and geographic proximity to the United States. It is impossible for other countries to duplicate Mexico's geographic proximity to the world's largest consumer market; however, they can more than compete with Mexico on the basis of low wages. Third, there is a serious shortfall in access to credit in Mexico. This constrains the growth of those nontradable economic sectors (producing goods that cannot be exported or imported) providing inputs for Mexico's tradable-goods (export) activities, which in turn raises the cost of doing business in the tradable-goods sector.

Investment Opening without Liberalization

The NAFTA offered foreign investors much stronger bases on which to defend their property rights in Mexico but the agreement did not remove all restrictions on investment. Several key economic sectors either remain largely closed to private investment or were privatized in such a way as to create lucrative, domestically owned monopolies. One notable example of these remaining restrictions on private investment is the electrical power industry. In principle, Chapter Six of the NAFTA allows private companies to build power generation plants for industrial consumers and to sell excess electrical power to the Federal Electricity Commission (CFE), which holds a monopoly on distribution.[39] In reality, however, regulatory constraints (such as a Mexican law that prohibits long-term sales contracts to the CFE) mean that only 3.3 percent of Mexico's electricity is privately generated.[40] Domestic demand for electricity has been expanding rapidly, and consumption would probably grow even faster if not for the fact that limited generation capacity means very high (and rising) electricity prices for

---

[39] Clarkson (2002), p. 239. In 1997 the administration of President Ernesto Zedillo Ponce de León (1994–2000) established the Long-Term Productive Infrastructure Program (PIDI-REGAS) as a way of channeling private investment to the energy sector. In the electrical power industry, the program allows private investors to build generating facilities that then sell their power to the CFE at fixed prices. After 30 years, the facilities are then turned over to the federal government. See World Bank (2005), p. 9.

[40] Tornell, Westermann, and Martínez (2004).

industrial producers and for individual consumers outside the Mexico City area.[41]

Petroleum exploration and production also remain almost entirely closed to private investment. Because of the historical political sensitivity of foreign involvement in the petroleum industry and continued strong public support for state ownership, private investors are forbidden from participating in either drilling for, or the basic refining of, oil and natural gas. Despite growing domestic demand for energy, overall petroleum production has stagnated because the state-owned Mexican Petroleum Company (PEMEX) has lacked sufficient capital to expand exploration and modernize its production facilities. Indeed, Mexico has become a net importer of gasoline and some other petroleum products. The administration of President Ernesto Zedillo Ponce de León (1994–2000) tried to attract private capital into "secondary petrochemicals," but the 1999 auction of petrochemical plants attracted no bidders.[42]

Although Mexico's telecommunications industry was privatized, the privatization process created a monopoly that raises costs both for individuals and for firms doing business in Mexico. In 1990, the government sold the Mexican Telephone Company (TELMEX) to private investors. Yet during its first 6 years of operation, TELMEX faced no competition at all because the government did not implement regulations defining how other telecommunications companies could access TELMEX's network. The regulations that were finally written in 1996 did little to prevent TELMEX from constraining competition. In 1997, therefore, federal regulators drew up more rigorous regulations designed to force TELMEX to open the market to competitors. TELMEX went to court to defend its position, thereby delaying the implementation of any new regulations until 2000. Even then, TELMEX continued to contest the rules on interconnection rates, service quality, and information given to consumers. As late as 2006, TELMEX still controlled approximately 90 percent of all fixed phone lines in Mexico and approximately 80 percent of the cellular phone market. The Organisation for Economic Co-operation and

---

[41] OECD (2002), p. 82; *Latin American Monitor: Mexico* 24, no. 3 (March 2007), p. 8.

[42] OECD (2002), pp. 81–2. The PIDIREGAS initiative allows PEMEX to pay private investors a fixed amount for a set period of time in return for developing a particular project, in effect allowing PEMEX to borrow from private investors off the books. To some extent, therefore, this partial (and quiet) form of privatization compensated for reduced public investment in the energy sector. See World Bank (2005), p. 9.

Development (OECD) estimated that Mexico had among the highest phone rates in the world, with calls costing 50 percent more than the average for OECD member countries.[43]

The Tax System and Public Investment

The NAFTA did not do anything to resolve Mexico's long-standing shortfall in public investment. The fundamental problem is an issue discussed at length in Chapter Two: Tax revenues constitute a very low proportion of GDP. Wealthy individuals regularly exploit loopholes and exemptions to reduce their tax burden, and the government has lacked mechanisms to tax lower-income people employed in the informal sector.[44] As a consequence, the Mexican government relies heavily on a 15-percent value-added tax (VAT), although many people avoid this tax by making their purchases in the large informal sector. Revenues from VAT collection, therefore, amount to less than 3 percent of the GDP. The net result is that in 2004 the government only managed to collect 10.7 percent of the GDP in taxes, a proportion that has held more or less constant since the mid-1970s. Oil taxes and royalties pushed total government revenues up to approximately 15 percent of the GDP in 2004, a proportion that has also held roughly constant since the early 1980s. As Figure 3.13 shows, by international standards the Mexican government is conspicuously underfunded. This is the case not just when comparing Mexico with other OECD member countries, but also when comparing it with other Latin American countries – even some of the very poorest ones, such as Honduras, Bolivia, and Nicaragua.

One major consequence of this low level of public revenue is a low level of public spending. Consider, for example, government spending on education. Measured as a percentage of GDP, Mexico spends only approximately half as much per student as Greece, Japan, or the United States.[45] Measured in absolute levels and adjusting for differences in purchasing power parity, the gap is even larger: Mexico's educational expenditures per student are only 30 percent of those in Greece, 18 percent of those in Japan, and 16 percent of those in the

---

[43] OECD (2002), pp. 81–2.

[44] The government has estimated that income tax evasion costs it revenue equal to 3 percent of GDP. *La Jornada Virtu@l*, 28 May 2007.

[45] OECD (2002), p. 72.

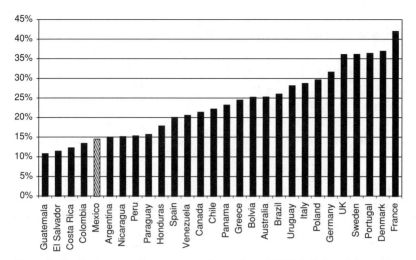

Figure 3.13: Government Revenues as a Proportion of GDP in Selected Countries, 2004. *Source:* International Monetary Fund (2006).

United States.[46] As a result, Mexico's levels of educational achievement, although improving, are still quite low. For example, in the year 2000 only 70.5 percent of Mexican workers in the tradable goods sector (mostly manufacturing activities) had more than 6 years of education. This was certainly an improvement on the 1987 figure of 55.9 percent, but it was still very low by international standards. Mexico has been even slower to increase the number of workers with at least a high school education; the percentage of such workers in the tradable goods sector rose only from 11.4 percent in 1987 to 15.1 percent in 2000.[47] When workers outside the traded sector are taken into account, in the year 2000 less than 20 percent of the population aged 25–64 years had graduated from high school. Indeed, only 60 percent made it past the sixth grade.[48]

A similar shortage of revenues has slowed the Mexican government's efforts to improve the country's road network. In the late 1980s and early 1990s, the Salinas administration attempted to overcome the problem created by the government's own lack of funds by encouraging private firms to build and operate toll highways. This program

[46] Authors' calculation using data provided by the OECD and Heston, Summers, and Aten (2002).

[47] Arenas Velázquez (2004), p. 13.

[48] OECD (2002), p. 71.

failed because the initial traffic loads proved too light to bear the construction and interest costs. Light traffic loads meant high tolls, which meant that traffic did not increase and thus tolls remained high. In 1995 the highway companies went bankrupt, and in 1997 the government nationalized the toll roads.[49] Although the program had succeeded in constructing 3,249 miles of modern limited-access toll highways, the eventual cost to the Mexican taxpayer was over US$12 billion.[50] The government has since continued to build toll highways by using its own revenues but at a much slower pace.[51]

The upshot of Mexico's continuing restrictions on foreign investment in some sectors and low levels of public investment is that FDI under the NAFTA has been concentrated primarily in manufacturing activities that employ workers with low skill levels. This outcome was not a surprise to the NAFTA's architects, who envisioned that low labor costs and geographic proximity to the United States would transform northern Mexico into a manufacturing export platform. It has, however, been a major disappointment to those who hoped that trade and investment liberalization would spark a more profound transformation of the Mexican economy.

The NAFTA did in fact stimulate Mexico's export-manufacturing sector. Indeed, manufacturing has typically accounted for more than 85 percent of Mexico's exports since the late 1990s. One must keep in mind, however, that manufacturing constitutes only approximately 20 percent of the Mexican economy. Moreover, the structure of the manufacturing sector is such that substantial growth in the volume of manufactured exports has not translated into rapid growth of the economy as a whole. More than half of Mexico's manufactured exports are produced in the *maquiladora* (in-bond processing) sector, in which firms import parts from the United States, assemble them in Mexico, and then re-export the finished product. On average, between 1993 and 2002 the maquiladora industry accounted for 44 percent of all Mexican exports, and during the same period the value of their gross output represented 12 percent of GDP (see Figure 3.14). By their very nature, however, maquiladora plants add little value in Mexico because

---

[49] OECD (2002), p. 81.

[50] Rachide et al. (2003), p. 1.

[51] In early 2007 the government announced that, as part of its effort to generate additional resources for road construction, some 70 percent of the nationalized toll roads would be auctioned to private investors. Those investors who had benefited from the earlier bailout were not be allowed to bid. See *La Jornada Virtu@l*, 1 March 2007, 23 March 2007.

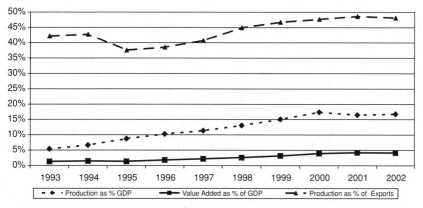

Figure 3.14: Economic Impact of Mexico's Maquiladora Industry, 1993–2002.
Source: INEGI, *Sistema de Cuentas Nacionales* (www.inegi.gob.mx).

the bulk of their output (79 percent) consists of imports of intermediate goods from the United States. As a consequence, the maquiladora industry added only 2.6 percent to Mexican GDP.[52] This value was certainly not insignificant but it was small.

Mexico's Credit Crunch

One assumption underlying Mexico's NAFTA strategy (and one of the central preoccupations of this chapter) was the crucial role of FDI in financing Mexican growth. The truth of the matter is, however, that foreign investment is not a substitute for domestic investment. As Figure 3.10 makes clear, FDI in Mexico has tended to cluster in the production of tradable goods, most particularly manufacturing. Much less foreign investment has flowed to the nontradable sector, such as construction, transportation, and services. This means that the nontradable sector of the economy must rely on domestic sources of capital and credit. The problem, as we shall discuss in Chapter Four, is that Mexico's banks have been retreating from credit markets since 1995. The direct effect of the shortage of credit has been to lower productivity in those sectors that are not major recipients of FDI – which is to say nearly all economic activities other than manufacturing.

The lack of credit has also had an indirect, but nonetheless serious, effect on the tradable-goods sector. As Tornell, Westermann, and

[52] INEGI, *Sistema de Cuentas Nacionales* (www.inegi.gob.mx).

Martínez (2004) have pointed out, roughly 25 percent of the production inputs for this sector come from the nontraded sector. Consider, for example, an automobile manufacturing plant financed with FDI. Its output of automobiles is tradable, and it consumes many tradable goods such as tires, windshields, brake linings, and cylinder heads. Yet it also consumes a wide variety of nontradable items, such as the construction of buildings, machinery repair and maintenance, and accounting and legal services. The workers in this automobile plant also consume a great variety of nontradable goods (for example, haircuts, restaurant meals, public transportation, and home construction and repair), and they must price their labor in accordance with the prices they pay in the nontradable sector. Thus, the firm's labor costs, as well as the cost of many of its production inputs, are determined by the productivity of the nontradable sector. If the growth of productivity in the nontradable sector is slow, then firms in the tradable sector will face higher prices than they would otherwise. These higher prices will, in turn, influence the prices that firms in the tradable sector must charge for their output. In short, the long-run performance of the economy hinges on the performance of myriad economic activities whose sources of finance are domestic.[53]

All of this begs a fundamental question: If there is demand for credit from firms, why does the domestic financial system not meet this demand? To answer that question, we turn to an examination of Mexico's banking system since its privatization in 1991.

[53] Tornell, Westermann, and Martínez (2004).

4

The Mexican Banking System:
The Politics and Economics of Financial Underdevelopment

In Chapter Three we discussed the surprisingly slow growth of the Mexican economy once it opened up to foreign trade and investment. We noted that one of the causes of Mexico's sluggish economic performance since the mid-1990s has been the scarcity of credit for firms and households. Indeed, whether we compare Mexico with other members of the Organisation for Economic Co-operation and Development (OECD) or with other Latin American countries, Mexico has an extraordinarily small banking system. As Figure 4.1 demonstrates, in 2005 the ratio of private credit to gross domestic product (GDP) in Mexico was the smallest of any OECD country. Moreover, it was the smallest by a very wide margin, even when compared with the economies of Southern and Eastern Europe. Mexico also does not fare well when compared with other Latin American countries. As Figure 4.2 shows, in 2005 Mexico's banking system, as a percentage of GDP, was dwarfed by those of Chile, Honduras, Uruguay, Bolivia, Costa Rica, Brazil, and even Nicaragua. It was even small by the standards of Ecuador, Peru, Colombia, and Guatemala. In fact, in 2005 there were only two countries in the region with banking systems that were appreciably smaller than Mexico's: Argentina and Venezuela.

Perhaps even more surprising is the fact that Mexico's banking system has been shrinking over time. As Figure 4.3 makes clear, the ratio of bank loans to GDP in Mexico declined drastically between 1994 and 2005. The result, as Figure 4.4 shows, is that Mexican business enterprises have found it increasingly difficult to mobilize capital. In 1998, Mexico's central bank, concerned about this problem, began to survey national firms to ascertain their sources of capital. During the 1998–2005 period, these surveys indicated that there was a monotonic decline in the ability of firms, regardless of their size,

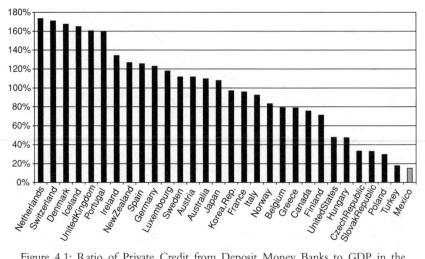

Figure 4.1: Ratio of Private Credit from Deposit Money Banks to GDP in the OECD, 2005. *Source:* World Bank Financial Structure Database.

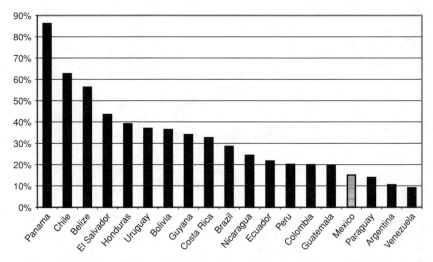

Figure 4.2: Ratio of Private Credit from Deposit Money Banks to GDP in Latin America, 2005. *Source:* World Bank Financial Structure Database.

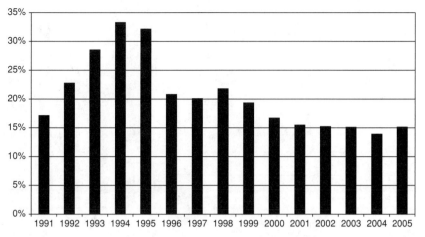

Figure 4.3: Commercial Bank Lending to Firms and Households as a Percentage of GDP in Mexico, 1991–2005. *Source:* Word Bank Financial Structure Database.

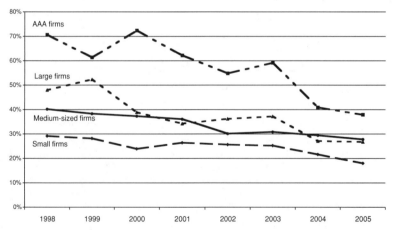

Figure 4.4: Proportion of Mexican Firms Using Commercial Bank Credit at Year's End, 1998–2005. *Source:* Banco de México (http://www.banxico.org.mx). *Note:* Firm size is defined in terms of sales in U.S. dollars in 1997: small, less than $12.5 million; medium, from $12.5 to $65 million; large, from $65 to $650 million; very large (AAA), more than $650 million.

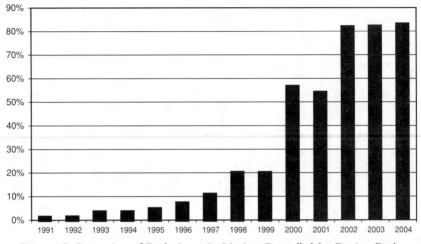

Figure 4.5: Proportion of Bank Assets in Mexico Controlled by Foreign Banks, 1991–2004. *Source:* Haber (2005), table 4; Haber and Musacchio (2005), table 1.

to mobilize capital from commercial banks. Consider the experience of small firms, for example. In 1998, 29 percent of small businesses mobilized capital from banks but by 2005 only 18 percent did. The pattern was similar for medium, large, and very large firms: sustained, significant declines in their use of the banking system.[1]

How could this possibly have been the case, inasmuch as Mexico privatized its banking system in 1991 and then in 1997 allowed foreign banks to enter the Mexican market without restriction? As Figure 4.5 indicates, 83 percent of the Mexican banking system, measured by assets, was foreign owned in 2004. Why, given the opportunities available to foreign banks in a capital-scarce economy, is Mexico not awash in bank credit?

Our answer to these questions draws on the theoretical framework we presented in Chapter One: The growth of Mexico's banking system is limited by institutions bequeathed by more than a century of authoritarian rule. Until 1997, when the Institutional Revolutionary Party (PRI) lost its majority in the federal Chamber of Deputies, the

---

[1] A November 2006 poll of individuals' financial practices similarly found that only 14 percent of respondents applied to banks for credit. The frequency with which individuals sought credit from the banking system varied inversely with their level of income. The results of this Parametría poll were published in *Excélsior*, January 29, 2007.

Mexican government had virtually unlimited authority and discretion, which put commercial banks at risk of expropriation. Mexico also lacked the institutions necessary to enforce contracts. The two sets of institutional arrangements were causally linked. As we shall see, however, reforming the first set of institutions did not automatically produce a reform of the second.

When Mexico's banks were privatized in 1991, the arrangements that compensated bankers for expropriation risk interacted with Mexico's weak contract-enforcement institutions to create incentives for reckless behavior by bankers. As a consequence, the banking system completely collapsed within a few years of the bank privatization. A subsequent government bailout of the banks required US$65 billion in taxpayers' money – a step that further discredited what little remained of PRI administrations' reputation for sound economic management. Voter and opposition party discontent with the privatization and bailout fiasco, coupled with the widespread political discontent that was unleashed by the generalized economic crisis caused by the collapse of the banking system in 1995, cost the PRI control over the lower house of Congress and the government of the Federal District in the 1997 midterm elections. With the Chamber of Deputies in the hands of opposition parties, the government lost the high degree of discretionary authority that had previously allowed it to compromise property rights virtually at will. Thus, when in 1997 the government sought to recapitalize the financial sector by permitting foreign banks to purchase controlling shares in Mexican financial institutions, both the North American Free Trade Agreement's (NAFTA) investor-protection provisions and radically different domestic political circumstances meant that foreign banks could move rapidly to expand their presence in Mexico without fear of expropriation.

Nevertheless, Mexico's banks continued to operate in an institutional setting still characterized by legacies of the country's authoritarian past, particularly the high cost of enforcing contracts. As we shall discuss later, many of these institutional weaknesses – including corrupt police, out-of-date and difficult-to-access property registers, a lack of adequate credit reporting, and inefficient courts – cannot be reformed at the stroke of a pen. The result is a banking system that is foreign owned and stable but that is still reluctant to advance credit to business enterprises. This situation has negative consequences for Mexico's rate of economic growth.

The Legacy of the 1982 Bank Expropriation

To understand the conditions that shaped the process of bank privatization in the early 1990s, we need to step back to the 1970s,
when Presidents Luis Echeverría (1970–1976) and José López Portillo
(1976–1982) began a stepwise expropriation of the banking system.
To fund government spending without increasing taxes, Echeverría
directed the central bank to expand the money supply, a policy that
continued during the López Portillo administration. The result was
an inflationary spiral that gained momentum with each passing year.
To fight inflation, and to direct credit into government-owned firms
or industries with large, unionized workforces that were politically
important, Echeverría and López Portillo imposed interest rate ceilings and raised bank reserve requirements. Those reserves could then
be directed to enterprises chosen by the central bank. The result, as we
saw in Chapter Two, was that the banking system began to contract
sharply in the late 1970s.

The situation facing bankers turned worse in the early 1980s. In
addition to printing money to fund their escalating deficits, Echeverría
and López Portillo borrowed heavily abroad. As we discussed in Chapter Two, the last years of the López Portillo administration found
Mexico caught in a debt trap: The public-sector debt and the interest
rate on U.S. dollar-denominated loans mushroomed; the government
then took out short-term loans to service long-term debt obligations; and the price of oil, which López Portillo believed would
rise indefinitely and allow him to continue borrowing, fell sharply.
López Portillo then had to scramble to avoid a foreign debt default.
He converted U.S. dollar-denominated savings accounts into pesos at
the official rate of exchange (which was approximately one-third less
than the rate on the parallel exchange market), thereby expropriating
the assets of individuals and firms holding dollar accounts. Next, he
declared that the government was temporarily suspending payments
on Mexico's foreign debt, a step that only exacerbated an already deteriorating foreign-exchange crisis. As pressure built on the peso:dollar
exchange rate, López Portillo blamed the bankers for its collapse and
expropriated their assets on September 1, 1982.[2] Bankers received only
limited compensation.[3]

[2] Del Ángel-Mobarak, Bazdresch, and Suárez Dávila (2005).
[3] Elizondo Mayer-Serra (2001), pp. 225-8.

For the next 7 years, Mexico's banking system existed in a near-vegetative state.[4] Banks continued to take deposits and clear checks, but they directed more than half of their lending to public-sector loans. As a consequence, firms and households were starved for credit. Indeed, by 1988 the ratio of private-sector loans to GDP was only 8 percent – roughly half its level in 1981 and the lowest level attained by Mexico in the entire post–World War II period.[5] Some large firms were able to compensate for the absence of a private banking system by raising capital through financial markets, sparking a vigorous but brief run-up in the value of shares listed on the Mexican stock exchange and the growth of brokerage houses and mutual funds. Nevertheless, the majority of Mexican firms were far too small to engage in stock offerings. As a result, they simply had no access to capital other than whatever meager profits they could reinvest.

There was, therefore, considerable pressure on López Portillo's successors to reprivatize the banking system. The administration of President Miguel de la Madrid Hurtado (1982–1988) had made a tentative step in this direction by returning brokerage operations to their previous owners, but the country was too mired in serious economic crisis during the 1980s for the government to contemplate selling the banks.[6] In fact, the government desperately needed to own the banks because they provided a mechanism through which the savings of individuals and companies could be turned into a source of finance for the government and its remaining state-owned firms.

Authoritarian Institutions and the Privatization of Mexico's Banks

Bank privatization was therefore left to President Carlos Salinas de Gortari (1988–1994). Salinas did, in fact, have strong incentives to accomplish this measure. Even though the de la Madrid administration had closed or sold off hundreds of money-losing public enterprises, the government was still saddled with many others. Selling these firms would allow the Salinas administration to pay down the domestic public debt and, by substantially lowering government interest payments,

---

[4] Yacamán (2005).

[5] International Monetary Fund, *International Financial Statistics*, various years.

[6] For de la Madrid's own views on the 1982 bank expropriation (which occurred when he was already president-elect), see de la Madrid Hurtado (2004), pp. 27–37.

reduce the drain on the federal budget and help bring inflation under control. This step would also provide some one-time revenues that could be used as partial funding for the social programs that were a crucial part of the PRI's strategy to win the 1994 presidential elections. There were two particularly valuable jewels in the government's crown of state-owned enterprises: the telecommunications sector and the banks. The Salinas administration therefore moved to privatize the banks in 1991.

In examining this episode, one should not underestimate the importance of the government's desire to raise as much revenue as possible as the fundamental driving force behind the sale of the banks. The government's primary goal was not to create a stable banking system; rather, it was to obtain the highest price possible. This decision had serious ramifications for the tragedy that was soon to follow.

Why, one might ask, would investors pay high prices for banks that the government had seized only 9 years before? Salinas and his principal cabinet officials may have been firmly pro-business in their policy orientation but there was no telling what their successors might do – and, as the 1982 bank expropriation had dramatically demonstrated, in Mexico's authoritarian regime there were few checks on presidential power. What would keep some future government from doing what the Echeverría and López Portillo administrations had done? This dilemma was resolved in much the same way that it had been solved in Mexico since the late nineteenth century – by raising rates of return high enough to compensate the owners of assets for the expropriation risk they faced. In this particular case, rates of return would have to be extremely high because a privatized banking sector would hold no particularly powerful leverage within the PRI regime should a future government decide to move against the banks.

The task that faced the Salinas administration and Mexico's potential bankers was extraordinarily difficult: They had to craft a deal that would raise the rate of return on capital and simultaneously allow the government to maximize the price that it received for the banks. These different interests were reconciled by creating a set of arrangements that limited competition and minimized the amount of capital that bankers actually placed at risk. These arrangements were not, however, established at a single stroke; rather, they emerged over time through a process of negotiation between bankers and the government. Yet when that process was complete, the future of the banking system was sealed: The owners of the banks actually had very little capital at risk, which seriously weakened their incentives to lend money in a prudent manner. The banking system was bound to fail.

To induce investors to offer high prices for the banks despite the possible risks they faced, the Salinas administration signaled potential bidders that they would not have to operate in a competitive environment. When privatized in 1991, the Mexican banking industry was composed of eighteen banks, four of which controlled approximately 70 percent of total bank assets. The government did not break up these banks; instead, it sold them "as is." In addition, the government made it clear that it would use its regulatory authority (obtaining a bank charter required the permission of the secretary of the treasury) to control entry into the banking industry.

The government also signaled potential bidders that they would not have to compete against foreign banks. Foreign banks were barred from the 1991–1992 bank auctions. Moreover, the 1994 NAFTA provisions governing banking severely limited the participation of foreign banks in the Mexican market. For instance, the NAFTA provided that U.S. and Canadian banks could own no more than 30 percent of a Mexican bank's capital. It further prohibited U.S. and Canadian banks from purchasing a controlling interest in any Mexican bank whose market share exceeded 1.5 percent, and it stipulated that the total market share under their control could not exceed 8 percent. Over a 6-year transitional period, the NAFTA allowed U.S. and Canadian banks gradually to hold larger market shares, up to a maximum of 15 percent by the year 2000. Yet the NAFTA allowed the Mexican government to block U.S. and Canadian purchases of Mexican banks for a 3-year period if foreign banks as a group controlled more than 25 percent of the market. Foreign banks remained subject to the rule that they could own no more than 30 percent of a Mexican bank's stock.[7]

Having reduced the competition that bankers would face and thereby raised their likely rate of return on capital, the Salinas administration then structured the auction process to maximize the prices that would be offered for the banks. The formal rules of the auction specified that bids would be sealed and that the managerial expertise of the bidding groups would be taken into account.[8] The notion that the government would take the quality of management into account was,

[7] Murillo (2005).
[8] Unal and Navarro (1999).

however, eviscerated by a decision to do so only if the second–highest bid was within 3 percent of the highest offer made.

The government also maximized the price it received by not bringing Mexico's accounting practices into line with generally accepted accounting standards. One of the most lenient of Mexico's bank accounting rules, dating from the period of government ownership, was that when a loan was past due only the interest in arrears was counted as nonperforming. The principal of such loans could be rolled over and counted as a performing asset. Moreover, the past–due interest could be rolled into the principal and the capitalized interest could then be recorded as income. Modifying this rule, as well as others that inflated bank capital and assets, would have lowered the banks' market value because it would have increased the ratio of nonperforming to total loans, lowered banks' reported rates of return, and decreased the book value of assets. How much lower the banks would have been valued is difficult to know. It is known, however, that the Salinas administration contracted outside consulting firms to provide it with a realistic valuation of the banks – but it did not make the results of those studies public.[9]

Rather than a single round of sealed bids, the Salinas administration sold the banks in six rounds of bidding between June 1991 and July 1992. This arrangement increased competition for the banks sold in the later rounds, thus creating a "cascade effect." The most important determinant of the price paid for a bank in terms of its bid-to-book value ratio (that is, the amount bid as a proportion of the bank's nominal value) was the bidding round in which it was purchased. All other things being equal in terms of the size of the bank, its profitability, and the number of bidders, each additional round of bidding pushed up the bid-to-book value ratio by .30.[10]

This set of institutional arrangements produced a weighted average bid-to-book value ratio of 3.04 and an income of US$12.4 billion for the Mexican government. Indeed, a bid-to-book value ratio of 3.04 suggests that bankers paid a substantial premium. In bank mergers in the United States during the 1980s, for example, the average bid-to-book value ratio was 1.89.[11] Moreover, on the basis of past-due loans, the return on banking assets, and the industry's capital-to-asset ratio,

[9] Unal and Navarro (1999).

[10] Haber (2005).

[11] Unal and Navarro (1999).

Mexico's government-owned banks were not healthy enterprises at the time that they were auctioned.[12] An analysis of the market value of traded shares around the time of the bank auctions is consistent with this view: The prices paid at auction carried a premium of 45 percent above the value of that equity as priced by the Mexican stock market.[13]

Why, given the risk of expropriation, would the purchasers of banks have been willing to pay three times book value for the financial institutions at auction? Why were they willing to pay a premium of 45 percent above the value of bank equity as priced by the Mexican stock market? The answers to these questions lie in a step the Salinas administration took that was highly unusual by the standards of bank privatizations: It allowed bankers to pay for their purchases with money that they borrowed, sometimes from the very same banks they were purchasing.[14]

The original payment plan devised by the government called for a 30-percent payment within 3 days after the announcement of the auction winner, with the remaining 70 percent due within 30 days. The bankers, however, convinced the Salinas administration to replace that plan with one that gave them time to finance their purchases with outside sources of funds. Under the new rules, the first payment was reduced to 20 percent, a second payment of 20 percent was to be paid 30 days later, and the remaining 60 percent was to be paid within 4 months after that. The bankers used the 5-month period between the auction and the final payment date to raise the necessary funds from outside investors.[15] These funds came from a variety of sources: small Mexican investors, bonds floated on the stock market, foreign banks, other Mexican banks, and, in some cases, the same bank that had been purchased. That is, some shareholders were able to finance or refinance their share purchases with a loan from the same bank they were purchasing, with the collateral for the loan being the shares that were being purchased. In one particularly well-documented case, a group of purchasers actually financed 75 percent of the cost of

[12] Gunther, Moore, and Short (1996).

[13] Unal and Navarro (1999).

[14] Mackey (1999), pp. 55, 61, 141, 216. The Salinas administration's reform of the National Worker Housing Institute (INFONAVIT) also raised the financial attractiveness of the banks. The legislation required mandatory financial contributions from employers and workers, which substantially increased bank assets. Advance word of this measure led investors to bid up the value of banks scheduled for privatization. See Middlebrook (1995), p. 416, n14.

[15] Unal and Navarro (1999).

acquiring a bank in this manner.[16] The government's policy in this regard was disastrous because it meant that bankers actually had very little of their own capital at risk. Hence, they had very weak incentives to monitor to whom the bank lent money and under what terms.

Who Monitored the Banks?

Preventing reckless behavior by banks typically requires monitoring by three groups: government regulators, bank directors, and bank depositors (particularly large corporations that have significant deposits at risk). We have already seen that bank directors themselves had weak incentives to monitor the banks. Mexico's bank regulators were also ineffective monitors, both because they were inexperienced and because the tools they had at their disposal were blunt in the extreme. Indeed, the National Banking and Securities Commission (CNBV) did not even possess the information technologies necessary to gather data from banks in a timely manner, and it did not have the authority and autonomy required to supervise banks properly.[17] Mexico's bankers may, in fact, have expected a high degree of regulatory forbearance because it was the government itself that had designed Mexico's extraordinarily permissive bank accounting standards.[18]

The lack of effective monitoring by bank directors and bank regulators meant that the only line of defense against reckless behavior by bankers was Mexico's bank depositors, who in fact faced considerable risk. Depositors were not, however, sheep to be fleeced. We do not know the political process through which they influenced the government but we do know the outcome: The government removed any risk that they faced, thereby also eliminating their incentive to monitor the banks.

Bank deposits were insured by the Bank Savings Protection Fund (FOBAPROA) up to the total amount of resources available to the fund. These resources were the premiums paid by banks and were very limited. As a practical matter, however, FOBAPROA had the ability to borrow from Mexico's central bank, the Banco de México. According to the Law of Credit Institutions, FOBAPROA's technical committee (on which sat representatives from the Ministry of the Treasury, the National Banking and Securities Commission, and the

---

[16] Mackey (1999), pp. 55, 61, 141, 216.

[17] Mackey (1999), p. 97.

[18] Gruben and McComb (1997).

Banco de México) made recommendations that were forwarded to the governor of the Banco de México, who then acted on behalf of the bank in its capacity as FOBAPROA's fiduciary trustee and legal representative.[19]

The Banco de México's guarantee was, moreover, not just implicit, as a consequence of its fiduciary responsibility to FOBAPROA. It was an unequivocal promise. The Banco de México was supposed to publish each December the maximum amount of obligations that would be protected by FOBAPROA during the following year. The statements that it published in the *Diario Oficial de la Federación* (Mexico's version of the U.S. Federal Register) in 1993 and 1994 did not, however, list actual amounts. Instead, they offered the following blanket commitment:

> Based on Section IV of Article 122 of the Law of Credit Institutions, and considering that it has been a tradition that Mexican financial authorities try to protect investors from any loss in case of insolvency of credit institutions, FOBAPROA's technical committee has decided to continue with this tradition. For this reason, it has been agreed that FOBAPROA will endeavor to honor all of the liabilities charged to the financial institutions that participate in the fund, provided that these liabilities are derived from their operations, excluding liabilities arising from subordinated debentures and those resulting from illicit, irregular, or bad-faith operations.[20]

In short, the Banco de México explicitly stated that it was guaranteeing virtually all bank liabilities. These included deposits made by individuals and business enterprises, as well as credits and loans made between banks. The only type of bank liability not covered was subordinated debentures (loans made to banks that are represented by a long-term bond and that confer certain legal rights on its holder).

Precisely because there was unlimited deposit insurance, bank depositors did not police banks by withdrawing funds from those institutions with risky loan portfolios. An analysis of changes in time-deposits and interest rates in Mexico from 1991 to 1996 found that various measures of banks' risk did not influence deposit growth through

---

[19] Mackey (1999), p. 44.

[20] Quoted in Mackey (1999), p. 53. Between 1995 and 1997 the statement was amended slightly by adding the following phrase: "and liabilities derived from loans granted between banking institutions participating in funds-transfer systems administered by the Bank of Mexico in order to back up obligations chargeable to the Bank of Mexico, as well as liabilities in favor of intermediaries belonging to the same financial group as the bank."

September 1995. Banks with riskier loan portfolios offered higher interest rates, and those rates attracted deposits.[21]

The danger posed by the absence of institutions capable of preventing reckless behavior by bankers now intersected with potential problems arising from another legacy of Mexico's authoritarian political economy: the weak state of institutional arrangements for enforcing contracts. If banks are to enforce contracts, they must be able to repossess collateral, whether that collateral takes a physical form (a house, a farm, an inventory of raw materials) or is reputational (the knowledge that failure to repay will preclude borrowing in the future). Although most borrowers do not think of it in these terms, when they take out an unsecured loan (such as when they use a credit card) they are pledging their reputation as collateral.

To repossess physical collateral, banks need access to well-organized property registries, clear legal codes, efficient courts, and honest police. These institutional arrangements emerge in societies *over time* because societies *choose* to invest in them. When property rights are excludable (that is, when the owner of an asset can prevent encroachment by other parties), the owners of assets have incentives to invest in these institutions. In the language of property rights theory, it is in their interest to make their rights transparent (that is, by registering a claim with the government). Their registered claims to property allow them to transfer the property (by sale, lease, or bequest) and to enforce those claims (using the courts and the police). When property rights are not excludable – because the government can encroach on them – the incentives run in reverse: Owners have incentives to hide their assets (by making them less transparent by not registering them) to protect them from confiscation. Moreover, they lack incentives to invest in efficient courts and police because the government can use those same institutions to encroach on an owner's claim to property. This strategy does, however, carry large risks: If owners cannot clearly demonstrate a registered claim to an asset and if the courts and police cannot be used to enforce that claim, then a bank will not accept that asset as collateral because it is not clear that the bank can take possession of it in the event of nonpayment of a loan.

Banks cannot repossess reputational collateral, but they can prevent borrowers from using their reputations as collateral in the future. Typically they do this through two means. First, banks themselves develop

---

[21] Martínez Peria and Schmukler (2001).

internal systems of credit–analysis reporting. Second, they share this information with other banks or with other creditors generally. Typically they do this through a credit-reporting agency.

In the early 1990s, neither system of collateral attachment was available to bankers in Mexico. Physical collateral was extraordinarily difficult to repossess. Mexico did not have an accurate real property register.[22] Although there was a commercial property register maintained by the Ministry of Commerce, it was not available to the public. It was, therefore, difficult for banks to use in their efforts to attach property. Moreover, in those cases in which bankers did move to foreclose, debtors could take advantage of Mexico's extraordinarily complicated bankruptcy laws and the political support of various organizations and movements defending debtors' rights. Even when banks won favorable judgments, the police did not always enforce them. As a consequence, collateral recovery rates were very low: 5 percent in 1991 and 1992, 7 percent in 1993, and 9 percent in 1994.[23]

Banks also found it difficult to attach reputational collateral. First, the banks themselves had weak internal systems of credit analysis – to the point that they were virtually nonexistent.[24] In most instances, internal analysis systems of this kind had been eviscerated during the period of state ownership because the government-run banks had little need for credit analysis, given that they lent primarily to the government. Second, banks could not rely on information gathered by other creditors because there was no adequate system of private credit reporting in Mexico.[25] Indeed, the country's first private credit bureaus were not founded until July 1993, and it was not until February 1995 that rules were established governing their operation.[26]

Poised for Collapse

Precisely because they had little of their own capital at risk, Mexico's new private bankers expanded credit at a prodigious rate. As Figure 4.6 shows, the compound rate of growth in bank lending between 1991

---

[22] Joint Center for Housing Studies of Harvard University (2004).

[23] Haber (2005). The situation was actually much worse than these figures indicate because Mexico's departure from generally accepted accounting practices lowered the reported levels of nonperforming loans.

[24] Mackey (1999), p. 56.

[25] Negrin (2000).

[26] Mackey (1999), p. 25.

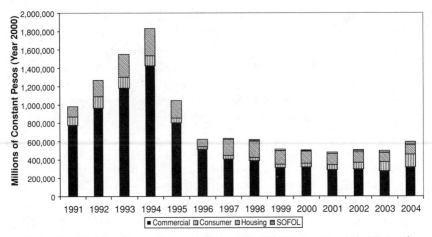

Figure 4.6: Bank Lending in Mexico by Type, 1991–2004. *Source:* Comisión Nacional Bancaria y de Valores, *Boletín estadístico de banca múltiple* (http://sidif.cnbv.gob.mx/ Documentacion/Boletines), various years. *Note*: Observations are at year's end. Nominal data have been deflated with the Banco de México's wholesale price index. SOFOLES are Limited-Objective Financial Societies.

and 1994 was on the order of 24 percent per year. Housing loans in particular grew phenomenally fast; from December 1991 to December 1994, inflation-adjusted lending for housing and real estate nearly tripled. This is, moreover, a lower-bound estimate of the growth in housing lending because it includes only performing loans (that is, loans on which the borrower makes principal and interest payments on schedule). Much of the housing portfolio was nonperforming, with the principal value and past-due interest on these loans continually rolled over into an accounting category called "rediscounts." Inasmuch as the value of rediscounts was nearly equal to the total value of housing loans in December 1994, the actual increase in housing loans might actually have been double the reported figures.

The growth in lending was not, however, matched by an equal growth in deposits. In 1993, 1994, and 1995, loans outstripped deposits by roughly 20 percent. The difference was funded through inter-bank lending, predominantly from foreign banks in foreign currency.[27] Foreign-denominated liabilities therefore grew rapidly, from 11 percent of total Mexican bank liabilities in December 1991 to 14.7 percent by December 1993, and to 27 percent by December 1994.[28] This meant that Mexican banks took on significant exchange-rate risk. The

[27] Mackey (1999), pp. 60, 98.
[28] Mishkin (1996).

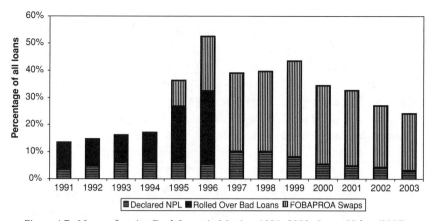

Figure 4.7: Nonperforming Bank Loans in Mexico, 1991–2003. *Source:* Haber (2005), table 3.

only way to have avoided this risk would have been to make loans in U.S. dollars to firms that had incomes in dollars.[29] Banks did make loans in dollars but most of those loans went to firms whose sources of income were in pesos. Thus, if the peso was devalued, many firms would be unable to service their debts, and Mexico's banks, in turn, would be unable to meet their own dollar-denominated liabilities.[30]

Even more rapid than the expansion of lending was the growth of nonperforming loans. Figure 4.7 presents data on the value of nonperforming loans based on different ways of treating the various rollovers and restructurings that were permitted under Mexican accounting rules. One way that banks handled past-due principal was to "rediscount" these loans, which meant creating a category of rollovers that reflected the low probability that the loans would be repaid. These rediscounts were neither listed in the portfolio of performing loans nor were they listed as being nonperforming. If we add these rediscounts to declared nonperforming loans, then the default rate jumps dramatically. For example, instead of the ratio of nonperforming to total loans being the declared ratio of 3.6 percent in December 1991, the ratio would have been 13.5 percent, and instead of being 6.1 percent in December 1994, it would have been 17.1 percent.[31]

In 1995 banks began to phase out the practice of "rediscounting" loans. Instead, they began to restructure unpaid principal, treating

---

[29] Mishkin (1996), p. 32.

[30] Krueger and Tornell (1999).

[31] In the case of U.S. banks, the ratio of nonperforming loans to total loans is typically well under 1 percent.

these rollovers as performing. Thus, rather than an official, reported ratio of nonperforming to total loans of 5.7 percent in December 1996, the actual ratio was 32.5 percent. Even this figure, however, is an underestimate because banks were allowed to swap many of their nonperforming loans for bonds from Mexico's deposit insurance system as part of the government bailout that took place in 1995. When the value of these FOBAPROA bonds is added to the value of declared nonperforming loans, rediscounts, and restructured or renewed loans, then the percentage of all loans that were nonperforming actually exceeded the percentage of loans that were in good standing. At its peak in December 1996, the nonperformance ratio would have been 52.6 percent.

The 1995 Banking Collapse and Bailout

It is commonly asserted that the Mexican banking crisis of 1995 was the product of the government's devaluation of the peso in December 1994. The evidence suggests, however, that the Mexican banking system would have collapsed even had the government avoided a dramatic devaluation. The overvaluation of the peso and the government's mishandling of the exchange rate merely hastened the banking system's demise.[32] The Salinas administration had adopted a so-called crawling-peg exchange rate policy (that is, the government held the peso within a stipulated range of values vis-à-vis the U.S. dollar, allowing a gradual devaluation over time) to help fight inflation, and it had been largely successful in accomplishing that goal. Given the fact that Mexican interest rates were considerably higher than U.S. rates, and given that the government was signaling its intention to maintain a stable (but overvalued) exchange rate, there were strong incentives for both Mexicans and foreigners to deposit funds in Mexican banks. There were also incentives for Mexican firms and banks to sign debt contracts denominated in U.S. dollars.

By late 1994 it was becoming increasingly clear that the exchange rate was seriously overvalued. Once this perception became widespread, bank depositors had every incentive to withdraw their funds and convert them to U.S. dollars before the government allowed

---

[32] See Krueger and Tornell (1999) for a discussion of the Salinas administration's exchange rate policy and its implications for the banking sector.

the currency to float freely; however, firms with dollar-denominated debts could not act so quickly. Once the peso:dollar exchange rate was allowed to fluctuate freely in December 1994, the peso value of their debts nearly doubled in the space of a few days.

The collapse of the exchange rate created two problems for the banking system. First, loans denominated in foreign currencies represented roughly one-third of all the loans made by Mexican banks. Many of these loans had, however, been made to firms without sources of foreign-currency income.[33] Second, the collapse of the peso gave foreign portfolio investors strong incentives to pull their funds out of Mexico. In fact, net foreign portfolio investment flows (that is, foreign funds invested in the stock market or in government bonds) turned negative in the last quarter of 1994 and stayed negative throughout 1995.[34] This required the Mexican government to adopt a tight monetary policy and raise central bank interest rates. The interbank loan rate (the rate charged by banks for short-term loans from one to another, which is dictated by the rate that the central bank sets for such loans) reached 114 percent at its peak in 1995. Interest rates on variable-rate mortgages jumped from 22 percent in November 1994 to 74 percent by March 1995.[35] The rapid rise in interest rates pushed small businesses and individuals with large consumer or housing debts into bankruptcy. As increasing numbers of loans went into default, the banks became insolvent.

Different measures of bank performance illustrate the dimensions of the collapse. Figure 4.7 reports different measures of the ratio of nonperforming to total commercial bank loans. If principal rollovers and the value of FOBAPROA bonds are included as nonperforming, then the ratio of nonperforming loans grew from 17 percent at the end of 1994 to 36 percent by the end of 1995, and to 53 percent by the end of 1996. As debtors stopped making payments, income from loans dropped precipitously. Net interest margins, which are the spread between what banks charge for loans and what they pay depositors, became negative because banks paid out interest on deposits but did not earn interest income from loans.[36] Not surprisingly, banks retreated from the loan business. The inflation-adjusted

---

[33] Krueger and Tornell (1999).
[34] Mishkin (1996), p. 31.
[35] Gruben and McComb (1997).
[36] Haber (2005).

value of lending to consumers and businesses contracted by 66 percent between December 1994 and December 1997 (see Figure 4.6).

President Ernesto Zedillo Ponce de León (1994–2000) responded with a bailout of the banking system to keep the entire economy from collapsing. First, the government opened a special U.S. dollar credit window at the Banco de México to provide banks with access to foreign currency and thus cover their dollar-denominated liabilities. Second, the administration sought to prop up the banks by lending them the capital necessary to maintain adequate reserves. The government's deposit insurance agency, FOBAPROA, used resources from the central bank to create the Temporary Capitalization Program (PROCAPTE). In exchange for 5-year subordinated debentures from the banks, this trust fund lent them capital sufficient to maintain a 9-percent capital:assets ratio. In the event of nonpayment, the debentures were convertible to ordinary stock in the banks that could be sold by the government. Moreover, during the period that they participated in the Temporary Capitalization Program, banks were enjoined from issuing either dividends or additional debt instruments to raise capital.[37]

Third, the government took measures to protect some borrowers, and, in so doing, it protected bank stockholders. These debtor-protection programs came in several forms. As time went on, however, the scope of these programs expanded and their terms gradually became more lenient. As a first step, the Zedillo administration created an inflation-indexed accounting unit (investment units, UDIs) designed to prevent an accelerated amortization of debts via inflation and allowed loans to be redenominated in these units. Banks were then allowed to transfer loans to a government trust fund, which converted them to UDIs bearing an inflation-adjusted interest rate of 4 percent plus a margin to reflect the borrower's credit risk. Additional programs soon followed, each of which targeted different groups of debtors (including consumers, the holders of home mortgages, small businesses, and farmers) and each of which was modified over time to offer debtors even larger discounts off their payments.[38] In 1996 there were roughly 1.75 million debtors who participated in various government-run debtor relief programs.[39]

---

[37] Mackey (1999), p. 65.
[38] Mackey (1999), pp. 82–6.
[39] Mackey (1999), p. 92.

Finally, the government cleaned the banks' balance sheets of nonperforming loans through a loan-repurchase program run by FOBAPROA. In exchange for their nonperforming assets, the banks received nontradable, 10-year FOBAPROA promissory notes that carried an interest rate slightly below the rate paid on the most common type of government bond. The bankers agreed that for each peso in FOBAPROA bonds they received, they would inject 50 centavos of new capital to recapitalize their banks. The government also made the banks responsible for collecting the principal and interest due on the loans transferred to FOBAPROA. As a practical matter, however, they did not do so.[40] The banks had little incentive to try to collect on loans that had a low probability of repayment – especially when they had converted those loans into low-risk government bonds.

The National Banking and Securities Commission intervened in banks that were in serious financial distress. In some cases, the CNBV conducted a de facto intervention in which it removed the bank's management and then arranged for another financial institution to invest in or acquire control of the bank. In all, the CNBV formally intervened in twelve banks; another three were placed under de facto intervention.

Mexico's bankers may have anticipated the government intervention and bailout. Given that Mexico had unlimited deposit insurance and that many of the banks were "too big to fail," it is in fact hard to see how they would not have expected the government to rescue them. It appears, however, that the anticipated intervention and bailout gave some bankers the incentive to make large loans to themselves – and then default on the loans.[41] One study found that roughly 20 percent of all large loans made between 1995 and 1998 went to bank directors. These insider loans carried rates of interest that were on average 4 percentage points lower than those on arm's-length loans, had a

[40] Krueger and Tornell (1999); Murillo (2005).

[41] Mexico's bankers had been engaged in related lending for more than 100 years before the failed related loans of the 1995–1998 period. Related lending during this earlier period was a rational response to the difficulty of enforcing contract rights through the legal system. There were, however, several reasons why related lending during the pre-1991 period did not result in bankers looting their own banks. First, bank directors monitored one another through complex networks of interlocking directorates. Second, shareholders developed mechanisms to monitor directors. Third, because there was no deposit insurance, depositors policed banks by withdrawing deposits from risky banks. See Maurer (2002); Del Ángel-Morarak (2002); and Maurer and Haber (2007).

33-percent higher probability of default, and had a 30-percent lower collateral recovery rate.[42]

It was a revision of the rules governing the FOBAPROA loan-repurchase program that made it possible for directors to loot their own banks. When the program was first instituted in 1995, the following types of loans were ineligible for repurchase by FOBAPROA: past-due loans; loans held by companies in bankruptcy; loans made in conjunction with government-operated development banks; loans denominated in UDIs; and loans to "related" parties. As the health of banking system continued to deteriorate, however, FOBAPROA's technical committee dropped these restrictions.[43] As a consequence, banks were able to transfer to FOBAPROA a large number of loans that were highly unlikely ever to be repaid, as well as loans made to the banks' own directors or to the directors' families or firms.

There were no general guidelines setting limits or restrictions on any of the FOBAPROA programs. Participation in them was determined on a case-by-case basis.[44] Moreover, the FOBAPROA bailout was not a one-time event as originally anticipated in early 1995. Instead, it became an open-ended mechanism, and banks transferred loans to FOBAPROA through 1999. For the same reason, bank interventions were also spread out from 1994 to 2001. As of June 1999, the total cost of the bailout programs was 692 billion pesos (US$65 billion), roughly 15 percent of Mexico's GDP.[45]

The fact that the banking system bailout involved an implicit transfer of large amounts of money from taxpayers to bank stockholders – including some of the country's wealthiest individuals – produced a political firestorm in Mexico. In point of fact, it fueled the expansion of a national debtors' protest movement (the most prominent manifestation of which was an organization known as "El Barzón," named for the yoke ring to which an ox-drawn plow is attached), and, in the run-up to the 1997 midterm congressional elections, it contributed to the further growth of opposition political parties, which capitalized on the fact that millions of small businesses and middle-class debtors were pushed into bankruptcy as a result of sharply increased interest rates

[42] La Porta, López-de-Silanes, and Zamarripa (2003).
[43] Mackey (1999), p. 70.
[44] Mackey (1999), p. 52.
[45] Murillo (2005).

and the collapse of the banking system.[46] Newly empowered congressional representatives from opposition parties subsequently insisted on an investigation into the mechanisms that had been used to rescue commercial banks before they would approve any further bailouts, a maneuver that held up approval of the 1999 federal budget for a full 9 months.

In 1998 the Congress disbanded FOBAPROA and replaced it with a new, more autonomous deposit guarantee agency, the Bank Savings Protection Institute (IPAB). Most FOBAPROA bonds were swapped for similar IPAB bonds, and the IPAB assumed responsibility for recouping and liquidating the assets backed by those bonds – a de facto admission that the loans that had originally been swapped for FOBAPROA promissory notes could not be recovered. Congress also insisted that the annual cost of the banking-sector rescue would be paid for by the government out of each year's budget.[47] This was a de facto admission that the new IPAB bonds had the status of sovereign debt.

Mexico's Financial Liberalization Experiment Since 1997

Saving the Mexican economy from a major collapse required the government to rescue the country's commercial banks, and the Zedillo administration chose to achieve this goal by bailing out depositors, bank debtors, and (in the case of the largest banks) bank stockholders. Having forestalled a complete meltdown at the taxpayer's expense, the government urgently needed to place the banks on a sounder long-term footing. The Zedillo administration, therefore, implemented a series of measures designed to improve monitoring and to recapitalize the banks. First, these reforms made it more difficult for banks to engage in insider lending. As of 1997, commercial banks are required to publish consolidated accounts that include the operations of their subsidiaries. They are also precluded from making loans to bank officers and employees that are not part of their contracted employee

---

[46] On the "El Barzón" debtors' movement, see Mackinlay (2004), p. 310, and Olvera (2004), pp. 425–6.
[47] McQuerry (1999).

benefits. Related-party loans are permitted, but their amount cannot exceed a bank's net capital.[48]

Second, banks are required to diversify risk. Since June 1998, bank loans to any individual cannot exceed 10 percent of a bank's net capital or 0.5 percent of the total net capital of all banks. The same law also enjoins banks from granting loans to companies that exceed 30 percent of a bank's net capital or 6 percent of the total net capital of all banks.

Third, the Zedillo reforms both increased capital requirements and introduced a regulatory system that establishes reserve minimums that vary in accordance with the risk level of a bank's portfolio. In particular, banks are required to access, via a credit bureau, the credit records of borrowers. Loans made without regard to this requirement, or loans made to a borrower whose credit record is poor, must be provisioned at 100 percent.[49]

Fourth, on January 1, 1997 Mexico adopted new accounting standards that more closely approximate generally accepted international accounting standards. For example, the reform brought the accounting treatment of past-due loans into line with generally accepted standards. In addition, stock repurchase agreements (contracts to buy and sell stocks at some future date) are no longer treated as assets, and interbank loans must be separately grouped in financial statements. Even so, Mexican banks still do not adhere to all features of generally accepted accounting standards. In particular, banks are still allowed to record deferred taxes as part of their capital base, an arrangement that may overstate the quantity and quality of the capital available to banks.[50]

Finally, the rules governing deposit insurance were reformed. Unlike its predecessor (FOBAPROA), the IPAB does not provide unlimited insurance. As of January 1, 2005, its operating rules limit insurance to 400,000 UDIs (approximately US$100,000). Moreover, the IPAB only insures bank deposits, rather than a broad range of bank liabilities.

The Zedillo administration also lifted all restrictions regarding foreign ownership of domestic banking institutions. The government began to remove restrictions on foreign bank acquisitions of Mexican

---

[48] Prior to 1995, Mexican law stipulated that related-party loans could not exceed 20 percent of a bank's total portfolio. In practice, however, loans of this kind often exceeded even this extremely permissive limit. See Mackey (1999), p. 141.

[49] Mackey (1999), p. 117.

[50] Mackey (1999), pp. 127–9.

banks in February 1995, when foreign institutions were permitted to purchase Mexican banks with market shares of 6 percent or less. Then, in 1996, the government removed all restrictions on foreign bank ownership, with the new regulations going into effect in 1997. As a result, foreign institutions quickly began to purchase controlling interests in Mexico's largest banks. In December 1996, just prior to the adoption of the new rules regarding foreign ownership, foreign banks controlled only 7 percent of total bank assets in Mexico. By December 1999, 20 percent of bank assets were controlled by foreign banks, and by December 2004 the share of Mexican bank assets under foreign control had increased to 83 percent (see Figure 4.5).[51]

Property Rights and Bank Strategies

The reform of accounting standards and the entry of foreign banks did not, however, resolve one of the crucial, long-standing problems of banking in Mexico: the weakness of contract rights. Since the late 1990s, therefore, Mexican banks and the Mexican government have advanced a series of reforms designed to make it easier to assess default risk and repossess collateral. A private credit bureau now exists, although it does not yet provide banks with the range or quality of information that is typically available in advanced industrial economies.[52] Banks, working with the government, have also undertaken institutional innovations whose purpose is to sidestep the country's inefficient bankruptcy courts by placing collateralized assets outside of an individual's or a firm's bankruptcy estate.[53]

Yet despite improvements such as these, Mexico remains a country with a difficult property-rights environment. Some assets are much easier to assign to creditors as collateral than others. For example, in the case of loans to finance the purchase of an automobile, the lending institution may write the contact in the form of a lease. Until the loan is repaid, the automobile is the bank's property, not the borrower's. Repossessing the car is a simple matter because an automobile is tangible, identifiable (by vehicle identification number), has ongoing

---

[51] In 2007, the five foreign banks whose subsidiaries dominated the Mexican market were (by market share, in descending order) Banco Bilbao Vizcaya Argentaria (Spain), Citigroup (United States), Banco Santander Central Hispano (Spain), HSBC Holdings (United Kingdom), and Bank of Nova Scotia (Canada). See Arai (2006), p. 15.

[52] Negrin (2000).

[53] These reforms are discussed further in Chapter Seven.

value, and can be sold in the used-car market. Moreover, the cost of repossessing the car is normally low relative to the value of the asset.

Commercial loan contracts are at the other end of the spectrum. Some types of commercial assets can be placed outside of a firm's bankruptcy estate through the same mechanisms as consumer loans for automobiles. For example, trucks, cranes, and earth moving equipment can be "leased" from the bank. These are tangible assets that are individually identifiable, depreciate slowly, have secondary (resale) markets, and can be repossessed by driving them off the borrower's property. Yet other commercial assets have characteristics that make them difficult to assign to a bank as collateral. Inventories of raw materials, for instance, are nearly impossible to identify individually, and in any event they are typically used up in production. Even most production machinery departs from the criteria for easy assignability. The machinery used in producing goods can, of course, be identified individually and tends to depreciate slowly. The problem, however, is that most machines are designed for particular tasks in a specific setting and cannot easily be sold on the secondary market. Moreover, much of the value of such machines is embodied in their installation, not in the cost of the machine per se. In short, much production machinery is expensive to remove relative to its resale value. Considerations such as these complicate commercial lending everywhere, but an inefficient and delay-prone legal system makes them intractable in Mexico.

Differences in the degree of assignability of collateral are compounded by differences in the ease with which banks can obtain information about borrowers' creditworthiness. Since 1995, Mexico's new private credit bureau has been gathering data on consumers and business enterprises. Nevertheless, it is far easier to track consumers than it is businesses. Consumers cannot (easily) change their identities. In contrast, business enterprises – especially small and mid-sized sole proprietorships and partnerships – can alter their corporate identities virtually at will.

Confronted by these constraints, Mexican banks allocate credit accordingly. They are relatively quick to make easy-to-enforce loans for automobiles and other consumer durable goods. Banks are much less eager to make loans on residential property (unless borrowers meet very stringent criteria), and they are extremely reluctant to grant credit for commercial purposes.

As a consequence, banks have reduced the size of their loan portfolios. Instead of making loans to firms and households, they lend to government entities or hold government bonds. Between December 1997 and December 2004, loans to households and business enterprises as a proportion of total bank assets fell from 50 percent to only 34 percent.[54] As Figure 4.6 demonstrates, this decline was not just relative to the size of assets; it was also an absolute decline in real terms – inflation-adjusted lending to firms and households in December 2004 was 6 percent below what it had been in December 1997. This result is particularly striking inasmuch as Mexico's banks in 1997 were still in the midst of recovery from the 1995–1996 collapse. Inflation-adjusted lending to households and business enterprises in December 2004 was less than one-third of its level in December 1994. The decline was even more marked in lending to businesses; from its peak in December 1994, lending for commercial purposes had declined by no less than 78 percent by December 2004. The purchase of Mexico's banks by foreign banking conglomerates did not reverse the sharp decline in lending for private purposes.[55] As a result, banks play only a small role in financing the (real) economy in Mexico. As Figure 4.3 shows, at the end of 2004 bank lending represented less than 15 percent of GDP, compared to 33 percent in 1994.

From the perspective of commercial banks, this lending strategy is quite rational. In an environment in which it is costly to enforce contracts, it makes economic sense to loan to the government, either by making direct loans to states and municipalities or by holding treasury bonds. It makes little sense to offer credit to business enterprises, especially small and mid-sized ones, which may present a risk of default followed by a prolonged and costly process of foreclosure.

Challenges for the Mexican Banking System

Creating an efficient banking system requires the crafting of three different sets of institutional arrangements. One set protects the property rights of bankers from expropriation by the government. A second set prevents bankers from behaving recklessly. A third set enforces the contracts made between bankers and borrowers.

Mexico has largely solved the first two institutional problems. Since the late 1990s Mexico has been a competitive electoral democracy, and since the year 2000 the country has experienced divided government

---

[54] Del Ángel-Mobarak, Bazdresch, and Suárez Dávila (2005).
[55] Haber and Musacchio (2006).

at the national level – that is, no party simultaneously controls both the executive and legislative branches of government. Thus, it is very unlikely that Mexico will return to the political conditions that permitted an unconstrained federal executive to hold bankers hostage to the threat of expropriation.[56] At the same time, other institutional reforms have made it more difficult for bankers to engage in reckless behavior; commercial banks are well capitalized, and depositors have only limited deposit insurance. There are, moreover, more stringent rules in place regarding the conditions under which bankers may lend to themselves.

Nevertheless, the third problem – the ability to enforce contracts – remains. To an extent, banks and the government have worked together to mitigate this problem. Recent reforms, for example, have removed the judiciary from the process of mortgage-loan foreclosure. Yet much remains to be done, particularly with regard to commercial credit. Thus, one of the principal challenges facing Mexico is the creation of the administrative capacity to enforce contracts. The emergence of a multiparty electoral democracy has resolved the underlying political issues, and, over time, the pressure of electoral competition may compel government authorities to undertake meaningful reforms in this area. Nonetheless, both significant political will and a substantial resource commitment will be necessary to develop an efficient system of property registries, competent judicial authorities, and an honest and reliable police force.

Until that happens, Mexico's banking system is unlikely to provide adequate credit to small and medium-sized businesses, farms, and households. As a consequence, the economy will grow more slowly than it otherwise would because the vast majority of Mexican firms are small businesses that cannot draw on the securities markets or international banks for finance. The lack of credit prevents them from investing in new plant and equipment, which has held back the growth of productivity, and, as we noted in Chapter Three, the high costs faced by these firms have weighed heavily on the large, export-oriented firms that purchase inputs from them.[57]

---

[56] Foreign banks are, moreover, safeguarded by the NAFTA's investment-protection provisions.
[57] Tornell, Westermann, and Martínez (2004).

5

The Transformation of Mexican Politics

The Institutional Revolutionary Party (PRI) paid a substantial political cost for the poor performance of the Mexican economy during much of the 1980s and 1990s. The party had legitimated its monopoly on electoral office in part by portraying itself as the architect of an "economic miracle" that had, over a span of several decades, industrialized the country and generated rising standards of living. As we discussed in Chapter Two, these claims had always been overstated. But more than a decade of recurrent financial crises and slow economic growth gradually undermined whatever validity they had. For the first time in its history, the PRI began to face serious competition from opposition forces on both the right and the left of the political spectrum.

There was nothing inevitable about the process by which Mexico democratized. In fact, progress toward electoral democracy in Mexico was gradual and halting. It is certainly true that long-term changes in Mexican society – increasing urbanization, the growth of an educated middle class, and the emergence of groups of students and intellectuals who were not easily co-opted – posed a challenge to Mexico's ruling party from the 1960s onward. These factors alone, however, cannot explain the PRI's eventual loss of national power. Electoral democratization owed as much – or more – to contingent economic and political developments.

Ironically, some of the strategies that PRI-led administrations adopted to forestall economic collapse, or to rekindle economic growth, undermined the coalition that had long supported the party's monopoly on power. The crisis of PRI hegemony began with President José López Portillo's (1976–1982) expropriation of the banking system in September 1982, an action that had a powerfully chilling effect on the alliance of convenience that had existed between PRI-led administrations and Mexico's business class. Owners of small and mid-sized businesses in particular therefore began to defect to the center-right National Action Party (PAN). The economic austerity measures and market-liberalizing policies that the Mexican government adopted in the wake of the 1982 debt crisis also gradually undercut the PRI's support among unionized urban and industrial workers, and they weakened the immense patronage machine in rural Mexico that had reliably mobilized millions of votes for the governing party. Even more consequentially, President Miguel de la Madrid's (1982–1988) program of trade liberalization and privatization of state-owned enterprises met strong opposition from left-leaning elements within the PRI. Indeed, the party fractured when these groups exited the party in 1987 and openly challenged the PRI's nominee in the 1988 presidential election. In time, this splinter group evolved into a unified left party, the Party of the Democratic Revolution (PRD), which became a contender for national power.

As opposition parties grew in strength, they joined forces with a broad range of nongovernmental organizations in concerted efforts to reduce governmental control over electoral institutions and ensure greater transparency in the casting and counting of ballots. Nevertheless, from the late 1980s through the early 1990s, Presidents Miguel de la Madrid and Carlos Salinas de Gortari (1988–1994) successfully implemented regressive electoral reforms that guaranteed the PRI control over the federal Chamber of Deputies even it if failed to win a majority of votes in a particular legislative election. It was only the political crisis provoked by the Zapatista Army of National Liberation's (EZLN) armed revolt in the southern state of Chiapas in January 1994 that compelled Salinas to accept a new federal electoral code that began to establish the institutional bases for equitable electoral competition. Even then, the PRI's candidate managed to win a convincing victory in the August 1994 presidential election. It took the financial crisis of 1994–1995 – and the widespread bankruptcies of families and small businesses that followed – to force President Ernesto Zedillo Ponce de León (1994–2000) to adopt a far-reaching reform of electoral rules and institutions that established conditions for free and fair elections. In the 1997 midterm elections, widespread voter discontent emanating from the 1994–1995 financial crisis finally brought to an end the PRI's dominance over the federal Chamber of Deputies and the Federal District government, and in the year 2000 the PAN broke the PRI's 71-year grip on the presidency.

The single most important consequence of Mexico's political transformation was to establish firmly the legitimacy of democratic formulas for winning and exercising political power, thus breaking decisively with the organizing principles of rent-seeking authoritarianism. Vigorous multiparty electoral competition, a more politically engaged civil society, and greater media freedom have substantially strengthened citizens' capacity to hold government officials accountable for their public actions. These changes have also heightened Mexican citizens' effectiveness in making demands for improvements in the quality of, and access to, social welfare benefits. However, as the country's post-2000 experience clearly shows, electoral democratization has not automatically strengthened the rule of law or brought about other changes required to consolidate liberal democracy. In fact, many legacies of Mexico's authoritarian past continue to weigh heavily on the country.

Maintaining the Façade of Democracy

Regularly scheduled but tightly controlled elections were a central feature of the PRI's long reign. Government resources were used to promote the party's candidates, and legal control over party registration permitted government officials to determine how many and which parties were eligible to run against the PRI. Moreover, the executive branch of government controlled the institutions that organized elections and certified their results.[1]

This is not to say, however, that elections in Mexico were meaningless. By demonstrating a symbolic commitment to popular sovereignty, they created a façade of democratic legitimacy. So long as they occurred on schedule and at least one legally registered opposition party participated in them, elections preserved the illusion of political competition and thus helped avoid the domestic and international criticism that would have arisen had the regime truly become a single-party system.[2]

Regular elections, coupled with constitutional restrictions on reelection in the executive and legislative branches of government, were also important in creating a predictable succession mechanism

---

[1] Crespo (2004); Gómez Tagle (2004). As Weldon (2004a) argues, these factors were also crucial to preserving the federal executive's dominance in Mexico's highly presidential system.

[2] Crespo (2004), pp. 57, 61.

and rotation in office among the PRI's leadership. This allowed dissidents within the party's ranks to be disciplined and loyal supporters to be rewarded.[3] Those who cooperated with the party leadership would be put forward for another elective post, or for a position in the government bureaucracy – both of which provided social status and, all too frequently, opportunities for illicit personal enrichment. Those who did not cooperate, however, would find themselves bereft of a political future. Needless to say, the PRI was noted for its high degree of internal discipline.[4]

The PRI's ability to generate overwhelming electoral majorities signaled political rivals that they would be better off cooperating with the PRI – that is, operating as a loyal opposition in exchange for various rewards, rather than working against it. Hence, of the three registered parties that operated during the 1950s and 1960s, only the center-right PAN actually represented an opposition voice. The other two principal "opposition" parties that were active during this period, the Authentic Party of the Mexican Revolution (PARM) and the Socialist Popular Party (PPS), were recipients of government support and almost always voted with the PRI in Congress. Indeed, perhaps the most telling fact about these two parties is that they failed to nominate their own candidates for the 1958, 1964, 1970, and 1976 presidential elections. Instead, they reliably backed the PRI's nominee.

Periodic and shallow electoral reforms helped preserve Mexico's hegemonic party system by enhancing its ability to respond flexibly to demands for political opening. An electoral reform orchestrated by the PRI in 1946 bolstered the party's position by bringing electoral processes under presidential control. Once the PRI had fully consolidated its electoral dominance, however, the most difficult problem the party's leadership faced was finding ways to encourage the opposition to compete against the PRI in the electoral arena (rather than through other forms of resistance), while simultaneously avoiding a genuine political opening that might actually allow the opposition to take power.[5]

In 1963, therefore, the government tinkered with the rules regulating elections for the federal Chamber of Deputies (Mexico's lower

---

[3] The Mexican constitution bars reelection of the president and (since 1933) immediate reelection to the same post in the federal Congress. State constitutions prohibit consecutive reelection of governors, legislators, mayors, and municipal councillors.

[4] Crespo (2004).

[5] Crespo (2004), pp. 63–7.

legislative chamber) to guarantee opposition parties a presence in the Congress. Until that time, all deputies had been elected in single-member districts, with the candidate who received a plurality of the votes winning the district's sole legislative seat (as occurs in the United States). The problem with this system was that the PRI, given its multiple advantages over other parties, won virtually all of the seats. The 1963 reform, although retaining the system of single-member districts, sought to keep the PAN from abandoning electoral competition by establishing a parallel system of proportional representation (the system that exists in most European parliamentary democracies, in which parties win seats based on the percentage of the vote they receive nationally).[6] Under what was known as the party-deputy system, a party receiving at least 2.5 percent of the total valid vote, but winning fewer than twenty single-member district seats, would receive five proportional-representation seats, plus one additional seat for each 0.5 percent of the vote in excess of 2.5 percent, up to a maximum combined total of twenty seats in the Chamber of Deputies.[7] Any party winning twenty or more single-member district seats was ineligible to receive proportional-representation seats. This clever formula meant that the PRI was ineligible for any proportional-representation positions, but no opposition party was likely to control more than 20 of the Chamber's 178 seats.

When these rules failed to generate sufficient seats for the PRI's satellite parties (the PARM and the PPS), a further electoral reform in 1972 reduced the representation threshold to 1.5 percent of the national vote and increased to 25 the maximum number of seats that could be held by an opposition party.[8] These measures succeeded in guaranteeing a larger opposition presence in the Chamber of Deputies. They did not, however, overcome opposition party resistance to an electoral system whose rules clearly remained stacked against them. Indeed, internal divisions within the PAN over whether to run a candidate or to promote widespread abstentionism prevented the party from nominating a presidential candidate in 1976 – leaving the PRI's candidate, José López Portillo, in the embarrassing position of facing no legally registered opposition candidate.[9]

---

[6] In 1958 the PAN had withdrawn its six federal deputies in support of its allegations of fraud in that year's presidential election. See Crespo (2004), p. 68.

[7] Molinar Horcasitas and Weldon (2001), pp. 210–11.

[8] Molinar Horcasitas and Weldon (2001), p. 211.

[9] Eisenstadt (2004), p. 169.

Significant (although still limited) political liberalization only began with the 1977 electoral reform. The authors of the Federal Law on Political Organizations and Electoral Processes sought to address a number of perceived challenges, including rising voter abstention in an electoral system without meaningful party competition. An even more important motivation, however, was the legitimacy crisis provoked by the "Tlatelolco massacre," an episode in which army troops killed or wounded several hundred of the student demonstrators gathered at Tlatelolco Plaza in Mexico City on October 2, 1968, to protest violations of university autonomy, the absence of democracy, and Mexico's vast social and economic inequalities.[10] The resulting public outcry from the country's urban middle class, the regime's most politically articulate constituency, marked a watershed in Mexico's political history and accelerated broad pressures for change.

In the wake of the Tlatelolco crisis and yet another instance of lethal violence against student groups on June 10, 1971 (the so-called Corpus Christi massacre, in which the government deployed armed thugs against student demonstrators), part of Mexico's leftist opposition concluded that peaceful reform efforts were futile. These elements subsequently organized various urban and rural guerrilla movements committed to overthrowing the PRI-led regime by force, a departure that provoked a systematic (and generally successful) government campaign to repress the guerrillas in a "dirty war" that was notable both for its violence and for the absence of serious coverage in either the domestic or the international media. At the same time, the administration of President Luis Echeverría (1970-1976) adopted a "democratic opening" policy toward nonviolent political opposition. The 1977 electoral reform built on these efforts by seeking to draw various unregistered groups into the legal party system.

The 1977 reform loosened party registration requirements, expanded opposition parties' access to the mass media, and guaranteed opposition political groups at least 25 percent of the seats in an expanded (400-seat) federal Chamber of Deputies.[11] The reform was judged

---

[10] Middlebrook (1986), pp. 126-9; Aguayo Quezada (1998b).

[11] For example, the 1977 reform permitted political parties to compete in elections on the basis of a conditional registration; if they then polled more than 1.5 percent of the total valid vote, their registration was confirmed. The legislation also introduced proportional representation in municipal councils in municipalities with more than 300,000 inhabitants (a principle that was applied to all municipalities beginning in 1983). For a detailed discussion of the 1977 reform and its longer-term implications, see Middlebrook (1986); Díaz-Cayeros and Magaloni (2001); Molinar Horcasitas and Weldon (2001); Weldon (2001); and Gómez Tagle (2004).

a success when two leftist parties (the Mexican Communist Party [PCM] and the Socialist Workers' Party [PST]) and one right-wing party (the Mexican Democratic Party, PDM) successfully sought legal recognition and competed against the PRI and other established parties (the PAN, PPS, and PARM) in the 1979 federal legislative elections.[12] Over the longer term, however, the PRI was the principal beneficiary of what remained a firmly controlled liberalization process. By giving legal registry to a range of political forces on both the left and the right, the 1977 reform preserved Mexico's democratic façade at a time of considerable political ferment by simultaneously reinforcing the party and electoral systems and confirming the PRI's dominant position at the center of the ideological spectrum.[13] Thus, while the reform increased the number and ideological diversity of the parties represented in the Chamber of Deputies (see Figure 5.1), it did not establish the conditions for free and fair elections and a multiparty electoral democracy.[14]

Economic Collapse, Political Crises, and Electoral Opening

The disastrous performance of the Mexican economy during much of the 1980s and 1990s radically altered the PRI's political fortunes. Mexico's hegemonic party was no longer concerned with maintaining a façade of democracy through the strategic allocation of seats to opposition parties. Instead, as voters began to defect from the PRI in significant numbers, the PRI's leadership dedicated itself to curtailing the growth of opposition parties.

One of the most significant blows to the coalition underpinning PRI rule was López Portillo's expropriation of the banking system in September 1982, an action that had a powerful, chilling effect on the alliance of convenience that had existed between Mexico's business

---

[12] As an additional incentive for former leftist guerrillas to channel their activism through political parties and elections, the government also decreed an amnesty for political prisoners and fugitives. See Gómez Tagle (2004), p. 85.

   Two additional leftist parties, the Social Democratic Party (PSD) and the Revolutionary Workers' Party (PRT), subsequently gained registration and participated in the 1982 general elections.

[13] Despite increased competition, the PRI won 69.7 percent of the total valid vote in the 1979 Chamber of Deputies elections and 68.4 percent of the vote in the 1982 presidential election. Middlebrook (1986), table 6.1.

[14] Expanding the size of the Chamber of Deputies made it possible to increase the political opposition's presence without sacrificing career opportunities for PRI representatives.

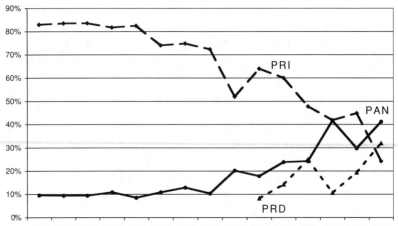

Figure 5.1: Proportion of Seats Held by Major Parties in Mexico's Federal Chamber of
Deputies, 1964–2006. *Source:* For 1964–1991, Craig and Cornelius (1995); for 1994
and 1997, Díaz-Cayeros and Magaloni (2001) and Klesner (2001); for 2003 and 2006,
Instituto Federal Electoral (www.ife.gob.mx). *Note:* See the List of Abbreviations and
Acronyms for political parties' full names.

class and the political elites who ran the PRI. That alliance had been
disturbed by President Luis Echeverría's radical rhetoric, inflationary
public finance, and stepwise expropriation of bank deposits. Yet the
bank seizure undermined whatever confidence Mexico's business class
still had in the PRI. Although the government managed to hold on
to the political allegiance of the country's leading entrepreneurs by
offering them debt bailouts and other policies intended to limit their
financial losses at a time of great economic hardship, the owners of
many small and midsized businesses did not similarly benefit from the
government's largess. Consequently, they began to shift their support
from the PRI to the center-right, pro-business PAN. In northern
Mexico, in particular, they joined the PAN in significant numbers,
channeled financial resources to the party, and frequently ran as its
candidates for state and municipal offices. Several of the PAN's most
important figures during the 1980s and 1990s, including president-
to-be Vicente Fox Quesada, came from private-sector backgrounds,
and entrepreneurs' organizational skills and financial support were key
elements in the party's growing electoral success.[15] The government's

[15] Arriola (1988), p. 31; Maxfield (1989), p. 232; Camp (1989), pp. 136–8; Mizrahi (1995),
pp. 83–5; Loaeza (1999), pp. 12, 17, 23; Bizberg (2003), pp. 164–5.

response to increasing discontent with the economy and rising support for opposition parties varied somewhat over time. In early 1983, the de la Madrid administration felt compelled to "balance" economic austerity measures with official recognition for a series of local-level electoral victories by opposition candidates, including PAN triumphs in five state capitals in central and northern states.[16] As the economic crisis persisted, however, the government hardened its position, resorting to conspicuous fraud to ensure that the PRI won a hotly contested gubernatorial election in Chihuahua in 1986.

The government also reversed the 1963-1977 trend toward more liberal election rules by adopting the first of several regressive electoral reforms. The 1987 electoral code abolished the conditional registry of political parties (making it more difficult for new parties to form), and it strengthened the executive branch's control over the electoral process. Although the new law increased the number of proportional-representation seats in the federal Chamber of Deputies from 100 to 200 (for a total of 500 seats), it gave the PRI access to these seats for the first time, effectively making it more difficult for opposition parties to gain representation in the Chamber. Most notably, the 1987 legislation introduced a "governability clause" stipulating that if no party obtained more than 51 percent of the total national vote in a particular legislative election, then the party that had received between 35 and 50 percent of the vote would receive compensatory proportional-representation seats so that it would have an absolute majority in the Chamber of Deputies. This arrangement ensured that the PRI would continue to hold a majority of seats in the Chamber even if it failed to win a majority of the votes actually cast in a given legislative election. Given the strong likelihood that the PRI would still prevail in presidential races, the governability clause implied that the PRI would dominate both the executive and legislative branches of government.[17]

The need to rely on the governability clause was reduced, however, by another component of the 1987 reform: It rewrote the rules governing the way that citizens voted in the proportional representation elections. Prior to 1987, citizens voted twice: once for the single-member district race and again for the proportional-representation seats. As of 1987, citizens voted once: Their vote in the single-member

---

[16] Middlebrook (1986), pp. 144–5.

[17] For more detailed analyses of the 1987 electoral law, see Molinar Horcasitas and Weldon (2001), pp. 214–17; Crespo (2004), pp. 69–72; Díaz-Cayeros and Magaloni (2001), pp. 282–3.

district race was automatically counted as their "party vote" for the proportional-representation seats. Given that the PAN and the principal leftist opposition party, the Mexican Unified Socialist Party (PSUM), only had the resources to take on the PRI in a small minority of Mexico's 300 electoral districts, this meant that the PRI would not only win an overwhelming number of the single-member district races but that it would also capture an overwhelming percentage of the proportional-representation seats.[18]

These maneuvers temporarily safeguarded the PRI's legislative majority. Nevertheless, the strains produced by the post-1982 economic crisis and the government's response to it eventually split the ruling party itself. Left-leaning, nationalist elements within the PRI strongly opposed de la Madrid's program of trade liberalization and privatization, and some prominent members contested the PRI's presidential nomination – a process that had traditionally been tightly controlled by the incumbent president, who "fingered" his successor in an act known as *el dedazo*. Porfirio Muñoz Ledo (a former PRI party president and cabinet minister) and Cuauhtémoc Cárdenas (a former PRI governor from the state of Michoacán and son of former President Lázaro Cárdenas, who had famously nationalized Mexico's petroleum industry in 1938) organized left-leaning PRI members into the "Democratic Current," an opposition group within the PRI itself.[19] In 1987, when President de la Madrid selected as his successor Carlos Salinas de Gortari (then secretary of budget and planning and one of the principal architects of trade liberalization and privatization), Cárdenas and Muñoz Ledo led their supporters out of the PRI. The "Democratic Current" subsequently joined with several small political parties (including the PARM and the PPS, which had traditionally backed the PRI's presidential candidate) to form the National Democratic Front (FDN) and support Cárdenas's 1988 presidential bid.

Cárdenas proved to be a very uncharismatic campaigner. Nevertheless, during the final phases of the race his challenge to PRI candidate Salinas ignited popular opposition to de la Madrid's austerity policies and the undemocratic practices of the PRI.[20] In fact, when federal

---

[18] Díaz-Cayeros and Magaloni (2001).

[19] Bruhn (2004).

[20] Public discontent with years of government budget cuts and prolonged stagflation was aggravated by yet another significant devaluation of the peso in November 1987 and the prospect of hyperinflation. In Mexico City, the government had been badly discredited by

electoral officials began counting ballots on the evening of July 6, 1988, the early returns (principally from Mexico City and the surrounding area, where anti-PRI opposition was strongest) placed Cárdenas firmly in the lead. Vote tallies arriving later from rural districts and other parts of the country favored the PRI, but Ministry of the Interior officials feared the worst, panicked, and claimed that a computer failure prevented them from releasing preliminary results. Even so, the PRI, in violation of a multiparty agreement reached before the elections, claimed victory for Salinas. When the Federal Electoral Commission announced official results a week later, it declared Salinas the winner (with a bare majority of 51.7 percent of the total valid vote, compared with 31.1 percent for Cárdenas and 16.8 percent for PAN candidate Manuel J. Clouthier) in what was widely regarded as the most fraudulent election in modern Mexican history.[21] The elections for the Chamber of Deputies were equally shocking to the PRI: Its candidates earned only 50.4 percent of total votes cast (see Figure 5.2), the lowest proportion in the history of the party.[22]

Legitimizing the outcome of the 1988 presidential election was a complicated and delicate affair. Indeed, the egregious fraud that took place was one of the reasons why the FDN became the PRD. Even though the PRI still controlled the newly elected Chamber of Deputies (which, along with the Senate, served as an electoral college constitutionally responsible for certifying the election results) and therefore had the capacity to certify Salinas's victory, it needed political support from the PAN. Had the PAN, whose candidate placed third in the presidential election, continued to side with Cárdenas's supporters in denouncing electoral fraud and seeking to block the certification process, the elections might have been viewed as completely illegitimate by both Mexican citizens and the international community. PRI leaders, however, offered the PAN a backroom deal: If the PAN would work with the PRI, then in exchange the government would henceforth respect the PAN's victories in gubernatorial, mayoral, and municipal council elections. In addition, Salinas agreed

its inept response to devastating earthquakes in September 1985. See Salinas de Gortari (2002), pp. 944–8; Camacho Solís (2006), pp. 199–201, 206.

[21] For former President de la Madrid's own remarkably inadequate explanation of the disputed vote count, see de la Madrid Hurtado (2004), pp. 814–25, 834. Salinas's defense appears in Salinas de Gortari (2002), pp. 949–65. For an analysis suggesting that Cárdenas may in fact have won more votes than Salinas de Gortari, see Castañeda (1999), pp. 327–8.

[22] PRI candidates for federal deputy positions had garnered 86 percent in 1964, 85 percent in 1976, and 69 percent in 1982. Klesner (1993), p. 189.

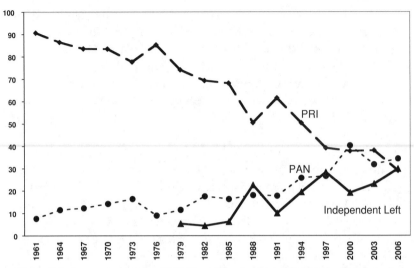

Figure 5.2: Proportion of the Valid Vote Won by Major Parties in Elections for Mexico's Federal Chamber of Deputies, 1961–2006. *Source:* For 1961–1994, Gómez Tagle (1997), pp. 67–72; for 1997–2003, IFE (www.ife.gob.mx); for 2006, IFE (2006). *Note:* The parties grouped as the "Independent Left" include: for 1979, the PCM and PRT; for 1982, the PSUM and PRT; for 1985, the PSUM, PRT, and PMT; for 1988, the PMS, PST, PARM, and PPS; for 1991–1997, the PRD and PT; for 2000–2006, the PRD, PT, and CD. In 2000 the PAN total includes votes for the PVEM. In 2003–2006, the PRI total includes votes for the PVEM. See the List of Abbreviations and Acronyms for political parties' full names.

to incorporate the PAN's pro-democracy demands in a new federal electoral code.[23]

Salinas made good on part of his agreement with the PAN, recognizing the party's electoral victories at state and municipal levels. He even went so far as to incur the wrath of conservative sectors of the PRI by displacing apparent PRI winners and allowing PAN candidates to take office in several particularly controversial elections.

Yet in the electoral code finally adopted in 1990, fears among the PRI leadership that opposition challenges would continue to grow (opposition parties already controlled 48 percent of the seats in the federal Chamber of Deputies) trumped whatever arrangements the party had made with the PAN after the 1988 election. The 1990 legislation did reintroduce the option of conditional registry for political

---

[23] Lujambio (2001), p. 78; Eisenstadt (2004), p. 176; Magaloni (2006), Chapter 8; Camacho Solís (2006), pp. 214–16.

parties. It also strengthened the federal electoral court (first established in 1987) charged with resolving election disputes, and it created a new agency called the Federal Electoral Institute (IFE) to oversee elections. For the first time in Mexico's history, the agency responsible for election supervision, with its own budget and staff, was legally independent of the government.[24] Nevertheless, the representational formula employed ensured that the PRI would retain its majority on the IFE's governing council, and the agency remained under the ultimate control of Mexico's secretary of the interior.

The 1990 electoral code also introduced a set of complicated rules for the allocation of proportional-representation seats that guaranteed the PRI a majority in the Chamber of Deputies so long as it met two criteria: It won more single-member districts than any other party, and it obtained at least 35 percent of the vote for proportional-representation seats. That is, even if the PRI did not actually win a majority of seats, the rules automatically allocated it sufficient proportional-representation seats to give it a majority. The new code also raised major obstacles to the formation of electoral coalitions like the one formed by Cárdenas in 1988.[25]

The bottom line was this: Even though the 1988 presidential election crisis had shaken the regime to its core, Salinas managed to regain the political initiative. The PRI retained its legislative alliance with the PAN, providing Salinas with the two-thirds majority in the Chamber of Deputies required for the constitutional amendments that permitted him to undertake, among other items on his reform agenda, the legalization of *ejido* land sales and the privatization of the banks. By renegotiating Mexico's external debt, and by accelerating the privatization of state-owned firms and using the proceeds to reduce the government's debt service payments, the Salinas administration succeeded in lowering the rate of inflation. Salinas also used a high-profile poverty-alleviation program, the National Solidarity Program (PRONASOL), to bolster his own popularity and undercut the PRI's electoral rivals by, for example, channeling funds to communities that had supported Cárdenas's candidacy in 1988.[26]

---

[24] Gómez Tagle (2004), pp. 87, 89–90.

[25] The rules for allocating proportional-representation seats also gave advantages to the smallest parties, thereby penalizing stronger opposition parties such as the PAN and PRD. See Balinski and Ramírez González (1996), pp. 205, 207; Molinar Horcasitas and Weldon (2001), pp. 217–19; Díaz-Cayeros and Magaloni (2001), p. 285.

[26] Molinar Horcasitas and Weldon (1994); Magaloni (2006), Chapter 4; Magaloni, Díaz-Cayeros, and Estévez (2006).

These moves allowed the PRI to recover some lost electoral ground. Opposition parties continued to make advances at state and municipal levels, the most spectacular of which was the PAN's victory in the 1989 Baja California gubernatorial race, the first time in six decades that the PRI had ceded control of a state government. In the crucial 1991 midterm legislative elections, however, opposition parties only managed to win 11 of 300 single-member district seats. The PRI took 61.4 percent of the valid vote (see Figure 5.2).[27]

Control of the legislature allowed Salinas to make yet another revision to the federal electoral code. The 1993 reform eliminated the much-criticized governability clause that gave the PRI a majority in the Chamber of Deputies even if it only won 35 percent of the vote.[28] At the same time, however, the 1993 legislation reinforced barriers against electoral coalitions (stating that if two or more parties nominated a single candidate for the presidency, they also had to coordinate their party programs and candidacies in all 628 congressional races) so as to prevent opposition parties from uniting behind a single challenger for the presidency.

In exchange for supporting these rule changes, the PAN obtained the PRI's consent to a long-standing demand for minority representation in the federal Senate. Before 1993, each of Mexico's thirty-one states, plus the Federal District, had two senators. Parties put up two-person tickets for each state, and voters would choose among these party tickets. That is, voters did not vote for candidates; they voted for parties, with the winning party taking both seats. This voting system worked overwhelmingly in favor the PRI. In fact, until 1988, it controlled all sixty-four Senate seats and in 1991 it still held fifty-nine seats (the PRD held four seats and the PAN one). The 1993 reform doubled the number of seats to four per state, which simultaneously created more opportunities for opposition parties while preserving career opportunities for PRI loyalists. Parties each put up a three-person ticket, and voters cast their ballots for party tickets. The party that won the most votes in the state received three Senate seats: The fourth seat was allocated to the runner-up party's lead candidate. This new rule ensured that the PRI would maintain a majority in the

[27] Molinar Horcasitas and Weldon (2001), p. 220.
[28] The formula employed for distributing single-member district and proportional-representation seats ensured that the PRI would retain a majority in the federal Chamber of Deputies in most instances, although it did not guarantee it. See Molinar Horcasitas and Weldon (2001), p. 220.

Senate (so long as it could win majorities in twenty-two of Mexico's thirty-two federal entities), and it provided the second largest party (at the time, the PAN) with a substantial number of Senate seats. In point of fact, the PAN would pick up twenty-four Senate seats in the 1994 elections.[29]

These changes in electoral rules were, however, soon overtaken by events. On January 1, 1994 – the very day on which the North American Free Trade Agreement (NAFTA) took effect – a guerrilla group named the Zapatista Army of National Liberation staged an armed revolt in the southern state of Chiapas to protest the lack of democracy in Mexico and the negative effects of market opening on the country's indigenous peoples.[30] The EZLN could deploy only a small number of armed fighters, and its forces were quickly surrounded by the Mexican army. Nevertheless, the rebellion reverberated across the nation and internationally. The crisis came at the outset of the 1994 presidential campaign, and as President Salinas struggled to maintain political control, the center-left PRD, the PAN, and other opposition parties banded together to extract concessions from the government over the rules that would govern the August 1994 general elections.[31] In fact, there was genuine fear that the PRD would abandon an opposition strategy based on electoral competition and instead take to the streets, in effect forming an alliance with the EZLN.

Recognizing that the PRI's continuing capacity to govern was at stake, Salinas conceded the necessity of yet another round of electoral reform – the third such initiative undertaken during his administration. Yet even before negotiators had finished drafting the new law, another major political crisis underscored the importance of reaching a broad agreement among rival political groups that would permit peaceful elections in August 1994 and encourage all the major parties to accept the results. On March 23, 1994, PRI presidential candidate Luis Donaldo Colosio was assassinated during a routine campaign stop in the northern border city of Tijuana – the first killing of a mainstream national political figure since the assassination of president-elect Álvaro Obregón in 1928. The gunman, a local factory worker, claimed

---

[29] Díaz-Cayeros and Magaloni (2001), pp. 278, 287–8; Díaz-Cayeros (2005), p. 1203.

[30] There is a very substantial literature on the EZLN. Two major works are Tello Díaz (1995) and Harvey (1998).

[31] Loaeza (1999), pp. 424–5. The January 1994 "Pact for Peace, Democracy, and Justice" was signed by seven of the eight registered parties (the PPS declined to join the initiative) and all eight presidential candidates (including the PPS's Marcela Lombardo).

that he had acted alone. That version of events was, however, heavily discounted by the Mexican public amidst rumors that elements of the PRI had a hand in the assassination.

With these dramatic events serving as the political backdrop, in May 1994 the Congress adopted new legislation to govern the upcoming general elections. It had three particularly salient features, all of which worked to the PRI's disadvantage.[32] First, the revised electoral code gave greater autonomy and credibility to the institutions responsible for organizing elections and certifying their results. Although the secretary of the interior continued to chair the Federal Electoral Institute's General Council (as he had since 1946) and control its day-to-day activities, the Council's other members were now six nonpartisan citizen representatives (*consejeros ciudadanos*) nominated by the major political parties and four representatives of the legislative branch. These changes gave opposition parties a total of eight of the eleven voting members of the Council. The reform also gave the Federal Electoral Tribunal and IFE's General Council responsibility for certifying elections for federal deputies and senators, although the Chamber of Deputies remained responsible for certifying the results of presidential elections. Moreover, the legislation provided for independent examination of voter registration lists and authorized international election observers, something that the Mexican government had strenuously resisted up until then.

Second, the 1994 reform legislation lowered the ceiling on campaign spending, and it forbade the use of public funds and government personnel to benefit a particular political party – which is to say that it forbade the PRI from funding its election campaigns out of the federal treasury. It also established a special prosecutor's office to investigate violations of the electoral code. Third, although the law did not alter the pro-PRI formula for the distribution of proportional-representation seats in the Chamber of Deputies, it did reduce to 60 percent the total number seats that could be held by any one party.[33]

These reforms, coupled with pro-democracy groups' electoral observation efforts and heightened international scrutiny of events in Mexico, reduced the risk of overt fraud in the 1994 general elections.

---

[32] Crespo (2004), p. 73; Molinar Horcasitas and Weldon (2001), p. 223; Gómez Tagle (2004), p. 91.

[33] The cap on a single party's share of Chamber of Deputies seats had been set at 75 percent in 1977, 70 percent in 1987, and 63 percent in 1993. See Molinar Horcasitas and Weldon (2001), pp. 215, 221.

Nevertheless, the PRI continued to derive enormous advantages from its status as the incumbent party. Its alliance of convenience with private broadcasters ensured that the PRI's candidates received disproportionate and highly favorable media coverage. The party also benefited (in violation of the provisions of the new electoral code) from both the direct use of government resources to support its candidates and from the largess provided to voters by social welfare programs such as PRONASOL and the Direct-Support Program for the Farm Sector (PROCAMPO), a program that provided direct subsidy payments to small-scale rural producers.[34] Moreover, the Banco de México's decision to adopt an exchange rate policy that systematically overvalued the peso helped the PRI because it raised the purchasing power of Mexican consumers by keeping foreign-produced goods remarkably inexpensive in peso terms – thus creating the impression that, from the point of view of the average consumer, trade liberalization was a resounding success. The PRI also played upon voters' fears of instability and radicalism by sensationalizing the PRD's contacts with the EZLN.

These advantages allowed PRI candidate Ernesto Zedillo to win the August 1994 presidential election with 50.2 percent of the valid votes cast. Although the PRI lost seats in both the federal Chamber of Deputies and the Senate to the PAN and the PRD, it retained majority control of both legislative chambers. The PRD initially refused to acknowledge its defeat, claiming that it had been the victim of the same fraudulent tactics employed against its candidates in 1988. Yet both domestic and foreign election observers agreed that, despite some recurring problems involving vote buying and coercion, the conduct of the elections and the vote count had been generally clean. Nevertheless, they did note – as did President-elect Zedillo himself, in a speech delivered to PRI leaders in late August 1994 – that the electoral playing field had not been level and that the PRI continued to enjoy substantial advantages over its political rivals.[35]

Unfortunately for President Zedillo (1994–2000), his moment of triumph did not last long. In September 1994 the PRI's secretary general, José Francisco Ruiz Massieu, was gunned down in Mexico City. The assistant attorney general appointed to the case, Mario Ruiz Massieu (the victim's brother), resigned only a few weeks into the

[34] Cook, Middlebrook, and Molinar Horcasitas (1994), p. 44.
[35] Molinar Horcasitas and Weldon (2001), pp. 223–4; Hernández Rodríguez (2003), pp. 55–6; Gómez Tagle (2004), pp. 91–2; Camacho Solís (2006), p. 240.

investigation, claiming that high members of the PRI were blocking his inquiries. **As if this accusation was not damaging enough, the investigation soon came to focus on Raul Salinas de Gortari (the former president's older brother), who was arrested in February 1995 and charged with masterminding the Ruiz Massieu murder.** The fact that José Francisco Ruiz Massieu had been married to the Salinas brothers'sister gave the charges a particularly macabre twist. Several days later, U.S. authorities arrested Mario Ruiz Massieu at the Newark, New Jersey Airport while he was en route to Spain with US$40,000 stuffed into a suitcase. Facing charges of money laundering in the United States and obstruction of justice in Mexico, he committed suicide. It was subsequently discovered that he held U.S. bank accounts containing 9 million dollars, a very large sum for someone whose only visible source of income was his salary as a public servant.[36]

Ruiz Massieu's overseas fortune was soon revealed to be a pittance compared to the US$130 million that Raul Salinas held in foreign bank accounts. To protest what he argued was the politically motivated arrest of his brother, Carlos Salinas briefly went on a hunger strike in March 1995 and then began a prolonged, self-imposed exile abroad. The public disgrace of the PRI redoubled President Zedillo's intention to maintain "a healthy distance" between his administration and the party.[37]

On top of this public display of murder and corruption at the highest levels of the PRI, in late 1994 Mexico faced another severe economic crisis. The Salinas administration's strategy of raising the purchasing power of consumers by overvaluing the peso came at a price: It made Mexican products expensive in U.S. dollar terms, thereby undercutting their competitiveness in international markets. It was not long before investors ceased to believe that the government would be able to maintain an artificially high exchange rate. Shortly after Zedillo took office on December 1, investors began to sell off their peso holdings. The Banco de México initially tried to control the slide of the peso via a modest devaluation of 15 percent vis-à-vis the U.S. dollar, but the "controlled adjustment" soon turned into a rout. Within days, the peso lost close to half its value. To defend the value of the peso, the Banco de México raised interest rates to astronomical levels in an attempt

[36] Preston and Dillon (2004), pp. 238–9, 313–14, 320–1; Pichardo Pagaza (2001), pp. 235, 274–6, 291, 295–8, 302.

[37] Pichardo Pagaza (2001), pp. 189, 199, 206, 288, 309; Hernández Rodríguez (2003), pp. 46, 54–5; Preston and Dillon (2004), Chapter 10; Camacho Solís (2006), pp. 263–4.

to encourage investors to purchase peso-denominated financial assets. As we discussed in Chapter Four, however, the sharp jump in interest rates forced households and businesses to default on their debts. Their defaults pushed Mexico's banks, many of which were already teetering on the edge of insolvency, into bankruptcy. This development, in turn, occasioned an economy-wide recession and a bank bailout whose ultimate cost was on the order of US$65 billion.

The 1994–1995 financial crisis was a severe blow to the PRI. The party's leadership had promised Mexican citizens that the NAFTA would significantly raise their living standards. Instead, the population was forced to endure an economic contraction even larger than that which had occurred in 1982–1983. Moreover, the rescue of the banking system involved large transfers of public funds to some of Mexico's richest individuals. The combination of economic collapse and financial scandal only served to strengthen the appeal of the PRD and PAN, which demonized the PRI, lambasting it as both incompetent and corrupt. Indeed, by 1997 voters no longer believed that the PRI was a more capable steward of the economy than the political opposition.[38]

With the country mired in recession and the PRI again on the defensive, opposition parties and civic organizations pressured the government into yet another round of electoral reform. The electoral code adopted in 1996 (lauded by President Zedillo as the "definitive" electoral reform, even though the PAN and PRD failed to support the final version submitted for congressional approval) eliminated government control over the organization of elections and ballot counting by establishing the Federal Electoral Institute as a fully autonomous body. Its president was elected by majority vote of its General Council members, all of whose nine voting members were independent citizens nominated by political parties but approved by a two-thirds vote of the Chamber of Deputies. The reform also made the federal electoral court (renamed the Electoral Tribunal of the Federal Judicial Branch, TEPJF) exclusively responsible for certifying the results of federal elections and strengthened its role in resolving allegations of electoral fraud. In addition, it gave opposition parties more equitable access to public funding and the mass media, and it established new oversight mechanisms for political party finances.[39]

---

[38] Magaloni (2006), Chapter 7; Buendía (2004), pp. 123–5.

[39] Gómez Tagle (2004), pp. 91–5; Molinar Horcasitas and Weldon (2001), pp. 225–7. The 1996 reform also provided for the direct election of the governor of the Federal District and gave full legislative authority to its representative assembly.

The 1996 reform also altered the way in which the Congress was elected. In the Chamber of Deputies, the legislation limited over-representation of the PRI by stipulating that a party's total proportion of Chamber seats could not exceed its share of the national vote by more than 8 percentage points.[40] In the Senate, a new formula for allocating the bloc of ninety-six senators gave two seats to the winning party in each state and one seat to the runner-up party. The remaining thirty-two seats (one for each state, plus the Federal District) were allocated according to the proportion of votes that each party received across the entire country. These rules worked to the disadvantage of the PRI, which would now receive two (rather than three) Senate seats for winning a plurality in a particular state. In contrast, the new arrangement favored the PRD (it had previously held very few seats in the Senate because the PAN had won most of the runner-up seats) because it was likely to capture a sizable share of the seats allocated via proportional representation.[41]

The 1996 reform culminated a political liberalization process that spanned two decades. PRI-led administrations, despite their stiff resistance and several modifications to the federal electoral code designed to preserve the PRI's dominance, were slowly forced to make the political system more competitive. In combination with significant civic mobilization and important changes in government-media relations, these modifications in the electoral code established the bases for free and fair elections.

The Rise of Civic Action

The reform of electoral rules and institutions during the 1980s and 1990s was driven forward in part by Mexico's increasingly mobilized citizenry. Many civic groups initially organized around other causes, including human rights and the environment.[42] In other instances,

---

[40] Thus, to gain a majority (251 seats) in the Chamber of Deputies, the PRI would have to win at least 166 of the 300 single-member districts and at least 42.2 percent of the national vote. See Molinar Horcasitas and Weldon (2001), p. 236.

[41] Klesner (1997); Díaz-Cayeros and Magaloni (2001), pp. 288–91; Gómez Tagle (2004), pp. 94–5. For statistical evidence that Mexican citizens' growing confidence in the electoral system during the 1990s had a positive impact on support for the PAN and the PRD, and that lack of credibility in the electoral process gradually became less important as a cause of abstention, see Buendía (2004).

[42] Aguayo Quezada (1998b), pp. 169–70; Lamas (2003); Olvera (2004).

civic groups emerged in response to government ineptitude in the management of specific crises, such as the government's incompetent response to the devastating earthquakes that struck Mexico City in September 1985, or its mismanagement of the economy and the collapse of the banking system in 1995.[43] Egregious electoral fraud during the 1980s was an important factor in bringing these groups together around the issue of electoral transparency.

The Roman Catholic Church played an important role in this process of societal awakening.[44] The church had long represented an exception to the PRI's near monopoly over the public sphere. From the 1960s onward, the church, in part responding to the doctrinal shifts associated with the Second Vatican Council (1962-1965), supported the formation of local-level associations focused on socioeconomic development problems. Despite the church hierarchy's overall conservatism, Jesuits and other religious orders were actively involved in the creation of nongovernmental organizations. In particular, Christian base communities devoted to "consciousness raising" proliferated during the 1970s, and over time they helped open public spaces for popular groups and shaped a new generation of leaders. In some areas, more conservative Catholic groups also constituted part of a network of organizations that increasingly questioned the legitimacy of Mexico's political order.[45] This was especially the case in the state of Chihuahua, where electoral fraud perpetrated by the PRI in the 1986 gubernatorial election galvanized the church into support of the PAN. Given the PAN's Catholic identity, the Church's more active role in promoting clean elections was of particular value to the party.[46]

There were areas in which a more active and politically engaged civil society directly intersected with the challenge to the PRI posed by opposition political parties. Civic organizations were often key constituents in the protest coalitions that the PAN and the PRD mobilized at state and municipal levels during electoral campaigns in the 1980s and 1990s. In some cases, regional resentment against political centralism was an important factor behind local support for opposition parties; in other instances, local groups had been alienated

---

[43] González Casanova (1994), p. 598; Olvera (2004), p. 416. On the impact of civic mobilizations by the 1985 Mexico City earthquake victims' movement, see Tavera-Fenollosa (1988) and Camacho Solís (2006), pp. 199-201.

[44] Camp (1997); Aguilar Ascencio (2000); Chand (2001); Olvera (2004).

[45] Aguayo Quezada (1998b); Olvera (2004), pp. 411, 413, 415–16.

[46] Loaeza (1999), pp. 352, 391; Chand (2001), Chapter 4.

by PRI-orchestrated electoral fraud, unpopular federal government decisions, or the especially egregious public conduct of PRI-affiliated government officials. The PAN in particular became the favored vehicle for middle-class groups alienated by economic instability and the federal government's reluctance to open electoral channels for the expression of discontent.

Effective two-party or multiparty competition at state and municipal levels became increasingly common during the 1990s in part because opposition parties were able to create or strengthen links to civic organizations whose demands frequently included electoral transparency.[47] These alliances often provided opposition parties with more durable constituent bases and helped build stronger party organizations, thereby allowing opposition parties to compete more effectively and demonstrate to the general public that they were a viable alternative to the PRI.

Civic organizations also became leading promoters of national networks of election observers. The de la Madrid administration's resort to fraud to contain opposition electoral gains at state and municipal levels in 1985 and 1986, as well as the blatant fraud committed in the 1988 presidential election, galvanized many of these groups into concerted action to ensure electoral transparency. For example, the Mexican Academy of Human Rights and other civic organizations established a network of observers to oversee the 1991 federal legislative elections, and in the 1994 presidential election some 400 civic groups and NGOs joined forces as the Civic Alliance. This initiative went beyond poll watching and the oversight of electoral officials on election day. It also included an assessment of media coverage (both news reporting and paid advertising), the monitoring of campaign spending, and efforts to inform voters of their rights. The Civic Alliance managed to create chapters in twenty-nine of Mexico's thirty-one states, and as many as 40,000 Mexican citizens (joined by some 900 "international visitors," as they were designated by the Mexican government) were involved in observing the 1994 elections.[48]

---

[47] For examples of PRD alliances with local civic organizations, see Bruhn (1997); for parallel examples of PAN alliances, see Middlebrook (2001).

[48] Olvera (2004), pp. 430–2. Aguayo Quezada (1998b), p. 179, places the number of election observers in 1994 at approximately 20,000. The Civic Alliance remained active throughout the 1990s, devoting its energies to state-level electoral observation, civic education, and the coordination of various popular referendums on political and social justice questions. It also organized an important electoral observation initiative around the 2000 elections, although its efforts were somewhat overshadowed by a now-independent and more vigorous Federal Electoral Institute.

The Mass Media and Democratization

Enhanced freedom of expression and greater political diversity in the print and electronic media played a particularly important role in Mexico's democratization. Government–media relations had long been characterized by cooptation, collusion, and censorship. PRI-led administrations framed the public agenda and ensured generally favorable coverage of the party and public officials through a combination of direct and indirect means. These included government censorship of newspaper and magazine content, administrative sanctions, political alliances with media owners, financial inducements, and the threat (and, all too frequently, the reality) of physical violence.

The relationship between the PRI and the country's most important television network, Televisa, illustrates the scope of Mexico's authoritarian rent-seeking coalition and gives a sense of how the government manipulated information for political purposes.[49] Most Mexicans receive the bulk of their information about political and economic issues from television news coverage. Until the mid-1990s, however, Televisa – a multibillion-dollar enterprise that controlled some 80 percent of television audiences and advertising revenues – was the only private television network in the country. The source of Televisa's monopoly was not difficult to discern: The government simply granted no other broadcast licenses. In a not-so-subtle quid pro quo, the network slanted news coverage heavily in favor of the PRI. Its anchormen and reporters typically extolled the virtues of PRI candidates and provided ample, flattering coverage of their campaign rallies. They also derided opposition candidates (or ignored them altogether). Indeed, Televisa went to far as to maintain a list of opposition political figures its reporters were not allowed to interview. Televisa's tacit alliance with the PRI was so close that it paid no taxes; instead, it provided 12.5 percent of its airtime to the government, free of charge. Emilio Azcárraga Jr., Televisa's long-time owner, took pride in making statements such as, "We are soldiers of the PRI" and "Televisa considers itself part of the governmental system."[50]

The print media were somewhat more difficult to control but not dramatically so. Because the government owned the only supplier of newsprint in Mexico, newspapers or magazines that were overly critical of the government could find themselves without paper, whereas

---

[49] Lawson (2002), pp. 29–30, 51–4, 96.
[50] Quoted in Lawson (2002), p. 30.

those publishers who reported favorably received newsprint at below its market price. In addition, the government provided a variety of direct and indirect subsidies to the print media, including payments for running "news articles" that had actually been written by government press agents and revenues generated by advertisements taken out by government agencies or the PRI. The government also engaged in the outright bribery of newspaper owners and reporters. When these tactics did not work, it threatened reporters and editors with physical violence, and it was prepared to make good on those threats.[51]

In the 1990s, however, both the print media and radio and television experienced major changes in their content and political behavior. Indeed, the growth of an increasingly mobilized citizenry made it more difficult for government officials to engage in direct media censorship or to intimidate dissident journalists with the threat of physical violence. The growing independence and pluralism of Mexico's media also reflected changes in journalistic norms, especially the gradual diffusion of stronger professional ethics – a development whose origins can be traced to 1976, when the government forced one of Mexico City's largest newspapers (*Excélsior*) to sack its editorial staff. Some of the individuals who were purged subsequently founded a politically independent news magazine, *Proceso*, which managed to survive despite a lack of government subsidies and occasional threats against its editor and publisher. Market forces reinforced these changes in professional ethics: An increasingly engaged public demanded more from journalists than merely serving as the PRI's mouthpiece. Equally important was the emergence of market competition *among* different media outlets. This was particularly true in radio, where station owners were reluctant to fire talk show hosts critical of the PRI because these personalities attracted listeners, thereby allowing the station to maintain market share and earn advertising revenues.[52]

The pace of change was less swift in television broadcasting. Televisa had a particularly close association with the PRI. Yet even Televisa was not immune from the effects of a more politically active citizenry and the vagaries of market competition. Pro-democracy groups began to protest strongly against the network's slanted and selective coverage of events. Then, in 1993, the privatization of a government-owned television network gave rise to a large and technically capable

[51] Lawson (2002), Chapters 3, 4.
[52] Lawson (2002), Chapter 5; Hughes (2003).

rival, Televisión Azteca. In making a decision that undercut Televisa's monopoly on private broadcasting, government officials may have assumed that they retained sufficient points of regulatory leverage to ensure the political loyalty of Televisión Azteca's owners.[53] In fact, the company's coverage of news events was initially as politically slanted as Televisa's. Over time, however, competition between the two networks for market share gave rise to higher-quality and less overtly biased coverage.[54]

These changes had very significant political consequences. Liberalization of the media contributed directly to democratization by ending the tradition of selective silence on such highly sensitive topics as government corruption, abuses of power, electoral fraud, and political repression.[55] The activities of pro-democracy groups were also further legitimated by the increased media attention they received. Equally important, the media provided much more balanced coverage of opposition political parties and candidates during election campaigns, a shift that greatly reduced the PRI's traditional electoral advantages. This departure was especially notable where television reporting was concerned, and by the 2000 general elections media coverage was generally quite equitable.[56]

The Consolidation of a Competitive Electoral Democracy

Mexico's transition was a staggered process, in which the PRI gradually lost control of different levels and branches of government – first at the municipal level, then state governorships and the federal Chamber of Deputies, and finally the presidency. Within this process the PRI's fortunes waxed and waned. Indeed, there were times (such as the 1991 and 1994 elections, when the PRI not only increased its congressional representation but also won the presidency in credible

---

[53] Calculations of short-term personal interest and the capacity of an incumbent president's close relatives to exploit political connections for private gain – a long-standing problem in Mexican public affairs – may have played a role in this politically sensitive privatization decision. Lawson (2002), p. 30, reports that one of the apparent conditions for the sale was that the new private owners take on Raul Salinas de Gortari, the incumbent president's elder brother, as a silent partner. See also Preston and Dillon (2004), pp. 306–8.

[54] Lawson (2002), Chapter 6.

[55] Morris (1999), pp. 631–2.

[56] Lawson (2002), Chapter 9.

fashion) when it seemed that the PRI might recover its dominance, a prospect that made it difficult for many observers to envision a transition to democracy in Mexico by electoral means.[57]

The PRI held several advantages in this protracted struggle. In addition to its tight grip on the mass media, the party's control over the federal government budget allowed it both to finance its campaigns from public funds and to use social welfare programs to buy votes. Moreover, the strong ideological split between the PAN and the PRD, as well as marked differences in their social bases of support, permitted the PRI to play the two main opposition parties off against one another in the process of drafting new electoral laws. On several occasions the governing party was able to make concessions that benefited the PAN in the short run, in exchange for the latter's acquiescence to provisions in the federal electoral code that safeguarded the PRI's majority in the Chamber of Deputies.[58] Yet over time, as political and economic crises sapped the ruling party's legitimacy, opposition parties and nongovernmental organizations together succeeded in gradually establishing more equitable conditions for electoral competition and nonpartisan institutions capable of ensuring free and fair elections.[59]

The PRI's own bases of organized support severely eroded over time. For instance, the economic crisis of the 1980s gradually weakened the political loyalty of unionized urban and industrial workers, who had been a bulwark of the party. As we discussed in Chapter Three, Mexican manufacturing workers saw their real incomes decline and their opportunities for economic mobility shrink dramatically after 1982. The government's decision to attempt to rekindle growth by unraveling the trade policies that had heightened job security for unionized industrial workers undermined their willingness to vote for the party's candidates. In the 1988 general elections, for example, PRI-affiliated labor leaders conspicuously failed to deliver their members' votes.[60] This is not to say that organized labor mobilized to bring about democratic regime change "from below."[61] Indeed, the leadership

---

[57] Middlebrook (2004), pp. 1 n2, 8, 14–15.
[58] Díaz-Cayeros and Magaloni (2001); Crespo (2004), pp. 69–74; Gómez Tagle (2004), pp. 86–92; Eisenstadt (2004), Chapter 6; Magaloni (2006), Chapter 8.
[59] For an evaluation of international (particularly U.S.) influences on democratization in Mexico, see Middlebrook (2004), pp. 21–2.
[60] Middlebrook (1995), pp. 293–4.
[61] Middlebrook (1997).

of Mexico's PRI-affiliated unions stood by the party all through the 1980s and 1990s. It is to say, however, that many rank-and-file union members came to the view that the PRI had broken its pact with them: The fiscal austerity, trade liberalization, and privatization policies imposed by the de la Madrid and Salinas administrations meant that labor leaders no longer controlled many of the patronage resources that had previously benefited them, and union membership no longer guaranteed stable, long-term employment. Thus, as opposition parties gained in strength and credibility, urban and industrial workers increasingly viewed them as viable electoral options.[62]

A similar, if more muted, phenomenon occurred in the countryside. From the 1930s onward, the government had built an immense patronage machine in rural Mexico that mobilized millions of votes for the PRI, even if those votes came at a cost to the economic efficiency of agriculture. The Salinas administration threw this machinery into disarray by ending land distributions to *ejidos* and by largely eliminating a complex system of price supports and production credits that helped sustain rural producers – and which had made them clients of the PRI.[63] The PRI continued to draw a substantial proportion of its electoral strength from the countryside, but between 1991 and 2000 the PAN more than doubled its support among rural voters.[64]

The impact of these changes was first visible at municipal and state levels. Indeed, given that the majority of seats in the federal Chamber of Deputies was allocated via single-member plurality districts in which the PRI was likely to prevail, the only practical way for the opposition eventually to gain control over the lower legislative chamber (even after the introduction of proportional-representation seats) was for it to build effective parties at the local level.[65] This meant that although opposition parties sometimes joined forces in broad anti-PRI coalitions, in most elections the ruling party faced off against whichever opposition party had built the most effective local organization. Generally speaking, the PAN was the principal rival to the

---

[62] In the year 2000 presidential election, for example, only 49 percent of all union members voted for the PRI's candidate. See Lawson (2000).

[63] Randall (1996); Pastor and Wise (1998), pp. 63–70; Mackinlay (2004).

[64] Buendía (2004), figure 4.2.

[65] Lujambio (2001), pp. 59, 62–3. One incentive for opposition parties to pursue this approach was the 1983 constitutional amendment introducing proportional representation in state legislatures and municipal councils. See González Casanova (1994), p. 593.

PRI in central-western and northern states, whereas the PRD was the main challenger in central and southern states.[66]

With increasing frequency during the 1990s, opposition parties were able to defeat the PRI in these local contests. Between 1988 and 1999, the PAN or the PRD took control, for a period of at least 3 years, of twenty-seven of the thirty largest municipalities in the country. In 1999 the PAN governed 33.1 percent of Mexico's population at the municipal level, and the PRD governed an additional 12.3 percent.[67] Data on elections to choose state governors tell a similar story. Federal authorities first recognized an opposition (PAN) gubernatorial victory in Baja, California, in 1989. In the years that followed, opposition parties rapidly expanded their base by winning eleven of the thirty-two gubernatorial elections held between 1993 and 1999 (including the governorship of the Federal District). Equally telling, the PRI won an absolute majority in only eight of the thirty-two gubernatorial contests held during this period.[68]

Local victories permitted opposition forces to build stronger party organizations, forge closer alliances with their constituencies, and gain valuable political and administrative experience. Equally important, an expanded presence in municipal and state government allowed the PAN and the PRD to demonstrate that they could perform effectively in office, thereby countering the PRI's claim that only it had the experience necessary to govern the country. Indeed, some of the policy reforms adopted by opposition parties once they took office (for instance, institutionalizing consultations with citizens about budgeting priorities and how best to deliver public services) reshaped voters' expectations regarding what could be achieved via partisan alternation in power.

Once PRI administrations could no longer control information, directly organize elections, count the votes, and certify the winners, the government lost the ability to determine electoral outcomes and the PRI's grip on national power began to slip rapidly. In the watershed

---

[66] Klesner (2003), table 5.2, reports that the proportion of two- or three-party-competitive districts in Chamber of Deputies elections rose from 37.7 percent in 1991 to 93.7 percent in 1997. See also Díaz-Cayeros (2004), pp. 219–24.

[67] Lujambio (2001), pp. 85–6. See also Moreno-Jaimes (2007), pp. 140–1.

[68] Díaz-Cayeros and Magaloni (2001), table 3. Six of these gubernatorial elections were won by the PAN operating alone, three by the PRD campaigning alone, and two by the PRD in coalition with smaller opposition parties.

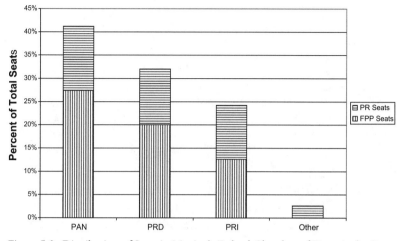

Figure 5.3: Distribution of Seats in Mexico's Federal Chamber of Deputies by Party and Seat Type, 2006–2009. *Source:* Instituto Federal Electoral (www.ife.gob.mx). *Note:* PR = proportional-representation seats; FPP = first-past-the-post seats. See the List of Abbreviations and Acronyms for political parties' full names.

1997 midterm elections (the first conducted under the terms of the 1996 electoral reform legislation), the PRI lost both its majority in the federal Chamber of Deputies and political control over the populous and strategically significant Federal District government. The PRI then saw its share of seats in the Chamber of Deputies shrink from 48 percent in 1997 to 42 percent in 2000, and to just 24 percent in 2006 (see Figure 5.1). Even more stunning, as Figure 5.3 demonstrates, nearly half of the PRI's 2006 victories in the Chamber of Deputies were allocated to it (ironically) via the proportional-representation formula that the party had initially created to appease the opposition; in its bread and butter single-district races, the party lost in overwhelming numbers. The 2006 results in the Senate were equally shocking to the PRI. As Figure 5.4 indicates, PRI party tickets only won five of thirty-two races (producing ten Senate seats). The majority of the PRI's Senate seats were allocated to it either as a result of placing second in a particular state (it obtained nineteen "minority party" seats), or via the proportional-representation system that had been introduced in 1996 to mollify the PRD (giving the PRI an additional ten seats).

The presidential election of 2000 was, nevertheless, the defining moment in the consolidation of a competitive electoral democracy

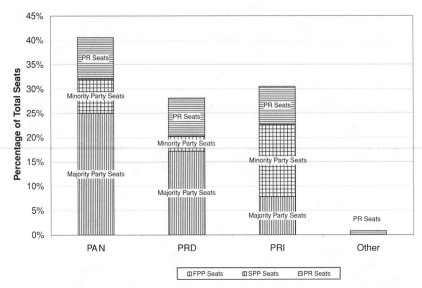

Figure 5.4: Distribution of Seats in Mexico's Federal Senate by Party and Seat Type, 2006. *Source:* Instituto Federal Electoral (www.ife.gob.mx). *Note:* FPP = first-past-the-post seats; SPP = second-past-the-post seats; PR = proportional-representation seats. See the List of Abbreviations and Acronyms for political parties' full names.

in Mexico. Despite the considerable advances embodied in the 1996 electoral reform, until an opposition candidate actually won the presidency there remained some doubt as to whether these changes had been sufficient to permit an opposition party or coalition to break the PRI's enduring control over the federal executive. On July 2, 2000, Vicente Fox (the candidate of the "Alliance for Change" coalition formed by the PAN and the Mexican Ecologist Green Party, PVEM) won the balloting with 42.5 percent of the total valid vote.[69] The margin of Fox's victory over PRI candidate Francisco Labastida Ochoa (who received 36.1 percent of the vote) was especially important because it made it difficult for old-line forces within the PRI to contest President Ernesto Zedillo's decision on election eve to recognize publicly Fox's triumph.[70]

---

[69] For an analysis of the 2000 elections, see Domínguez and Lawson (2003); Moreno (2003).

[70] The third major candidate, Cuauhtémoc Cárdenas, received 16.6 percent of the vote as leader of the center-left "Alliance for Mexico" coalition that grouped the PRD, the Labor Party (PT), the Democratic Convergence (CD), the Nationalist Society Party (PSN), and the Social Alliance Party (PAS).

The Fox Administration: Mexico's First
Opposition Government

Vicente Fox (2000–2006) took his oath of office on December 1, 2000, amid extremely high public expectations. During the 2000 presidential campaign he had promised voters, simply but powerfully, to bring about "Change Now!" ("¡Cambio Ya!"). His clear-cut victory over the PRI delivered on a major portion of that promise. Fox had, however, also assured voters that he would quickly resolve the festering political crisis in Chiapas resulting from the 1994 Zapatista rebellion, promote rapid economic growth and job creation, raise educational levels, and bring about substantial reductions in poverty. In his first months in office Fox did in fact succeed in enacting a Law on Indigenous Rights and Culture (albeit one that failed to win the support of the EZLN and its allies), and in 2002 the Congress approved a Federal Law on Transparency and Access to Governmental Public Information.[71] Nevertheless, Fox was unable to secure congressional approval for several of the reforms that, he argued, were essential to Mexico's long-term economic development and international competitiveness. These included a major tax reform, measures permitting foreign direct investment in electrical power generation and the petroleum industry, and a reform of the federal labor code. Fox's personal popularity remained high throughout his presidency, but, over time, the growing public sense that Fox had failed to achieve his most important policy goals cast a shadow over his administration.[72]

The fundamental problem was the PAN lacked a legislative majority in either house of Congress, and forging a coalition with either the PRI or the PRD proved elusive.[73] Three factors contributed to this state of affairs. These include particular features of Mexico's electoral system, partisan calculations by opposition parties that they could make future electoral gains by blocking the Fox administration's legislative initiatives, and the ineffectiveness of Fox's own tactics and governing style.

---

[71] The 1977 electoral reform had included a constitutional right to freedom of information but the necessary enabling legislation had never been passed. See Gómez Tagle (2004), pp. 85, 103.

[72] Public perceptions of this kind were politically important. As Magar and Romero (2007) correctly note, however, PRI administrations with unified control over both the presidency and the Congress had also failed to enact significant energy, tax, and labor reforms.

[73] The PAN began the 58th Congress (2000–2003) with 206 seats (41.2 percent) in the Chamber of Deputies and 46 seats (35.9 percent) in the Senate.

The coordination problems inherent in Mexico's multiparty democracy posed a barrier to Fox's ability to build the majority coalitions
required to enact his top-priority legislative proposals. Successive PRI
administrations, assuming that there would always be one dominant
party (the PRI) controlling the presidency and both legislative chambers, had accommodated minority party demands for representation
by creating an electoral system that combined single-member plurality
districts with a parallel system of proportional representation. Electoral
systems composed exclusively of single-member legislative districts
(like that which exists in the United States) generally tend to have
only two parties because voters have incentives not to "waste" their
ballots by supporting third-party candidates who have little chance
of winning. In contrast, proportional-representation systems tend to
promote the formation of multiple parties. Votes are not "wasted" in
these systems because legislative seats are allocated on the basis of the
percentage of the vote that a party obtains.[74] Thus, even parties with
a minimal number of adherents can gain seats in the legislature.[75]

To be sure, mixed-member electoral systems (those combining single-member plurality districts with proportional representation) like
Mexico's can, at least in parliamentary democracies, capture the best
features of both majoritarianism and proportional representation.[76]
Nevertheless, there is also substantial evidence indicating that the
multipartism promoted by proportional-representation arrangements
is problematic when it coexists with presidentialism (a system in which
there is an elected president).[77] In parliamentary systems, a single party
(or a coalition of parties) names a prime minister, and the government

---

[74] Proportional-representation systems vary in terms of the way these percentages are calculated.
Some allocate seats on the basis of the percentage of votes that a party received nationally,
some on the basis of the percentage of votes received regionally, and yet others on the basis
of the votes that a party received at the state or provincial level.

[75] PRI administrations actively sought to ensure the representation of opposition parties on
both the left and the right of the ideological spectrum as a way of safeguarding the PRI's
position as the majority party in the political center. Indeed, provisions in several versions
of the federal electoral code penalized the strongest opposition party while favoring the
smallest ones. Díaz-Cayeros and Magaloni (2001), p. 283; Weldon (2001), pp. 464–6.

[76] Shugart and Wattenberg (2001), pp. 571, 578, 582, 591, argue that mixed-member electoral
systems can successfully promote two-bloc competition and legislators' accountability to
constituents based on single-member plurality districts, while simultaneously ensuring the
representation of smaller parties and encouraging (through party elites' control over the
formulation of candidate lists) the development of disciplined national parties. As Weldon
(2001), p. 470, notes, two-party competition did emerge in a number of Mexican states
with mixed-member electoral systems.

[77] Mainwaring (1993), pp. 199–200, 207–8, 213.

he or she leads can only function for as long as it can maintain its legislative majority. In multiparty presidential systems, however, the strong likelihood that there will be more than two parties with seats in the legislature reduces the odds that a single party will have a majority. It reduces even further the odds that one party will simultaneously control both the executive and the legislative branches of government. When different parties do control the executive and the legislature in a situation of divided government, legislative coalitions are more difficult to sustain and must often be assembled issue by issue. As a consequence, executive–legislative deadlock frequently occurs.

The chances of forming majority legislative coalitions are lower in multiparty presidential democracies in part because there is likely to be considerable ideological distance among rival political parties,[78] and this element did indeed constitute a second factor complicating matters for the Fox administration. Opinion polls have found substantial distance between PAN and PRD party leaders on a left–right ideological spectrum, a distance that is in fact greater among party elites than among those members of the electorate who identify closely with the two parties.[79] This gap between party leaders and supporters is important because the 1996 federal electoral code allowed parties to nominate as many as sixty candidates on both their single-member plurality and their proportional-representation slates,[80] thus increasing the odds that (more ideological) PAN and PRD party leaders will be elected and hold a prominent position in their respective congressional delegations.

Ideological divisions between the PAN and the PRD have deep roots in the two parties' distinctive histories and in party leaders' different backgrounds and socialization experiences. The PAN was formed in 1939 to protest the radical educational and land-reform policies pursued by President Lázaro Cárdenas (father of PRD founder Cuauhtémoc Cárdenas), and the support the PAN has received from Catholic activists clearly differentiates it from the strongly secularist PRD (as well as the PRI). During the 1980s and 1990s, these differences were reinforced by the contrasting positions the PAN and the PRD took with regard to the Salinas and Zedillo administrations' economic policies. The center-right PAN – long a defender of private

---

[78] Mainwaring (1993), pp. 200, 213.
[79] Bruhn and Greene (2007); Lawson (2007), p. 47.
[80] Weldon (2001), p. 457.

property and a consistent opponent of an expansive state – was, of course, the PRI's principal legislative ally in enacting the constitutional reforms necessary to liberalize Mexico's trade and investment regimes and to privatize state-owned firms, and it sanctioned the controversial bank bailout after the 1994–1995 financial crisis. The PRD, in contrast, had been founded in part to protect the system of state-owned enterprises and trade protection that had developed in Mexico before the de la Madrid administration. Some of its leaders also resented the PAN's role in enacting the legislative program of an administration (Carlos Salinas de Gortari) whose electoral legitimacy they impugned. Several of the legislative initiatives promoted by Fox and the PAN (especially energy-sector reform) went to the very heart of these ideological divisions. Thus, although the PAN and PRD could find common ground on such matters as legislation that greatly expanded health insurance coverage and on democracy-enhancing measures such as a federal freedom-of-information law designed to promote transparency and accountability in public administration, it was impossible for them to do so on a range of economic policy issues.

The PRD and some elements of the PRI also perceived that cooperation with the PAN was not in their long-term partisan interests. From the outset of the Fox administration, the PRD announced that it was not going to cooperate with "a government of the Right," and rarely did it depart from this stance.[81] Although some PRI members were strongly opposed to Fox's proposed constitutional reforms, such as those that would have permitted foreign investment in the electrical power and petroleum industries, the party did not reject in principle the idea of supporting some PAN initiatives. Indeed, the Fox administration apparently decided to forego high-profile prosecutions of former PRI government officials for corruption and human rights abuses in order to promote a PAN–PRI legislative alliance. In time, however, PRI strategists took the view that the party's chances of regaining the presidency in 2006 would be greater if Mexican voters perceived the Fox administration to have failed.[82] The fact that ideological and partisan differences precluded a PAN–PRD alliance gave the PRI considerable leverage in this regard.

---

[81] Langston (2007), pp. 21–2; Bruhn and Greene (2007), p. 37.

[82] The PRI's inclination to obstruct the Fox administration's legislative program may have been bolstered by its electoral recovery in the 2003 midterm elections, in which it won 34.4 percent of the valid vote and 44.8 percent of the seats in the Chamber of Deputies. It also won gubernatorial elections in Colima, Nuevo León, and Sonora in 2003, and in Chihuahua, Durango, Oaxaca, and Veracruz in 2004.

Finally, these obstacles to the PAN's capacity to implement its legislative agenda were exacerbated by the inadequacies of Fox's own
tactics and governing style. Even though Fox had been a charismatic
and highly effective presidential candidate, once in office he proved to
be an ineffective chief executive. The fundamental problem was that
he could not figure out how to cut deals with the leaders of opposition parties' congressional delegations. Instead, he sought to sidestep
his congressional opponents and build support for his legislative program by appealing directly to the Mexican people via weekly radio
broadcasts and aggressive public relations campaigns. This tactic might
have borne fruit in another institutional context. In large part because
of Mexico's "no reelection" rule, however, legislators had only weak
ties to their constituents. They were, nevertheless, extremely sensitive to the preferences of their party leaders, who could determine
a politician's chances of future electoral success through the position
they assigned her or him on the party's list of proportional-representation candidates.[83] Fox's direct appeals for public support were, therefore, generally ineffective in influencing legislators' behavior.

The interaction of these factors – institutional and ideological legacies from Mexico's past, partisan calculations of the possible electoral
advantages to be derived from obstructionism, and the ineffectiveness of President Fox's own tactics and governing style – produced
executive–legislative gridlock on the Fox administration's leading legislative initiatives.[84] Perhaps the most significant casualties of this situation were the administration's proposals for fiscal and tax reform.
Fox first submitted this legislation to the Chamber of Deputies in
2001.[85] Some provisions, including those designed to make financial
transactions more transparent (for example, barring insider trading and
regulating conflicts of interest and the use of privileged information in
stock market transactions) and modify the federal budgetary approval
process so that executive–legislative disagreements did not jeopardize

---

[83] Weldon (2001), pp. 472–3.

[84] Overall congressional productivity during the 2000–2006 period (measured as the number
of bills enacted into law) compared very favorably to productivity rates during the era of PRI
dominance. Approval rates for executive-sponsored bills also remained robust (for example,
72.1 percent in the Chamber of Deputies for the September 2003–December 2005 period,
and 89.7 percent in the Senate for the September 2000–December 2005 period). The federal
executive did, however, submit fewer bills than in the past, and greater political pluralism
in the Congress encouraged deputies and senators to propose far more bills than they had
during the period of PRI hegemony. See Weldon (2004a), pp. 150–65; Weldon (2004b),
pp. 10–13; Weldon (2006), pp. 7, 17, 30, 33.

[85] See Middlebrook and Zepeda (2003), pp. 43–5, for details.

continued governmental operations at the end of each calendar year, were easily enacted into law. Yet the heart of the measure – a proposal to increase taxes by the equivalent of approximately 2 percent of GDP, in part by extending the 15 percent value-added tax to previously exempt categories of food and medicines – sparked intense political opposition. Despite sustained lobbying by the Fox administration, the legislation that was finally approved limited tax increases to approximately half of what had initially been proposed and retained the tax exemption on food and medicines.[86] The defeat of Fox's proposed tax reform denied the government badly needed revenues to fund education and other social welfare initiatives.

The Controversial 2006 Elections

In the July 2006 general elections, the PRI hoped to retake the presidency by building on its string of electoral successes in the 2003 midterm elections and in gubernatorial races held during 2003 and 2004.[87] PRI candidate Roberto Madrazo Pintado was, however, badly tarnished by campaign spending fraud in his 1994 Tabasco gubernatorial victory and hampered by serious factional divisions within the PRI. The race therefore centered on the bitter rivalry between the PAN's Felipe Calderón Hinojosa and the PRD's Andrés Manuel López Obrador.[88] Calderón denounced López Obrador as a "danger to Mexico" and compared him to Venezuela's populist President Hugo Chávez, claiming that López Obrador's proposed social justice programs would endanger the country's hard-won financial stability. Calderón lagged in public opinion polls throughout much of the race. Late in the campaign, however, he closed the gap through the highly effective use of negative television advertising, the benefits he derived

---

[86] In a second attempt at tax reform in 2003, the Fox administration's initiative (in which government officials stubbornly insisted on levying the value-added tax on food and medicines) failed when efforts to build an alliance with the head of the PRI's delegation in the Chamber of Deputies fell victim to a rank-and-file revolt by PRI deputies and feuding among PRI leaders. Insufficient coordination between Ministry of Finance officials and the PAN's congressional delegation also hampered the negotiations. See Musacchio (2003); Weldon (2004b), p. 15; Langston (2007), p. 22.

[87] For analyses of the 2006 elections and their aftermath, see Estrada and Poiré (2007), Klesner (2007), Middlebrook (2007), Moreno (2007), and Schedler (2007).

[88] López Obrador led the "Alliance for the Good of All" coalition, which included the PRD, the Labor Party (PT), and Democratic Convergence (CD).

from President Fox's massive (and much-criticized) media campaign touting the achievements of his administration and advocating political continuity, and López Obrador's own political errors. These included López Obrador's personal attacks on the still-popular President Fox, as well as his decision not to participate in the first of two nationally televised debates among the candidates – an absence that his rivals exploited by placing an empty chair on the debating platform.

The balloting on July 2 occurred without major problems, but the very narrow difference in the vote totals for Calderón and López Obrador quickly led to controversy as both candidates claimed victory. When the Federal Electoral Institute announced that Calderón held an extremely tight lead, López Obrador demanded that the Electoral Tribunal of the Federal Judicial Branch (TEPJF) order a ballot-by-ballot recount. Claiming that the entire electoral process had been tainted by the Fox administration's partisan actions in support of Calderón and by massive irregularities on election day, López Obrador sought to pressure electoral authorities by announcing a national campaign of civic resistance that included the blockade of one of Mexico City's main boulevards and an occupation of the Zócalo, the public plaza facing Mexico's National Palace.

In a highly charged political environment, TEPJF magistrates agreed to examine ballots in approximately 9 percent of all polling places but they unanimously rejected demands for a full recount. Then, in early September, the TEPJF declared Calderón president-elect with 36.7 percent of the valid vote, compared with López Obrador's 36.1 percent (a difference of just 233,831 of the 41,557,430 ballots cast).[89] López Obrador refused to accept his defeat and later proclaimed himself president of an alternative, parallel government. Nevertheless, the 2006 election outcome was highly significant in political terms both because the PAN won a come-from-behind victory to retain the presidency for a second consecutive time, and because Mexico's electoral institutions survived a severe test of their authority in what had become a remarkably competitive electoral environment.

---

[89] The PRI's Madrazo won 22.7 percent of the vote, and Patricia Mercado Castro (representing the Social-democratic and Peasant Alternative Party, PASDC) and Roberto Campa Cifrián (representing the New Alliance Party, PANAL) won 2.8 percent and 1 percent, respectively. The TEPJF's final ruling also criticized President Fox and private-sector groups for their sustained efforts to undercut López Obrador's presidential candidacy and sway voters' opinion in favor of Calderón. See Middlebrook (2007).

What had not changed as much, however, were the challenges facing any Mexican executive searching for a way to raise the revenues needed to fund health care, education, retirement pensions, and housing. How the Fox administration, like the Zedillo administration before it, was forced to make a series of difficult tradeoffs when it came to funding those public priorities, and the consequences of those trade-offs, are the focus of the next chapter.

6

Health, Education, and Welfare in Mexico Since 1980

Mexico has experienced significant changes in social welfare policy since the early 1990s. The administrations of Ernesto Zedillo Ponce de León (1994–2000) and Vicente Fox Quesada (2000–2006) redesigned programs providing basic health care, housing, education, and retirement pensions in order to broaden access to these services. In some instances (particularly the partial privatization of health care and the creation of privately managed retirement pensions), meeting the goal of expanded program access in the context of continuing revenue shortages required the government to shift part of the responsibility for welfare provision from the public sector to individuals and families. The Zedillo and Fox administrations also adopted more selectively targeted programs aimed at reducing poverty in Mexico.

One key element underpinning these changes was a marked shift in the political logic shaping welfare policy making.[1] In the social welfare model that developed during the period of Institutional Revolutionary Party (PRI) hegemony from the late 1930s through the 1980s, select constituencies gained access to public services as a form of patronage. Indeed, there was a wide gap between an official rhetoric proclaiming the federal government's constitutionally mandated responsibility to cover the basic welfare needs of all Mexican citizens, and actual

---

[1] Some analysts argue that various initiatives adopted by the Zedillo and Fox administrations also reflected a significant rethinking of the philosophical underpinnings of social welfare policy in Mexico – a shift away from an assumption that the federal government has a responsibility to cover the basic needs of all Mexican citizens, and toward a view emphasizing individual and family responsibilities and the role of the market in promoting competition and efficiency in the delivery of health insurance, housing, retirement pensions, and other welfare programs. See, for example, Laurell (2003).

policy practice. Programs such as President Carlos Salinas de Gortari's (1988–1994) main poverty-alleviation initiative, the National Solidarity Program (PRONASOL), were notably politicized.[2]

The onset of real electoral competition in Mexico has, however, pushed political parties, regardless of their stated ideologies, both to increase spending on social welfare programs and to broaden access to those programs.[3] Certainly by the time the Fox administration took office (if not before), political parties viewed the amount and focus of social welfare spending as a basis on which to appeal for votes. For example, in September 2004 a coalition of the PRI, the Party of the Democratic Revolution (PRD), and the Mexican Ecologist Green Party (PVEM) actually rewrote the budget that the Fox administration had submitted to Congress, raising social welfare expenditures beyond what President Fox had proposed.[4] When their revised budget was subsequently passed (over Fox's objections), they took out a paid advertisement in one of Mexico's leading news magazines that featured the signature phrase "The Chamber of Deputies Comes Through for You" ("La Cámara de Diputados te cumple").[5] Similarly, in order to fund increased social expenditures, the administration of President Felipe Calderón Hinojosa (2006–2012) – led by the market-oriented National Action Party (PAN) – adopted a minimum tax on business enterprises and thereby distinguished itself as the first government in Mexican history to tax corporate income effectively.

The shift toward expanded public access to welfare provision does not necessarily mean that incumbent government officials have been willing to forego opportunities to administer those programs so as to maximize their own partisan advantages. Similarly, changes in the scope of welfare programs do not mean that Mexico is rapidly becoming a West European-style welfare state. Not all of the welfare reforms undertaken by recent governments have produced the outcomes envisioned by their architects, and social welfare initiatives remain constrained by the fact that the federal government's revenues as a proportion of gross domestic product (GDP) are only one-third to one-half as large as in West European countries (and comparatively low even by Latin American standards). Nevertheless, a nuanced analysis of the

---

[2] See, for example, Molinar Horcasitas and Weldon (1994).

[3] In some instances, the advocates of welfare policy reform explicitly sought to undermine the clientelist arrangements that had long sustained rent-seeking authoritarianism in Mexico.

[4] La Jornada Virtu@l, 18 November 2004.

[5] Proceso, no. 1466 (5 December 2004), p. 13.

transformation of social welfare policy in Mexico strongly suggests that elected officials now confront a political imperative characteristic of all democracies: If they do not deliver public goods, citizens will vote for other parties that promise to do so.

The Demographic Parameters of Social Policy

Before we assess how shifts in policies affected changes in social welfare outcomes, we must consider two underlying demographic trends that influenced patterns of social spending. The first is Mexico's rapidly falling birthrate, which has aided government efforts to provide health care and public education to more people. The average number of children borne by each woman fell from 6.7 in 1970 to 2.2 in 2005.[6] Had Mexico's fertility rate remained at its 1970 level, the country's population would have been 154 million people in the year 2000.[7] In fact, Mexico's population totaled only 97 million in that year. The number of children younger than age 19 has been roughly constant since 1990.

A falling birthrate made it easier for policy makers to expand access to childhood health care and basic education. The proportion of Mexicans aged 5–19 years declined from 40 percent of the population in 1970 to 31 percent in 2005, and United Nations projections anticipate that the proportion of Mexicans in this age bracket will fall even further to 22 percent by 2030.[8] If Mexico can simply maintain its level of educational spending as a percentage of GDP, then per-student spending will increase.

Falling fertility rates have, however, placed pressure on the retirement pension system. The proportion of the Mexican population older than age 65 grew from 1.8 percent in 1970 to 5.5 percent in 2005, and the United Nations projects that the elderly as a proportion of the total population will rise to 10.9 percent by 2030.[9] The

[6] The data for 1960 are from Tuirán, Partida, Mojarro, and Zúñiga (n.d.), figure 2. The data for 2005 are from INEGI, "Tasa global de fecundidad, 1976 a 2005," available at www. inegi.gob.mx.

[7] Consejo Nacional de Población (CONAPO) (2001a), p. 20. Indeed, as late as 1978 the Mexican government estimated that the population would reach 132 million by 2000. See Alba (1984), p. 17.

[8] INEGI, "Población total por grupos quinquenales de edad según sexo, 1950 a 2005," available at www.inegi.gob.mx; Espinosa-Vega and Sinha (2000), p. 5.

[9] Espinosa-Vega and Sinha (2000), p. 5.

growing number of elderly people will have to be supported by their relatively less-numerous children.

What caused Mexico's fertility rate to decline so rapidly? One significant source of Mexico's demographic transition was increasing urbanization. The urban portion of the population (defined as residents in population centers with more than 2,500 people) grew from 59 percent to 77 percent between 1970 and 2005.[10] Mexico's urbanites tend to have smaller families.[11] Thus, as the urban proportion of the population grew, family sizes shrank.

Increasing urbanization is, however, only part of the story; birthrates fell in both rural and urban areas. The total fertility rate of urban women declined from 4.0 children per woman of child-bearing age in 1980 to 2.3 children in 1996, and the rate for rural women dropped from 6.8 children to 3.5 children.[12] In both urban and rural areas, rising female educational levels contributed significantly to falling birthrates. The fertility rates of women with no formal education have been persistently twice as high as those of women who have graduated high school. Yet the proportion of all females aged 15 to 45 years with no formal education declined from 44 percent in 1960 to 12 percent in 2000, and the proportion of females in this age bracket who had attended some high school increased from 7 percent to 50 percent during the same period.[13] Birthrates declined commensurately.[14]

Rising female educational attainment coincided with (and contributed to) a large-scale movement of women into the labor force.[15] Between 1970 and 1990, Mexico's female labor force participation rate rose from 18 percent to 32 percent, and in 2003 it reached 38 percent.[16] Growing opportunities for women in the labor market have helped depress female fertility rates because they have raised the cost (in foregone income) of having children.

---

[10] INEGI, "Porcentaje de la población que reside en localidades con 2,500 y más habitantes, 1900 a 2005," available at www.inegi.gob.mx.

[11] Mexico's rural birthrates in the 1970s were 48 percent higher than urban birthrates. See CONAPO (2001a), p. 37.

[12] INEGI (2001a), p. 43.

[13] Dirección General de Estadística (1962); INEGI (2001b); INEGI, "Indicadores seleccionados sobre nivel de escolaridad, promedio de escolaridad, aptitud para leer y escribir y alfabetismo, 1960–2000," available at www.inegi.gob.mx.

[14] Because access to education is much greater in cities than in the countryside, it is very difficult in practice to disentangle the impact of urbanization per se on fertility rates from the effect of rising educational levels.

[15] Giugale, Lafourcade, and Nguyen (2001), p. 449.

[16] Hanson (2003), p. 32; Parker and Pederzini (2001), p. 13.

Access to contraception provides a further piece of the puzzle concerning Mexico's declining average birthrate. In 1976, only 30 percent of adult Mexican women reported using contraception. By 1987, aided by large-scale government programs designed to promote the knowledge and use of contraception, this figure had risen to 53 percent. By 1997 slightly more than 68 percent of adult Mexican women reported using contraception.[17]

Social policy makers have also had to take account of a second major demographic trend in Mexico: the gradual weakening of the traditional family. Although Mexicans overwhelmingly continue to live within family units (in 2005, families constituted 92 percent of all households in Mexico, compared with 68 percent in the United States), the characteristics of the family unit have changed.[18] One of the most obvious shifts has been in age at first marriage. In 1970, the average age of women at first marriage or cohabitation was 21.3 years; in 1990 it was 22.4 years, and in 2004 it was 24.7 years. The data for men tell a similar story: the average age at the time of first marriage or cohabitation was 24.3 years in 1970, 24.6 years in 1990, and 27.5 years in 2004.[19] As a result, the median age at which Mexican women had their first child rose quickly, jumping by a full 3 years (from 22 to 25 years) during the 1990s.[20]

There has also been a substantial rise over time in family instability. One measure of this phenomenon is the growth in female-headed households, which as a proportion of all households increased from 12 percent in 1960 to 13.5 percent in 1976, 15.3 percent in 1990, 20.6 percent in 2000, and 23.1 percent in 2005.[21] The increase in

---

[17] INEGI, "Porcentaje de mujeres unidas en edad fértil usuarias de métodos anticonceptivos, 1976 a 1997," available at www.inegi.gob.mx.

[18] INEGI, "Distribución porcentual de los hogares por tipo y clase de hogar para cada sexo del jefe, 1950 a 2005," available at www.inegi.gob.mx. Data for the United States are from Roberts (2004), p. 27.

[19] The data for 1970 are from CONAPO (2003b), p. 172; data for 1990 are from United Nations, *World Marriage Patterns*, available at www.un.org/esa/population/publications/worldmarriage/worldmarriage.htm; data for 2004 are from INEGI, "Edad media al matrimonio por entidad federativa de residencia habitual de los contrayentes según sexo, 2002, 2003 y 2004," available at www.inegi.gob.mx. During the 1990s cohabitating couples rose from 14 percent to 19 percent of all couples.

[20] Authors' estimate calculated from data in INEGI, "Promedio de hijos nacidos vivos de las mujeres de 12 años y más por grupos de edad, 1970–2005," available at www.inegi.gob.mx.

[21] The data for 1960 are from INEGI, "Hogares por sexo del jefe, tipo y clase de hogar, 1950–2005," available at www.inegi.gob.mx. The data for 1976, 1990, and 2000 are from CONAPO, "Sostienen las mujeres 5.6 millones de hogares," available at www.conapo.gob.mx/prensa/2002/2022mzo02.htm. The data for 2005 are from INEGI, "Conteo de población y vivienda, 2005," available at www.inegi.gob.mx.

the number of female-headed families mainly reflects higher rates of divorce and abandonment. Indeed, although still low by European and U.S. standards, the proportion of marriages ending in divorce in Mexico rose from 4.4 percent in 1980 to 7.4 percent in 2000, and to 11.3 percent by 2004.[22] In addition, since the 1990s growing numbers of men have abandoned their families (possibly temporarily) to seek work in the United States.

A skeptical reader might argue that the rising rate of family dissolution in Mexico is a side effect of the aging of the population. The logic behind this position is that the longer people live, the more likely their marriages are to end in divorce rather than death, and so the divorce rate is increasing in line with Mexican lifespans. The data, however, do not support this hypothesis. Indeed, dissolution rates have risen fastest among new families. In married and cohabiting couples that formed before 1967, there was only a 7.4 percent chance of dissolution before 10 years had passed, whereas a couple that formed in 1987 (the last year for which data are available) had a 14 percent chance of breaking up before 10 years had passed.[23]

An even more skeptical reader might argue that an increase in the proportion of "extended families" (households in which uncles, aunts, cousins, brothers and sisters, and elderly grandparents live with a nuclear family composed of parents and their children) among Mexican households indicates that the Mexican family is as strong as ever. Between 1990 and 2000 the proportion of all family households defined as "extended" rose from 20.7 percent to 26.3 percent.[24] It

---

[22] The divorce rate is thought to understate the actual rate of family dissolution because cohabiting couples are more likely to break up than married ones. Divorces in Mexico are still less common than in Catholic European countries. In 2002, for example, the divorce rate was 12.9 percent in Ireland, 15.4 percent in Italy, and 19.9 percent in Spain. In comparison, in the year 2000 the lowest divorce rate in the United States (for the state of Massachusetts) was 27 percent. The rate for the United States as a whole was 51 percent. See United Nations, *World Marriage Patterns*, available at www.un.org/esa/population/publications/worldmarriage/worldmarriage.htm.

[23] CONAPO, "Cerca de 4.5 millones de 'madres solas'," available at www.conapo.gob.mx/prensa/2002/2002may01.htm. Because the survey was conducted in 1997, the 10-year divorce rate for marriages initiated in 1997 was not yet available at the time we undertook this analysis.

[24] The figure reported for 2005 was 25.7 percent. See INEGI (1999), pp. 3, 133. The "extended household" category includes both "amplified [*ampliado*] households" (those having a head of household with or without spouses or children, but containing relatives of the head of household such as uncles, cousins, brothers-in-laws, and parents) and "composed [*compuesto*] households" (those having a head of household with or without spouse, children, or relatives, but with other nonrelated persons present). In a household survey conducted in 1994, the

is equally likely, however, that this increase was an artifact of the inter-action between economic distress and rising rates of single-parenthood and couple dissolution. Indeed, in the year 2000 some 60 percent of single mothers and 28 percent of female divorcees with children lived in "extended families" (that is, with their parents).[25]

Health Care Reform

One of the sharpest departures in Mexican social policy after 1980 was in the health care sector. During most of the period in which the PRI monopolized power, access to publicly funded health care depended mainly on the political clout wielded by particular social groups, rather than on criteria such as income level or medical need. The Mexican Social Security Institute (IMSS) provided health insurance to formal-sector workers, and a panoply of separate social insurance programs covered public-sector employees (via the Social Security Institute for State Workers ISSSTE), workers at the Mexican Petroleum Company (PEMEX), and military personnel. The Ministry of Health was responsible for providing health care to everyone else – that is to say, to the bulk of the population. By the 1990s, 3 percent of the population used private health insurance and another 47 percent relied on the various public health schemes; the remaining half the population had no insurance coverage and depended on the Ministry of Health.[26] The result was a three-tier system in which Mexicans with sufficient resources to purchase their own health insurance enjoyed top-quality care, those enrolled in the principal public schemes (IMSS and ISSSTE) received care that was generally within the standards found in the developed world, and the majority of the population depended on the chronically underfunded efforts of the Ministry of Health.[27]

The Zedillo administration sought to alter both the source and the extent of health care delivery. Despite continuing budgetary

---

INEGI found that 75 percent of the 18 million households in Mexico were composed of a nuclear family and 25 percent were defined as extended families. Of this latter group, some 97 percent were "amplified" households and 3 percent were "composed" households.

[25] CONAPO, "Información con motivo del Día de las Madres," available at www.conapo.gob.mx/prensa/2002/2002may02.htm.

[26] Frenk et al. (2003).

[27] OECD (2005), pp. 19–21.

constraints, between 1994 and 2000 the Zedillo government increased spending on health care by 11.2 percent in real (inflation-adjusted) terms.[28] The problem was that this growth began from a very low base, so that by the end of Zedillo's term in the year 2000 total health care spending in Mexico represented only 4.3 percent of GDP. This compared to 7.3 percent of GDP in Brazil, 8 percent in Chile, 9 percent in Costa Rica, and an average of 7.5 percent in Organisation for Economic Co-operation and Development (OECD) member states.[29]

One aspect of the Zedillo administration's strategy was to privatize part of health care delivery to concentrate government spending on the mass of the population without access to health insurance. Part of this privatization occurred via a 1995 legal reform that allowed many private employers to opt out of the public health care system. As a consequence, the number of people using private health insurance increased by 60 percent between 1995 and 1999, rising to 3.5 million individuals.[30] Further privatization occurred de facto as resource shortages caused the quality and accessibility of the health care provided by the IMSS and the ISSSTE to decline. Several studies indicate that, by the end of Zedillo's term, as much as one-quarter of the population with access to the IMSS or the ISSSTE chose to use private physicians instead.[31]

The Zedillo administration used the public funds saved through partial privatization to expand minimal health care coverage of Mexico's large uninsured population. The first component of this initiative was the Coverage Expansion Program, which offered a basic package of services for people living in extremely poor communities.[32] The second component was the Program for Education, Health, and Nutrition (PROGRESA), established in 1997. PROGRESA (continued by the Fox administration under the name Oportunidades "Opportunities") was a means-tested program that provided health services to individual families in extreme poverty.[33] Spending on the program grew by 8.4 percent per year (in inflation-adjusted terms)

---

[28] Authors' calculations based on data in OECD (2005), p. 30.

[29] Giugale, Lafourcade, and Nguyen (2001), pp. 414–15, 447–78.

[30] Giugale, Lafourcade, and Nguyen, (2001), pp. 412, 416, 447–78.

[31] Giugale, Lafourcade, and Nguyen, (2001), pp. 412, 416, 447–78.

[32] In 2003 the Fox administration transferred responsibility for the Coverage Expansion Program to state governments.

[33] OECD, (2005), pp. 35–7.

over the course of the Zedillo administration and by 9.8 percent per year between 2000 and 2003.[34]

The Fox administration supplemented these initiatives with a program named People's Insurance (Seguro Popular), a government-subsidized, voluntary health insurance program designed in part to provide coverage for Mexico's large number of informal-sector workers. Most of the program's cost is borne by federal and state governments; participating families pay a premium linked to their income, which is set at zero for the poorest one-fifth of the population.[35] By mid-2006 approximately 3.7 million families (15 percent of all households) had been enrolled in the program. Of the families enrolled, 95 percent were from the bottom income quintile (representing 72 percent of all families in that income range).[36] The government hopes to have half the target population enrolled in the program by 2010.[37]

Children were among the greatest beneficiaries of the reallocation of health care resources under the Zedillo and Fox administrations.[38] In 1993, only 30 percent of children younger than 1 year of age received standard infant vaccinations; by the year 2000 that proportion had grown to 90 percent. If we broaden the sample to include children aged 1 to 4 years, the proportion of vaccinated children grew to 98 percent by the year 2000. There were similar improvements in the quality of care at birth. In 1985, one-third of all births were not attended by trained medical personnel; by 2000 that proportion had fallen to one-fifth.[39]

These programs, in conjunction with improving economic conditions after the mid-1990s and related increases in average consumption levels, helped bring about significant declines in infant and child mortality.[40] In 1980 Mexico's infant mortality rate was 53 deaths per 1,000 live births. This rate rose briefly between 1986 and 1990, perhaps

[34] World Bank (2003), p. 35.

[35] OECD (2005), p. 110. In 2006, annual premiums ranged from US$59 for families in the third-poorest income decile to $936 for families in the top income decile. Recipients of income transfers via the government's Opportunities program were exempt from payment; *La Jornada Virtu@l*, 9 April 2007.

[36] These data are from the Ministry of Health, available at http://www.seguro-popular.gob.mx.

[37] Rodríguez (2006). Even if this goal is met, however, as many as 14.4 million families would remain without health insurance; *La Jornada Virtu@l*, 9 April 2007.

[38] Technological advances (the use of oral rehydration, for example) were also important in this regard. See Boltvinik (2003), p. 433.

[39] INEGI (2001a), pp. 153, 187.

[40] See Boltvinik (2003), pp. 429–32, on the relationship between mortality rates for infants and school-age children and overall economic and consumption trends.

as a consequence of deteriorating economic conditions in the early 1980s[41] By 1995, however, it had fallen to 30 deaths per 1,000 live births. The rate then continued falling in a monotonic fashion, reaching 25 deaths per 1,000 in 1999 and 19 deaths per 1,000 in 2004. These results placed Mexico's infant mortality rate below the Latin American average (24 per 1,000 live births in 2004). They also implied that the infant mortality rate fell faster in Mexico than it did in the rest of Latin America between 1990 and 2004; in 1990, Mexico's infant mortality rate was 90 percent of the rate for the rest of Latin America, whereas in 2004 it was 78 percent of the Latin American rate.

Even more striking, whereas in 1980 some 41 percent of infant deaths occurred during the first 30 days after birth, by 2004 that proportion had risen to 62 percent. This suggests that a substantial proportion of infant mortality in contemporary Mexico is related to genetic causes, poor maternal diets, or poor neonatal care, rather than to infectious disease, as it had been in the past.[42] The evidence also suggests that broad-based inoculation programs had a large, positive effect on the survival of children aged 1 to 5 years. In 1980, the death rate from infectious diseases for children aged 1 to 5 years was 2.8 per 1,000, but by 1997 that proportion had been driven down to 0.3 per 1,000.[43] As a result, the overall rate of child mortality fell sharply, from 3.4 deaths per 1,000 children in 1980 to 0.9 in 1999.[44]

The decline in infant and child mortality had a significant effect on Mexico's overall public health profile. One obvious change was a dramatic decline in the death rate from communicable diseases, which tend to have a disproportionate impact on the young. As Figure 6.1 shows, in 1995 Mexico's mortality rate from communicable diseases was 72 per 100,000 population. By 2002, it had fallen to 49 per 100,000 inhabitants. This was a much faster rate of improvement than in the rest of Latin America, where the rate fell from 81 to 64 per 100,000 people during the same period. In 1995, the Mexican rate was 89 percent that of the rest of Latin America; by 2002 it had fallen to 77 percent of the Latin American rate.

[41] Boltvinik (2003), p. 429.
[42] *Revista Salud Pública de México* 46, no. 1 (2004), p. 77.
[43] Giugale, Lafourcade, and Nguyen (2001), p. 411.
[44] INEGI (2001a), pp. 65–6. It is important to note in this context that children of poor women have a significantly higher mortality rate than those of nonpoor women. Child mortality rates are also higher in rural areas than in urban areas. See Boltvinik (2003), pp. 425–8.

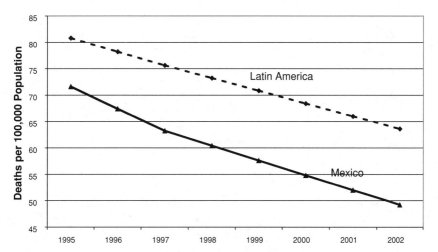

Figure 6.1: Mortality Rate from Communicable Diseases in Mexico and Other Latin American Countries, 1995–2002. *Source:* Pan American Health Organization (www.paho.org).

A second important change was a marked decrease in the crude death rate and a concomitant increase in life expectancy. In 1980, the overall crude death rate in Mexico was 6.5 deaths per 1,000. By 2001, the rate had fallen to 4.2 deaths per 1,000.[45] Life expectancy rose from 66.5 years in 1980 to 71.2 years in 1990, 74 years in 2000, and 75.4 years in 2005. As Figure 6.2 indicates, this was a much faster rate of improvement than in the rest of Latin America. In fact, by 2005 Mexico's average life expectancy was just 2 years below that of the United States.[46]

Education

Government efforts since the 1980s to improve the quality of public education have met with less success. Because education is highly labor intense, improving the quality of educational outcomes in Mexico requires far greater resources than recent governments have been able to muster.

[45] *Revista Salud Pública de México* 46, no. 1 (2004), "Estadísticas de mortalidad relacionada con la salud reproductiva, México, 2002," table 1.
[46] CONAPO, "Indicadores demográficos básicos, 1990–2030," available at www.conapo.gob.mx.

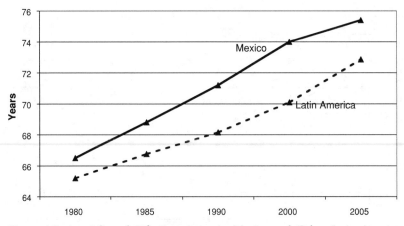

Figure 6.2: Age-Adjusted Life Expectancy in Mexico and Other Latin American Countries, 1980–2005. *Source:* INEGI (1994), p. 65; Oxford Latin American Database; Pan American Health Organization (www.paho.org).

Despite government promises to provide free public education to all citizens and some periods of innovation in educational policy, before the 1970s Mexico's overall level of educational attainment was very low. Between 1910 and 1960, for example, the population's average years of schooling crept up from 1.6 to 2.8 – a number that was low even by Latin American standards. As Figure 6.3 indicates, Mexico's

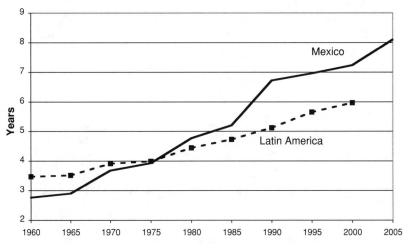

Figure 6.3: Average Years of Education in Mexico and Other Latin American Countries (Population Age 15 and Older), 1960–2005. *Source:* For 1960–2000, Barro and Lee (2000); for 2005, INEGI (www.inegi.gob.mx).

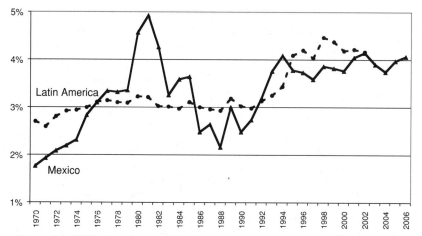

Figure 6.4: Public Spending on Education as a Percentage of GDP in Mexico and Other Latin American Countries, 1970–2006.   *Source:* Oxford Latin American Database; Centro de Estudios de las Finanzas Públicas (2005, 2006); Economic Commission for Latin America and the Caribbean, Estadísticas e Indicadores Sociales Web site.

average level of educational attainment in 1960 was only 80 percent of the average for the rest of Latin America (a regional average of 3.5 years).[47] The principal reason for this lagging performance was that in 1960 Mexican government spending on public education was equivalent to only 1.3 percent of the GDP – roughly half the level of government spending in the rest of Latin America.[48]

Changes in Educational Spending

During the 1970s, however, the Mexican government began to spend more heavily on education. The upward trend began during the administration of President Luis Echeverría (1970–1976) as part of a general increase in social spending, and it accelerated still more under Echeverría's successor, José López Portillo (1976–1982). As Figure 6.4 demonstrates, educational spending as a proportion of GDP increased from 2.1 percent in 1972 to 4.9 percent in 1981. As a result, by the late 1970s Mexico's average years-of-schooling for the population older than age 15 pulled ahead of the Latin American average. By 1990 (when the last of the students who entered the educational

[47] Barro and Lee (2000); Cohen, Macchiavelo, and Soto (2001).
[48] Oxford Latin American Economic History Database.

system during the 1973–1981 budgetary expansion turned 15), the average educational attainment of the population older than 15 years had reached 6.7 years, 16 percent above the Latin American average (see Figure 6.3).

The onset of Mexico's debt crisis in 1982 meant, however, that the burst in educational spending could not be sustained. Spending on public education collapsed after 1981, so that by 1988 it was only 2.2 percent of GDP – less than half its level just 7 years earlier. Confronted with this challenge, the Salinas government reallocated spending as a way of recovering past momentum in education.[49] The percentage of federal government spending (including education-related transfers to state governments) allocated to education rose from 9 percent in 1990 to 16 percent in 1993. Federal spending on education as a proportion of GDP rose from 2.5 percent to 3.8 percent during this same period, and it jumped to 4.1 percent in the presidential election year of 1994 (see Figure 6.4).

Where did the Salinas administration get the funds to increase educational spending? The main sources were the savings resulting from reduced interest payments on the country's foreign debt and investment cuts in the energy industry. By successfully renegotiating Mexico's foreign debt, the government reduced interest payments from a staggering 9.4 percent of GDP in 1990 to less than 2.9 percent by 1993. Four-fifths of the savings were allocated to eliminating the country's chronic public deficit. Some of the remainder was, however, available to expand educational spending.[50] Moreover, Salinas cut public spending on the petrochemical industry and on electrical power generation and transmission from 5.4 percent of GDP in 1990 to 3.5 percent in 1994, steps that also made additional revenues available for education.[51]

Despite continued low tax revenues, both the Zedillo and the Fox administrations maintained substantial levels of educational spending (close to the Latin American average) by further cutting energy spending (see Figure 6.4).[52] Moreover, these administrations went further than Salinas and also reallocated spending *within* the education sector.

---

[49] See Villa Lever and Rodríguez Gómez (2003) for an overview of other aspects of educational reform during the Salinas and Zedillo administrations.

[50] Authors' calculations based on data in Centro de Estudios de las Finanzas Públicas (2005), table A.9.2.

[51] Centro de Estudios de las Finanzas Públicas (2005), table A.9.2.

[52] Centro de Estudios de las Finanzas Públicas (2005), table A.9.2.

Between 1990 and 2002, the share of public educational spending allocated to primary schools rose from 32 to 49 percent.[53] Over the 2000–2006 period the share received by primary schools rose again, to an astonishing 65 percent of all public educational spending.[54] Presidents Zedillo and Fox were aided in their attempts to increase the resources available to primary schools by the fact that Mexico's birthrate was falling. This meant that the number of children aged 6–12 years grew by only 1.8 percent over the 1990–2005 period – slightly less than the average *annual* growth rate in same age group during the 1970s and 1980s.[55] In fact, there were 44,000 *fewer* public primary school students in 2005 than in 1990.[56] As a cumulative result of the increase in the amount of public resources channeled to education, the rising share of educational spending going to primary schools, and reduced growth in the number of primary school students, spending per primary school student rose by approximately 130 percent between 1990 and 2005.[57]

The reallocation of public educational spending to benefit primary schools meant that the government allocated spending away from higher education. Real (inflation-adjusted) government spending on primary education rose at an annual rate of 11 percent between 1990 and 2002, whereas real spending on postsecondary education rose by a rate of 8.5 percent per year during this same period.[58] During the Fox administration, overall growth in federal educational spending slowed but the spending disparity between primary schools and universities widened. Indeed, primary school spending rose at a real annual rate of 3.3 percent over the 2000–2006 period, whereas funding for university and postgraduate education rose at an average rate of only 1.3 percent per year.[59]

---

[53] United Nations Development Programme (2005), table 11.

[54] Centro de Estudios de las Finanzas Públicas (2006), p. 5.

[55] Authors' calculations from data presented in INEGI, "Población en edad escolar de 3 a 24 años por sexo y grupos de edad, 1950 a 2005," available at www.inegi.gob.mx.

[56] Secretaría de Educación Pública (2005). See also Villa Lever and Rodríguez Gómez (2003), pp. 278–9.

[57] Authors' calculations from data presented in INEGI, "Recursos humanos, materiales y financieros por nivel educativo, 1950 a 2005," available at www.inegi.gob.mx.

[58] Authors' calculations from data on spending shares in United Nations Development Programme (2005), table 11, and data on inflation-adjusted GDP from the Economist Intelligence Unit (Country Data), available at www.eiu.com.

[59] Authors' calculations based on data in Centro de Estudios de las Finanzas Públicas (2006), p. 6.

The relative decline in public funding for universities amounted to
a de facto privatization of higher education in Mexico.[60] The private
school student population as a proportion of total enrollment changed
little at lower educational levels (K–12) over the 1990–2005 period,
creeping upward from 8.3 percent to 9.7 percent.[61] The student population in private universities, however, rose from 18.1 percent of
total university enrollments in 1990 to 21 percent in 1994 – and then
exploded during the Zedillo administration, reaching 28.8 percent
in the year 2000. By 2005, private universities accounted for 31.7
percent of all university enrollments.[62] As a result of the growth in
private higher education, the proportion of total educational spending
coming from the private sector rose from 8.1 percent in 1990 to 21.7
percent in 2000 and 23.1 percent in 2005.[63]

What use did the federal government make of all the new public
funding on primary education? First, it built more schools and hired
more teachers. The number of students per primary school declined
from an average of 179 in 1990 to 150 in 2000, where it remained
throughout the Fox administration. At the same time, the student–
teacher ratio in primary schools declined from an average of thirty-one
in 1990 to twenty-seven in 2000 and twenty-six in 2005.[64]

Second, as part of the PROGRESA/Oportunidades program the
government provided targeted support to 80 percent of the rural poor
and a growing number of urban families to encourage them to keep
their children in school. The program gave poor families cash grants
in return for keeping their children enrolled and for sending them to
clinics for regular health check-ups.[65] Indeed, it was the program's
success at increasing primary school enrollment in rural areas that

---

[60] In 1993, a reform of Article 3 of the Constitution gave private and public institutions equal
   access to state subsidies for higher education and authorized public universities to charge
   students tuition. See Laurell (2003), pp. 322–3. The reform of Article 130 of the Constitution
   that same year also permitted the Catholic church to expand its private educational system.

[61] For the 1990–2000 period, authors' calculations based on data in Kent (2004), p. 29. The
   2005 data are from the Secretaría de Educación Pública (2005).

[62] For the 1990–2000 period, authors' calculations based on data in Kent (2004), p. 29. The
   2005 data are from the Secretaría de Educación Pública (2005). See also Villa Lever and
   Rodríguez Gómez (2003), pp. 305, 311, 314–15, and table 8.6, on the expanding role of
   private higher education.

[63] Authors' calculations based on data in INEGI, "Recursos humanos, materiales y financieros
   por nivel educativo, 1950 a 2005," available at www.inegi.gob.mx.

[64] INEGI, "Recursos humanos, materiales y financieros por nivel educativo, 1950 a 2005,"
   available at www.inegi.gob.mx.

[65] Giugale, Lafourcade, and Nguyen (2001), p. 588.

prompted the Fox administration to expand it first to poor urban families and then to all low-income families with children aged 14 to 20 years enrolled in secondary schools.[66]

Third, and in quantitative terms, most significant, the federal government sought to improve teacher quality by significantly raising teachers' salaries. In 1993 the Salinas administration created the Teaching Career (Carrera Magisterial) scheme to provide financial rewards for teachers who upgraded their professional qualifications and skills.[67] This program, along with other government initiatives, helped raise average salaries for primary and secondary school teachers by 139 percent in real terms between 1996 and 2003. By 2003, the average annual starting salary for a Mexican schoolteacher was US$10,784 ($12,688 in purchasing-power-parity terms), and salaries for primary school teachers with 15 years of experience averaged $14,210. These salaries were still only one-third as high as average U.S. levels. Nevertheless, average Mexican primary school teaching salaries were 8 percent higher (in purchasing-power-parity terms) than those in Chile, 43 percent higher than those in Brazil, and an astonishing 84 percent higher than those in Argentina.[68] Even more relevant, a starting teacher's pay was slightly more than double the average annual salary in Mexico (US$5,007 in 2004).[69]

These important advances in teacher salaries did, however, outstrip increases in the overall public education budget. Thus, salaries accounted for 90 percent of all federal government educational spending in 2004. As a consequence, there was relatively little budgetary support for textbooks (which are free at the primary school level but not for secondary school students), computers, libraries, or school lunches (a very important consideration in poor areas).[70]

Educational Outcomes

Because of significant shifts in the amount and focus of public spending on education, levels of educational achievement rose markedly

[66] World Bank (2003), p. 41.

[67] Salinas de Gortari (2002), pp. 638–40; Vegas and Umansky (2005); Navarro (2005). The scheme was fully implemented by 1996.

[68] OECD (2006), table D3.1.

[69] Authors' calculations based on data in INEGI, "Pagos al personal remunerado en las unidades económicas por sector de actividad y personal ocupado en las unidades económicas por sector de actividad," available at www.inegi.gob.mx.

[70] Santibáñez, Vernez, and Razquin (2005), pp. 8, 12.

between 1990 and 2005. The average educational attainment of the population older than 15 years of age increased from 6.7 years of schooling in 1990 to 8.1 years in 2005. Illiteracy dropped from 12.6 percent to 8.5 percent of this population group during the same period.[71]

Mexico's principal educational gains have been concentrated among primary school students and college graduates. Most of the country's increased educational attainment came from enrolling more students in primary school and ensuring that they graduated. The proportion of all children aged 6–12 years who were enrolled in school rose from 89 percent in 1990 to 96 percent in 2005, and the proportion of children who graduated from primary school within 6 years of enrollment rose from 70 percent in 1990 to 90 percent in 2005.[72]

Moreover, Mexico closed the enrollment gap and the achievement gap between male and female students. For the entire school-age population aged 6–19 years, in 2005 there were slightly more girls than boys enrolled in school.[73] With the caveat that much of this age cohort had not yet completed its formal schooling, in 1999 young women in the 15–19-year age group had completed an average of 8.2 years of education, compared with 8 years for their male counterparts.[74] Among individuals aged 20 to 24 years (who had completed most of their formal schooling), the achievement gap was small: 9 years of education for men, and 8.9 years for women.[75]

Mexico also managed to increase significantly the proportion of its population enrolled in institutions of higher education. Indeed, the proportion of all university-age students enrolled in some form of higher education rose from 14 percent in 1991 to 18 percent in 1999, and to 25 percent in 2004.[76] In 2005, 16 percent of all Mexicans aged 24–35 years possessed a university degree, and an additional 2.7 percent held associate degrees.[77] By that year Mexico had pulled ahead of most of Latin America in terms of the proportion of its citizens who were university graduates. In fact, by this measure Mexico had

---

[71] INEGI, "Indicadores seleccionados sobre nivel de escolaridad, promedio de escolaridad, aptitud para leer y escribir y alfabetismo, 1960 a 2005," available at www.inegi.gob.mx.

[72] Tamez Guerra, Zúñiga Molina, and Freyre Martínez (2005).

[73] INEGI, "Porcentaje de la población de 5 y más años que asiste a la escuela por grupos de edad y sexo, 1970 a 2005," available at www.inegi.gob.mx.

[74] Giugale, Lafourcade, and Nguyen (2001), p. 449.

[75] Giugale, Lafourcade, and Nguyen (2001), p. 449; Parker and Pederzini (2001).

[76] United Nations Educational, Scientific, and Cultural Organization (UNESCO), Institute for Statistics, Mexico Country Profile, available at http://www.uis.unesco.org.

[77] OECD (2006), table A1.3a.

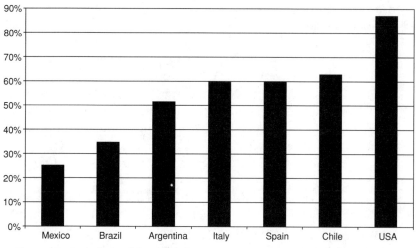

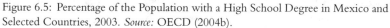

Figure 6.5: Percentage of the Population with a High School Degree in Mexico and Selected Countries, 2003. *Source:* OECD (2004b).

surpassed OECD member states such as Italy and Portugal, and it was closing in on Spain.

Nevertheless, despite these achievements, the Mexican educational system still faces serious shortcomings. One of the greatest challenges is at the middle levels of the educational system (junior high and high school). Three-quarters of Mexicans never graduate high school. Indeed, attrition occurs at every level past primary school. Approximately 95 percent of students who complete primary school enroll in junior high; however, only 78 percent of junior high school students graduate. Of those who do, only 85 percent enroll in high school, and only 60 percent of these students eventually graduate. In other words, in 2004 only one-third of the students who left primary schools were expected to graduate high school. Although this was an improvement over the 1996 rate of 26 percent, it was stunningly low by international standards.[78] In fact, as Figure 6.5 shows, in 2003 only 25 percent of the Mexican population aged 25 to 34 years had graduated high school. This rate was not only low compared with Mexico's North American neighbors, Canada and the United States, but it was also low compared with Southern European nations and with the other large countries of Latin America. Even Brazil, which has a notoriously

[78] Authors' calculations based on data presented in INEGI, "Indicadores sobre permanencia escolar y deserción por sexo, 1996 a 2004," available at www.inegi.gob.mx.

inadequate public education system, had a significantly higher high
school graduation rate.

A second major problem is that the quality of Mexico's primary
schools is very low. Quantitative evidence concerning the quality of
Mexican primary education came from the Programme for International Student Assessment examination that the OECD administered
to 30,000 Mexican students in 2003. In reading, 24.9 percent of those
taking the test scored below Level 1, meaning that they had at most
learned "very basic reading skills."[79] The equivalent percentage for the
United States (one of the lowest-performing members of the OECD)
was 6.5 percent. In fact, only one country (Brazil) scored lower than
Mexico.[80] In mathematics, Mexican students did even worse: 38 percent scored below Level 1, compared with 10.2 percent in the United
States and an OECD average of 8.2 percent.[81] Perhaps even more troubling, even the best Mexican students fared poorly when compared
with students from other countries. The 95th percentile of Mexican
15-year-olds ranked 34th in reading, 36th in science, and 38th in
mathematics.[82] Only 4.8 percent of Mexican 15-year-olds qualified
for the two highest categories of reading achievement, a figure that
compared very poorly with an OECD average of 29.6 percent.[83]

Scarce resources appeared to be a factor in Mexico's comparatively
poor record of educational attainment. In 2003 the student–teacher
ratio in Mexican secondary schools was 29 students per teacher, almost
twice the OECD average of 15.[84] Teaching loads were, moreover, very
high. Teachers in Mexican secondary schools were expected to give
an average of 1,182 hours of instruction each year, compared with
an OECD annual average of 714 hours per teacher.[85] Yet even with
such high teaching loads, many students still lacked physical access to a
teacher. Approximately 1 million junior high school students in rural
areas (one-fifth of all junior high school students in Mexico) received
their lessons through television programs broadcast by satellite as part
of the Telesecundaria program.[86]

[79] OECD (2004b), p. 79.
[80] Hagerstrom (2006), p. 12.
[81] OECD (2006), table A4.1.
[82] Jackson (2005).
[83] Hagerstrom (2006), p. 12.
[84] OECD (2004b), p. 330.
[85] OECD (2004b), p. 390.
[86] Giugale, Lafourcade, and Nguyen (2001), p. 463.

Issues of educational access and quality are important not least because of the increasingly strong relationship between educational achievement and earnings in Mexico. Workers who had failed to complete secondary school saw their inflation-adjusted earnings decline throughout the 1980s and 1990s, whereas employees who had completed high school or had some university education made real gains.[87] As of 2002, the World Bank estimated that graduating high school yielded a 40-percent gain in earnings, and completing university produced an additional 91 percent gain in income.[88]

Given the obvious implications of education for economic growth, there is a strong imperative to improve access to, and the quality of, primary and secondary education.[89] Considering, however, that Mexico's 2006 federal budget devoted 27 percent of all discretionary spending to education (the highest percentage in the OECD), it is unclear whether Mexico will have much success in further improving its public education system without significantly increasing tax revenues.

Housing Policy

For decades Mexico's difficult property-rights environment discouraged private commercial banks from entering the mortgage market. As a consequence, between 1965 and 1982 private banks financed the construction of fewer than 14,000 houses per year.[90] The "market failure" caused by weak property rights created a need for government-run housing programs – and an opportunity for the PRI and its affiliated labor organizations to use those programs as a form of patronage.

For three decades following its creation in 1972, the National Worker Housing Institute (INFONAVIT) was the federal government's principal means of providing subsidized housing for formal-sector workers. Nevertheless, because the agency had long been controlled by the Mexican Workers' Confederation (CTM, the PRI's official labor sector) as a source of patronage for its affiliates,

---

[87] Salas and Zepeda (2003), pp. 545, 547; Villa Lever and Rodríguez Gómez (2003), p. 282.

[88] López-Acevedo (2006), p. 29.

[89] Access to public secondary schools has been free of charge since 1992. See Parker and Pederzini (2001), p. 11.

[90] The data for the 1965–1979 period are from INEGI (2000), p. 159; the 1980–1982 data are from the Dirección General de Política y Fomento al Financiamiento de la Vivienda.

INFONAVIT had little incentive to become an efficient homebuilder. Thus, even with a 5-percent levy on private employers' wage bills, the government only managed to build an average of 56,783 housing units per year during the 1970s, a decade in which Mexico's population grew by an average of 1.86 *million* people per year. Although the government's output of new houses rose to an average of 253,000 per year during the 1980s, even this increased output barely managed to dent the housing shortfall.[91]

In an attempt to make INFONAVIT's operations more transparent, in September 1992 the Salinas administration pushed through legislation (against opposition from the CTM) that substantially reduced patronage abuse by unions in the distribution of housing units.[92] The new rules gave all formal-sector workers employed by private firms direct personal control over individual housing accounts. Accumulated funds could be used to secure a mortgage on any house or apartment available on the open market. In addition, INFONAVIT ended its direct involvement in housing construction.

The Salinas administration's reprivatization of banks briefly stimulated a significant increase in private housing finance. The number of commercial housing loans rose by 105 percent between 1990 and 1994, and the real (inflation-adjusted) value of commercial housing loans more than tripled. Mexico's bank-financed housing boom foundered on the fact that, when borrowers failed to meet their mortgage obligations, private financial institutions found it almost impossible to repossess property via the legal system. Thus, when mortgage defaults multiplied rapidly during the 1995 recession, private provision of housing credit almost disappeared.[93] Indeed, by 1996 the real value of new commercial housing loans had fallen to 3.5 percent of its 1994 level, and it continued to decline thereafter. By the year 2000, the inflation-adjusted value of new commercial housing loans stood at

[91] Dirección General de Política y Fomento al Financiamiento de la Vivienda. Data concerning the proportion of houses with access to piped-in water (a good measure of the quality of housing construction because most formal-sector homes have such access, while many informal, self-built houses do not) suggest that INFONAVIT did not make much of a contribution to the quality of Mexico's housing stock. In 1980, 49.9 percent of all houses had access to piped-in water; by 1990, the proportion had only risen to 50.2 percent. See INEGI, *Censos de Población y Vivienda*, 1970 and 1980, available at www.inegi.gob.mx.
[92] Middlebrook (1995), p. 297.
[93] Haber (2005).

less than *1 percent* of its 1994 level, and the number of new mortgages had dropped from 85,198 in 1994 to 865 in 1999.[94]

The failure of the housing finance system had very real consequences for the well-being of Mexican families. Without access to credit, they were thrown back on their own resources to construct houses. The resulting explosion of informal settlements meant that, after decades of steady decline, the proportion of one-room houses in the total housing stock rose from 10.5 percent in 1990 to 23.1 percent in 2000.[95] Fully 62 percent of all new housing built during the 1990s consisted of one-room structures.[96]

One of the measures the Zedillo administration adopted to address this problem involved a further reform of INFONAVIT. Legislation enacted in July 1997 converted the organization into a combination forced-savings scheme and mortgage lender. Under the new rules, account holders could use accumulated funds as the down payment on a home or a home-improvement loan from INFONAVIT up to a specified maximum (US$24,436 in 2006).[97] Moreover, the 1997 reform permitted them to combine the INFONAVIT loan with loans from other financial institutions, so long as the value of the property being financed was below a maximum amount specified by INFONAVIT (in 2006, US$47,560 in Mexico City and $40,766 elsewhere).[98] Placing a limit on the value of the properties that could be financed with INFONAVIT funds made the program redistributive. To the extent that higher-income workers wish to finance properties worth more than the maximum permitted value, money in their accounts in essence becomes capital from which INFONAVIT can make mortgage loans to lower-income families.

The Fox administration recognized that further expanding access to housing finance would both address a pressing social need and strengthen the PAN. The more widely the government could distribute the benefits of modern-quality homeownership, the better the

---

[94] Dirección General de Política y Fomento al Financiamiento de la Vivienda.

[95] Joint Center for Housing Studies of Harvard University (2004), p. 24.

[96] Authors' calculation based on data presented in Joint Center for Housing Studies of Harvard University (2004), pp. 12, 24; INEGI, *Censos de Población y Vivienda*, 1990 and 2000, available at www.inegi.gob.mx.

[97] In 2006 the maximum value of the loan was set at the equivalent of 180 minimum wages.

[98] The maximum value of the property was 517,848 pesos for Mexico City properties and 443,870 pesos for properties elsewhere.

odds that the PAN would be able to expand its electoral base and retain national power. Indeed, analyses of the 2006 general elections suggest that the success of the Fox administration's housing program directly contributed to the PAN's presidential victory.[99]

The Fox administration undertook two major initiatives in the housing sector. First, it substantially expanded the INFONAVIT mortgage credit program – a step that was particularly important to improving the housing market because the agency dominated the issuance of home mortgages (accounting for 73 percent of the value of all mortgage loans in the year 2000).[100] Between 2001 and 2006 the agency granted more than 1.88 million mortgages, a full 47 percent of the 4.04 million mortgages INFONAVIT had provided during the course of its entire history.[101] In 2006 alone, the agency granted 421,745 mortgage credits worth an average of US$22,620 each.[102]

One potential weakness of the INFONAVIT mortgage program, however, is that it may encourage excessively risky behavior by borrowers. Other than insurance against the permanent total incapacitation or death of the employee, INFONAVIT loans are secured through two main sources: the house itself and the 5-percent payroll tax paid by employers. Yet the payroll tax provides only limited protection for the lending agency against the risk that the borrower will default, and the majority of INFONAVIT borrowers owe mortgage payments that exceed 5 percent of their income by a wide margin. In addition, should a borrower lose her or his job (or choose to work in the informal sector), then INFONAVIT will have no payroll tax revenues to attach in the event that the borrower defaults on the loan. The only recourse left to INFONAVIT would be to repossess the house. This course of action might be politically possible when the number of repossessions is low, but in the event of a macroeconomic shock that causes default rates to rise, the government would be confronted with the prospect of repossessing large numbers of houses owned by voters. The government would then have one of two choices: repossess the

---

[99] Middlebrook (2007); Moreno (2007), p. 16.

[100] By 2005, INFONAVIT's market share had fallen to 45 percent, but it was still by far the largest issuer of mortgage credit in the country. It especially dominated the market for low-value housing loans. Authors' calculations based on data from the Dirección General de Política y Fomento al Financiamiento de la Vivienda.

[101] Authors' calculations based on data provided in INFONAVIT, "Créditos ejercidos por delegación, 1972–2006," available at www.infonavit.org.mx.

[102] The value of the average loan in 2006 was 248,500 pesos. See INFONAVIT, "Ejercio crediticio 2006: valor de los créditos al otorgamiento," available at www.infonavit.org.mx.

houses in question (and face a political firestorm), or write off the loans by transferring funds from the treasury to INFONAVIT in what would constitute a taxpayer-financed bailout of home owners.

The Fox administration's second major innovation in the housing sector was the 2001 reform of the Federal Mortgage Society (SHF), which converted "a previously obscure quasi-governmental body" into an important mortgage guarantor and financier.[103] The measure granted the SHF a federal guarantee that allows it to raise capital by borrowing on the open market (or from multilateral organizations such as the World Bank) on the same terms as the Mexican government. The SHF then acts as a second-tier lender, repurchasing loans made by private corporations called Limited-Objective Financial Societies (SOFOLES) that engage in housing construction and finance. The SHF provides a partial guarantee of the repurchased loans and then sells them to private investors.

Once the reformed SHF began operations, the scale of lending activities undertaken by the SOFOLES expanded very rapidly. By 2005, these corporations accounted for 20.4 percent of the mortgage market, making 98,898 loans with an average value of US$31,500 each.[104] Because the expansion of SOFOLES lending greatly increased competition in the mortgage market, the average down payment required to secure a mortgage declined from approximately 35 percent of the home sale price to 10–13 percent.[105] During the 2003–2006 period, the amount that a person earning an annual salary of US$1,379 (approximately Mexico's minimum wage at the time) could borrow increased by 350 percent.[106]

One could imagine that the loan repurchases made by the SHF would provide the SOFOLES with incentives to lend inefficiently and irresponsibly. That does not, however, appear to have been the case; indeed, the SOFOLES have enjoyed much higher rates of repayment than either INFONAVIT or private commercial banks.[107] As a matter of fact, the SOFOLES have a very strong incentive to lend responsibly

[103] Joint Center for Housing Studies of Harvard University (2004), p. 33; *The Economist*, 28 August 2004, p. 41.

[104] The peso value of the average loan was 343,291. Dirección General de Política y Fomento al Financiamiento de la Vivienda.

[105] *The Economist*, 28 August 2004, p. 41.

[106] This calculation holds the effective interest rate constant. The peso value of the annual minimum wage was 15,000. See "Ejemplo a seguir, la reactivación del crédito bancario a la vivienda" (2006).

[107] Joint Center for Housing Studies of Harvard University (2004), pp. 35–6.

because, if they fail to maintain high rates of repayment, they will lose access to the stream of cheap capital provided by the SHF.

To maintain access to SHF funds, the SOFOLES have developed a range of special techniques designed to minimize delinquency in mortgage payments. For example, the SOFOLES allow borrowers to demonstrate their creditworthiness and accumulate a down payment by paying an amount equal to their desired monthly mortgage payment into an account for a period of time. The SOFOLES also deliver mortgage statements in person, rather than by mail, and they apply personal pressure when a borrower fails to make a payment on time. In point of fact, they often pay delinquent borrowers to vacate a house, rather than go through the legal processes of foreclosure and eviction – processes that can be drawn out for months or years by determined debtors. These methods do increase administrative costs. They mean, however, that the SOFOLES have much lower rates of loan delinquency than other financial institutions in Mexico.[108]

The Fox administration's plan was that the SHF would gradually be replaced by private mortgage reinsurers and a market for mortgage-backed securities, and that by 2009 the SHF would no longer be engaged in house financing.[109] The SOFOLES have indeed been able to access private credit; in fact, by 2005 about half of their loans were backed by non-SHF sources.[110] Even if the private market does not take up all of the rest of the slack, there is no reason why Congress could not reauthorize the SHF to continue operating as a second-tier lender. The risk, of course, would be the possible dilemma confronting the government as a creditor: In the event of widespread mortgage defaults caused by an economic crisis, the government might find itself in the unenviable position of repossessing homes owned by voters.

Retirement Pensions

One of Mexico's least successful welfare reforms involved the retirement system. In 1995, the Zedillo government decided to shift the country's public pension program from a U.S.-style "pay as you go"

---

[108] Joint Center for Housing Studies of Harvard University (2004), pp. 35–6.

[109] "The War between Banks and 'Sofoles' Propels Mexican Real Estate," *Universia-Knowledge@Wharton*, 2 August 2006.

[110] These are the authors' calculations from data provided by the Dirección General de Política y Fomento al Financiamiento de la Vivienda.

system to a system of private accounts funded by mandatory payroll taxes collected from the wages of current workers. This new system went into effect in September 1997.[111]

Mexico's pension reform had three main goals. First, the Zedillo administration wanted to bring the great mass of Mexico's informal-sector workers into the public pension system. The government hoped that informal (and self-employed) workers would choose to participate in the new system. Second, the government hoped to raise Mexico's low savings rate. Under the reform, formal-sector workers would be required to save a substantial portion of their incomes. Moreover, savings would increase further as informal-sector workers voluntarily entered the system and began to contribute to their accounts. Third, the government knew that the old system would require payroll tax hikes within a few years to remain solvent. The new system would also require tax hikes but the government believed that these increases would be more palatable if they were linked to the new system of private accounts.[112]

Unfortunately, Mexico's pension reform ran aground. In a move reminiscent of the privatization of the telephone system and the banks, the Zedillo government designed the system in such a way as to allow the private pension funds to charge very high commissions on the flow of contributions into their funds.[113] High commissions, in turn, had the effect of undercutting the government's goals for the reform: Pension coverage fell and the savings rate did not rise. High commissions created, in effect, a tax on new contributions. Informal-sector workers, therefore, did not rush to join the new system. High commissions also ate into the returns that formal-sector workers expected to receive from their accounts. Reforms in 2007 finally imposed limits on some of these commissions. Yet whatever effects these changes might have, a decade of high commissions means that most formal-sector workers will probably end up earning less from their accounts than the amount that they would receive from the government's guaranteed minimum pension. The government, therefore, may need to top up their pensions at taxpayer expense.

---

[111] In March 2007, President Calderón secured congressional approval for legislation that modified the ISSSTE retirement pension system and established a funded pension scheme for public-sector employees. See Muñoz (2007).

[112] On the goals of Mexican pension reform, see Grandolini and Cerda (1998), p. 3; Sales-Sarrapy, Solís-Soberón, and Villagómez-Amezcua (1996).

[113] Sinha (2001); Whitehouse (2000); Mitchell (1999).

In the pages that follow, we explore the logic and evidence behind this bleak assessment of the first decade of Mexico's pension reform. To do so we must first step back from the Mexican case and explain how pension systems work.

Public Pension Systems

Public pension systems exist to guarantee workers a retirement income commensurate with their earnings during their working years. Such systems fall into three categories. The first are pay-as-you-go ("paygo") defined-benefit schemes such as the U.S. Social Security system. In this type of system the government collects mandatory contributions from current workers. Those contributions go into a public fund, which is invested in government bonds. The fund is then used to pay the pensions of current retirees. An individual worker's pension benefits are linked to the contributions that worker has made into the system during the course of his or her working life. Once a worker retires, however, his or her pension benefits are fixed (except for an adjustment for inflation). In addition, most paygo systems include a small redistributive component for low-income retirees.

In essence, workers in a paygo system invest in a defined-benefit security whose payoff is loosely linked to the level of wages in the economy, inasmuch as a worker's individual wages are linked to the overall level of wages. Imagine, for example, a paygo system in which worker contributions exactly equal the benefits paid out to retirees. If the wages of contributing workers rise relative to the number of retirees (or if the number of workers paying into the system rises relative to the number of retirees), then more contributions will be paid into the paygo system than the system will pay out in benefits. The paygo system, therefore, will accumulate a surplus, generally held in government bonds. These bonds can later be liquidated should the system run a deficit. Conversely, if the wages of contributing workers rise more slowly than the number of retirees (or if the number of workers paying into the system falls relative to the number of retirees), then the paygo system will pay more in benefits than it receives in contributions. Such deficits must be financed in one of three ways: Past surpluses (if any) can be liquidated; the government can use regular tax revenues to subsidize pension payments; or, the government can cut the benefits paid to current retirees.

In a second type of system (used in China, France, Germany, and Sweden, among other countries) benefits are allowed to vary with the amount of current contributions paid into the system. These systems are called "Non-financial Defined Contribution" (NDC) schemes.[114] In an NDC system, workers make mandatory contributions into a public fund. The public fund then pays benefits to current retirees. The initial level of benefits that a retiree receives is, as in a paygo system, linked to his or her wages during his or her working life span. Unlike a paygo system, however, benefits in an NDC system are variable. If contributions into the system rise (because wages rise or because the number of workers paying into the fund rises), then the benefits paid out to current retirees increase. If contributions fall, then the benefits paid out to current retirees also fall.[115] Workers in an NDC scheme, in effect, invest in a variable-benefit security tightly linked to the overall level of wages in the economy.

In the third type of pension system, called a "funded system," workers make mandatory contributions that are then used to purchase stocks and bonds. Retirees receive benefits funded from the liquidation of their holdings of stocks and bonds. The value of those stocks and bonds is linked to the level of the profits of the companies in which they have invested. If profits rise, then the value of the securities held by retirees will rise, and they will enjoy higher benefits. If profits fall, however, then the value of the securities held by retirees will also fall, and they will enjoy lower benefits. Workers, in effect, invest in a variable-benefit security linked to the overall level of profits in the economy.

What, then, are the differences among the three kinds of systems? The first difference involves governance. In NDC and funded systems, benefits are directly linked to contributions. In paygo systems, however, benefits are not directly linked to contributions. The potential exists, therefore, for paygo systems to run persistent deficits if governments promise benefits without collecting enough contributions to pay for them.

The second difference involves linkage. In paygo and NDC systems, benefits are linked to the overall level of wages in the economy, whereas

---

[114] Among poorer countries, Brazil, Latvia, and Poland also use NDC systems. See Lindemann, Robalina, and Rutkowski (2006).

[115] Moss, Dias, and Stephann (1999), p. 5.

in funded systems, benefits are linked to the overall level of profits (including interest payments) in the economy. In addition, in some funded systems workers can choose which companies or economic sectors they wish to invest in. That is, they can link their benefits not to the overall level of profits, but to the level of profits in a particular set of companies. Of course, doing so exposes workers to more risk. This approach, however, also allows them the possibility of realizing returns on their invested account, and hence a larger retirement pension.

Mexico's Pre-1997 Social Security System

Prior to 1997, Mexico had a paygo system, run by the IMSS. The IMSS collected an 8.5 percent payroll tax from private employees working in the formal sector and it used these contributions to fund pension, health care, and disability benefits for retirees.[116]

Mexico's system was very badly governed, in the sense that there were weak links between payments into the system and retirement benefits paid from the system. As a consequence, the IMSS system became less and less financially viable. Formal-sector workers became eligible to receive full IMSS benefits after approximately 10 years of full-time work. For example, a minimum-wage worker who was employed in the formal sector for 10 nonconsecutive years and who retired at age 65 would earn the minimum wage as a pension. No additional amount of work would increase that pension. A worker who earned 6.5 times the minimum wage in the formal sector for 10 nonconsecutive years and who retired at age 65 would, however, only earn 23 percent of her or his salary upon retirement. Even worse, a worker earning the same salary – 6.5 times the minimum wage – who was employed in the formal sector for 30 years (three times longer) would earn only a pittance more: 25 percent of her or his salary upon retirement.[117] In short, the system provided workers with few incentives to remain in the formal sector beyond 10 years. Employees would, therefore, often drop out of the system after a decade of formal-sector work and either seek employment in the informal sector (and henceforth avoid the 8.5 percent IMSS tax) or find an employer who was willing to pay salaries off the books.[118]

---

[116] Grandolini and Cerda (1998), p. 4.

[117] Serrano (1999).

[118] Espinosa-Vega and Sinha (2000), p. 5.

The collapse of the Mexican economy after 1982 placed serious pressure on the pension system. As wages and employment fell, payroll contributions to the IMSS declined but pension payments remained fixed. For a time during the 1980s, higher rates of inflation eased this problem by increasing the nominal value of wages (and contributions), even when the amount of pension payments remained stable. In 1989, however, the federal government indexed IMSS benefits to inflation, although contributions remained linked to the minimum wage. Because the value of the minimum wage rose more slowly than the rate of inflation, IMSS contributions began to fall relative to the amount of benefits to be paid.[119]

As a consequence, analysts expected that Mexico's public pension system would fall into deficit around the year 2000 and that the deficit would then continue to grow over time.[120] Indeed, the country's declining birthrate was bad news as far as the pension system was concerned because demographers projected that the number of workers per retiree would fall from 11.1 to 5.5 between 1995 and 2030.[121] A 1996 estimate indicated that unless economic growth in Mexico accelerated, pension system deficits would grow to 3.5 percent of GDP by 2022 and 4.4 percent by 2047.[122] Under such circumstances, the government would either have to use its limited tax revenues to cover pension system deficits or cut pension benefits.[123]

The 1997 Pension Reform

The problems affecting Mexico's former paygo pension system do not fully explain why the Zedillo administration chose to replace it. The deficits that the system faced in the near term were small, and even if the most pessimistic demographic forecasts proved accurate, the time frame involved stretched well beyond incumbent officials' political horizons. In fact, the Zedillo government had two other principal goals: It wanted to expand the coverage of the pension system to cover all workers (not just those in the formal sector), and it wanted to raise Mexico's dismally low savings rate. In addition, spreading the

---

[119] Espinosa-Vega and Sinha (2000), p. 4.
[120] Giugale, Lafourcade, and Nguyen (2001), pp. 227–8.
[121] Espinosa-Vega and Sinha (2000), p. 5.
[122] Sales-Sarrapy, Solís-Soberón, and Villagómez-Amezcua (1996), table 9.
[123] Sinha and Yañez Acosta (2006a).

benefits of the public pension system to the mass of the population could pay obvious electoral benefits.

Switching to a funded system could solve both the coverage and savings rate problems. First, informal-sector workers might be persuaded to participate in a system of tax-free private accounts. After all, they would not have to depend on the government to administer directly such a system. Rather, they would depend on privately administered funds to handle their money.[124] Second, the contributions from those workers would go into the financial markets. As long as the government could continue to pay the pensions of current retirees without running deficits, national savings would rise. In fact, a 1996 study estimated that national savings would rise by 2 percent of GDP in the year of the reform.[125]

The pension reform involved a significant rise in payroll taxes on existing formal-sector workers. It required workers to deposit a mandatory contribution of 6.5 percent of their wages in a private pension account managed by a Retirement Fund Administrator (AFORE).[126] Workers paid an additional 4 percent to IMSS to provide for publicly funded health, disability, and life insurance. The bottom line was that mandatory pension contributions rose from 8.5 percent to 10.5 percent of wages.[127]

These reforms implied significant transition costs to the public treasury. First, the government needed to continue paying benefits to current pensioners. Given the considerable cost of paying these benefits, the government needed to redirect general revenues equal to roughly 1.5 percent of GDP per year to funding those still covered by the old government-administered paygo pension system.[128] Second, the government promised to top up the contributions of low-income workers via a "social quota" payment equal to 5.5 percent of the federal minimum wage for Mexico City. The social quota cost an additional 0.3 percent of GDP.[129]

---

[124] Giugale, Lafourcade, and Nguyen (2001), pp. 227–8.
[125] Sales-Sarrapy, Solís-Soberón, and Villagómez-Amezcua (1996), table 10.
[126] The reform entitled workers to make additional voluntary contributions to their AFORE accounts.
[127] Giugale, Lafourcade, and Nguyen (2001), pp. 225–6.
[128] Laurell (2003), p. 328.
[129] Grandolini and Cerda (1998), table 10.

The Performance of the New Pension System

Over its first decade of operation, Mexico's pension reform was not a success. One of its most significant failings was that it did not attract many informal-sector workers. In fact, the system's coverage actually declined over time; the size of the labor force grew by 12 percent between 1997 and 2005 but the number of workers contributing to the new pension system increased by only 8 percent.[130] As a consequence, the national savings rate did not rise. In 1997, the year the reform took effect, Mexico's gross savings rate was 24 percent of GDP, whereas in 2005 it was only 20 percent of GDP.[131] It was equally unclear 10 years onward whether the AFOREs had solved the problem of future deficits. The returns on these funds had not proved sufficient to provide most participating workers with a pension above the minimum government guarantee. The government may, therefore, still have to top up some retirees' pensions at taxpayer expense.

There were two reasons why the AFOREs did not attract significant numbers of contributors from the informal sector. First, even though private retirement accounts are tax-free, withdrawals from AFORE funds incur a 20-percent penalty if they are made prior to the contributor's retirement.[132] Most contributors would, therefore, face substantial penalties should a family or health emergency require them to access their savings before retirement.

The second reason why the AFOREs were not successful at attracting contributors from the informal sector was that, in a situation reminiscent of the government's privatization of the telephone system and the banks, the Zedillo administration structured the market in such a way as to allow private pension funds to charge very high commissions

---

[130] Pension Research Council (2006); Sinha and Yañez Acosta (2006b), pp. 10–11. Many observers have been misled by statistics regarding the number of AFORE "affiliates." According to the National Commission on Retirement Savings (CONSAR), the government agency charged with regulating the funds, 36.3 million individuals were affiliated with AFOREs as of June 2006. That number is misleading, however, because most of those individuals do not actively contribute to their accounts. Rather, they are registered with an AFORE and thus could contribute if they obtain formal-sector employment or choose to do so voluntarily. In practice, only 14.6 million of the 36.3 million affiliates listed in 2006 actively contributed to their accounts.

[131] These data are from the Economist Intelligence Unit (Country Data), available at www.eiu.com.

[132] Sinha and Yañez Acosta (2006b).

(a de facto tax) on contributions made to them.[133] Indeed, during
their first years in operation, the AFOREs charged an average fee
of 19.5 percent on the flow of contributions to private retirement
accounts. That is, for every peso a worker contributed, only 80.5
centavos were actually credited to her or his account; the remainder
went to the AFORE's management. In fact, because most AFOREs
had management-fee structures providing for lower commissions the
longer that a contributor remained with the fund (so as to discourage
contributors from switching to rival funds), the average commission
charged first-time contributors was 21.1 percent. Even worse, as of
2006 the AFOREs also charged a management fee equal to 0.39 percent of the current balance in a worker's account in addition to the
commission charged on the flow of new contributions into it.[134]

Management commissions and fees of this magnitude were very
substantial disincentives for informal-sector workers to contribute voluntarily to an AFORE. Their size was especially noteworthy inasmuch
as most AFOREs were not very actively managed (that is, their man-
agers did not generally seek to evaluate and select individual companies
as investment options). In principle, an AFORE can invest a portion of
its total portfolio (up to 30 percent, as of 2008) in Mexican and foreign
equities (shares of stock in publicly listed corporations) and 20 percent in foreign government bonds. Because the law requires AFOREs
to protect their principal against market risk, however, most of their
investments (83 percent in 2005) have been in government bonds,
with almost all of the remainder in Mexican corporate bonds.[135]

By creating a de facto tax on contributions that discouraged
informal-sector workers from joining the new pension system in significant numbers and by eating into the returns that formal-sector
workers could expect to receive from their accounts, high commissions and fees seriously undercut the Mexican government's main
goals of expanding pension coverage and raising the national savings
rate. Readers might well ask, therefore, why AFOREs could levy
such high charges. One reason was that many retirement savers, who
were accustomed to receiving a government-provided pension and

[133] Mitchell (1999); Whitehouse (2000); Sinha (2001).
[134] These are the authors' calculations based on June 2006 data provided by CONSAR, available
at www.consar.gob.mx. The average is weighted by market share.
[135] Sinha and Renteria (2005); Ragir and Attwood (2007); "The Afores Story" (2007), p. 3;
International Herald Tribune, 21 April 2005, p. 15; 22 August 2007, p. 12.

inexperienced in managing their own retirement finances, lacked the financial sophistication to determine which AFOREs offered them better long-term returns. In this context, AFOREs were able to compete successfully for clients on the basis of prizes and other marketing techniques. Indeed, these tactics were so effective that a substantial proportion of those retirement savers who switched their account from one firm to another actually moved to an AFORE charging higher commissions and fees than the one they had left behind.[136]

Over the longer term, AFOREs may not compete very hard against each other on the basis of fees because of the way in which the government structured the retirement-savings market. On the grounds that it wished to prevent the emergence of a monopoly, the Mexican government capped any single AFORE's share of the market at 20 percent. Ironically, however, the caps actually may have the effect of limiting competition. The largest AFOREs may have little incentive to lower their management commissions and fees to attract more contributors because their capacity to expand their market share is limited. Moreover, the caps may discourage foreign firms from entering the market because the potential profits from a limited share of a small market will probably not be large enough to interest major U.S. fund-management companies such as Fidelity, T. Rowe Price, or Vanguard.

Recognizing the problems that had arisen from the Zedillo administration's pension reform, the Fox administration took some steps to increase competition in the AFORE market. For example, the government made firms' entry into the market easier, and in 2003 it abolished the penalties incurred by workers who switched AFOREs. These measures did produce an increase in the number of AFOREs, from eleven in 2002 to twenty-one in 2006.[137] Nevertheless, they did not have a sizable impact on AFORE commissions and fees. One reason may have been the incentive structure created by the government's commitment to a minimum guaranteed pension: 50 percent of the contributors do not expect to receive a pension

---

[136] Authors' communication with Vicente Corta, former director of CORSAR; 5 December 2007.

[137] At the end of 2006, AFORE accounts totaled US$66.7 billion, equivalent to 8 percent of Mexico's GDP. The AFOREs market was dominated by the leading financial institutions operating in Mexico, including Banamex, Bancomer, and Banco Santander Central Hispano. See "The Afores Story" (2007), pp. 1, 3.

from their account that is more than the minimum guaranteed by the government. They therefore have weak incentives to care about the fee structure. As a result, only 9.4 percent of account holders switched their accounts from one firm to another in 2004.[138]

The high fee structure of the AFOREs therefore limited the viability of the new system. Calculations by World Bank economists in 2005 indicated that a worker earning twice the minimum wage (a total of US$3,030 per year in 2005) – that is, about half of all AFORE contributors – would have needed to earn an inflation-adjusted annual return of 8.3 percent over 40 years of uninterrupted contributions to accumulate sufficient assets to receive an AFORE pension above the guaranteed minimum.[139] Returns of this magnitude are highly unlikely.

Responding to this problem, in 2007 the Mexican Congress passed legislation that finally eliminated commissions on contributions to individual retirement accounts. The Congress did not, however, restrict commissions on account balances, leaving open the possibility that the AFOREs will seek to raise commissions on account balances to compensate for the loss of income from the elimination of commissions on contributions.[140]

Regardless of whether the 2007 legislation drives down AFORE commissions – and thereby raises the rate of return to contributors – Mexico's pension system will almost certainly require infusions of taxpayer money to meet the government's commitment to a minimum guaranteed pension. The 1997 pension reform created a guaranteed minimum pension equal to the 1997 minimum wage, indexed to inflation. (In 2005, the guaranteed minimum pension came to US$1,496 per year, roughly 30 percent of the average wage in Mexico and roughly half the median wage of AFORE contributors.)[141] The government will top up the pension benefit of any worker whose pension is less than the minimum, as long as that worker has contributed to an AFORE for at least 25 years during his or her working lifetime.[142]

[138] Sinha and Yañez Acosta (2006a, 2006b).

[139] Azuara (2003).

[140] González Amador (2007).

[141] These are the authors' calculations, using data on inflation, average manufacturing wages, and exchange rates from the Banco de Estadísticas Económicas of the INEGI (www.inegi.gob.mx). The 2005 guaranteed minimum pension data are from Sinha and Renteria (2005).

[142] Azuara (2003).

Inequality, Poverty, and Government Policy

Advances in health care coverage, housing, and education since the late 1980s have benefited millions of Mexican families. Nonetheless, inequality and poverty remain serious problems. The data on income distribution are not of high quality, making meaningful comparisons across time difficult. There is a broad consensus, however, that the distribution of income improved significantly between the early 1960s and the early 1980s and then deteriorated over the next two decades.[143] Indeed, the World Bank's 1999 assessment of income distribution in ninety-six countries found that only twelve countries had a more unequal distribution of income than Mexico.[144]

Poverty remains an especially serious problem in Mexico. The year 2000 census found that 10 percent of all homes did not have running water, 13 percent of homes had dirt floors, and an astonishing 22 million people (23 percent of the national population) lived in housing that had no indoor plumbing for treating sewage. There certainly had been considerable improvement over time; for instance, in 1970 only one-third of all homes had durable roofs and only 44 percent had durable walls, whereas in the year 2000 two-thirds of all homes had durable roofs and 79 percent had durable walls.[145] Yet even by Latin American standards, at the beginning of the twenty-first century Mexico still ranked badly in terms of both rural and urban poverty.[146]

Mexico also suffers from sharp regional variations in the incidence of poverty. All social indices show a generalized level of poverty in a group of states running from Yucatán and Chiapas north though Oaxaca, Guerrero, Puebla, and Veracruz. This zone of poverty also extends into parts of Guanajuato, Hidalgo, Michoacán, San Luis Potosí, and

---

[143] See, for example, Soares et. al. (2007). Government wage policy had a significant impact on poverty and welfare trends in Mexico during the 1980s and 1990s. The same political and administrative controls that permitted government decision makers considerable flexibility in implementing economic stabilization measures and pursuing far-reaching economic reforms hamstrung workers and their organizations in efforts to defend wages and fringe benefits. See Middlebrook and Zepeda (2003), pp. 33–5.

[144] Cited in Griffin and Ickowitz (2003), p. 592.

[145] CONAPO (2001a), p. 216; INEGI (2001b), table 9; INEGI, "Características físicas de la vivienda," available at www.inegi.gob.mx.

[146] As measured by the United Nations' Human Development Index, in the year 2000 Mexico was still considerably behind the standards of well-being in such Latin American countries as Chile, Costa Rica, Argentina, and Uruguay. See INEGI (2002b), table 2.17.

Zacatecas.[147] Not surprisingly, these are among Mexico's most rural states; extreme poverty in Mexico is predominantly a rural phenomenon. Northern states and those in the environs of the Federal District clearly form the country's wealthiest zone, with indices for health, education, and standard of living above the national norms. [148]

The Salinas administration's National Solidarity Program made some attempt at addressing poverty in Mexico. It was, for example, innovative in its effort to promote community-level participation in the design and delivery of poverty-alleviation programs. The initiative was, however, widely criticized for an absence of clear guidelines for identifying extreme poverty and setting spending priorities, the strong personal influence that Salinas exercised over it, and the extent to which the distribution of PRONASOL resources reflected partisan political calculations rather than more objective criteria such as the actual incidence of poverty in a particular state or region.

The architects of the Zedillo administration's Program for Health, Education and Nutrition responded to these criticisms by pursuing a more integrated approach to poverty alleviation and by adopting stricter targeting guidelines.[149] The program's stated goal was to break the intergenerational character of poverty in rural areas by focusing benefits on the education, nutrition, and health of children, thereby augmenting poor families' long-term human capital. PROGRESA awarded scholarships to poor children younger than 18 years of age with the goal of stimulating school attendance and keeping children enrolled in grades 3–12. The amount of the scholarship (which included the cost of school supplies) increased with school level and was calculated to replace the monetary contribution that children might have made to household income.[150] The health care and nutritional components of the program expanded basic health care coverage and emphasized aspects such as prenatal care, as well as providing monetary subsidies for food purchases if beneficiary families had regularly scheduled medical checkups and participated in health and hygiene training sessions. The number of families enrolled in the

---

[147] Alarcón (2003), p. 459. Much of Mexico's substantial indigenous population is concentrated in this zone of poverty.

[148] Regional inequalities decreased from 1960 through the late 1980s but then worsened during the 1990s. See Díaz-Cayeros (2004), pp. 204–5.

[149] See Alarcón (2003), pp. 459–67, for a comparison of PRONASOL and PROGRESA. See also Laurell (2003), pp. 338–44.

[150] Alarcón (2003), pp. 464–5; Soares et al. (2007), pp. 10–12. The program gave girls slightly larger scholarships in an effort to close the gender gap in rural education.

program grew rapidly, from 300,000 in 1997 to 2.6 million in 1999, or the equivalent of 40 percent of all rural families.[151]

The Fox administration relaunched the program in 2002 as Human Development Opportunities ("Oportunidades") and extended it to include both the rural and the urban poor. By 2002 the program reached 4.2 million families, and during the 2004–2007 period it encompassed 5 million households and 25 million individuals, making it the most extensive targeted antipoverty program in Latin America.[152] Evaluations of PROGRESA/Oportunidades confirmed that its spending quite accurately targeted the poor; 56 percent of its funding reached the poorest 20 percent of the population, and 80 percent of income from the program reached the poorest 40 percent of the population. Moreover, it was effective at keeping children (especially girls) in school and improving their health and nutrition, lowering the incidence of poverty (the proportion of the population living in extreme poverty fell from 32.6 percent in 2000 to 24.4 percent in 2004), and even reducing somewhat the overall level of income inequality in Mexico.[153] Yet even so, in 2007 Mexican government officials estimated that 19 million individuals (equivalent to 18.2 percent of the entire population) still lived in extreme poverty.[154]

Inequality and poverty remain, then, major challenges for Mexico. In the era before truly competitive national elections, the government had few incentives to provide public services efficiently or universally. The PRI maintained its dominance by allocating benefits primarily to politically powerful groups whose support was vital to the survival of the regime. As a result, during most of the twentieth century Mexico lagged behind other Latin American countries on many indicators of social well-being.

In a democratic Mexico, however, the stark reality of these problems has become increasingly important in political terms. Indeed, public debate during the 2006 presidential campaign focused to a substantial degree on how best to address the country's unresolved

---

[151] Rocha Menocal (2001), p. 520; Levy (2006). One of the program's novel features was to designate the female heading the household the recipient of cash transfers.

[152] Molyneux (2006), p. 28; Notimex (2007). In 2007 the Oportunidades program had a total budget of approximately US$1.3 billion.

[153] See Skoufias and Parker (2001); Hoddinott and Skoufias (2004); Soares et al. (2007), pp. 21–2, 28, table A1. Soares et al. (2007), pp. 28, 31, conclude that conditional cash transfers under the PROGRESA/Oportunidades program accounted for about one-fifth of the decline in inequality (a drop of approximately 5 percent) that occurred between 1996 and 2004.

[154] Notimex (2007).

social challenges. Many voters were prepared to set aside their doubts about the personality and leadership style of PRD candidate Andrés Manuel López Obrador because he (campaigning under the slogan "For the benefit of all, the poor first") appeared to be the candidate who was most seriously committed to addressing them. So long as important segments of the electorate continue to believe that the benefits of economic growth are inequitably distributed, issues of poverty and inequality will remain politically salient. The capacity of government officials to address these problems will depend, however, on the resources available to them. The constraints imposed on them by Mexico's tax system are one of the subjects of the next chapter.

7

Democracy and Development in Mexico:
Future Challenges and the Legacies of
Authoritarian Rule

Since the early 1980s Mexico has experienced momentous economic, political, and social change. Of the various transformations examined in the preceding chapters of this book, the consolidation of a competitive electoral democracy was particularly important because it ended well over a century of authoritarian rule and established essential (albeit insufficient) bases for a liberal-democratic order. The combination of free and fair elections, intense multiparty competition for power, and heightened media scrutiny of political developments has significantly increased Mexican citizens' capacity to hold government officials accountable for their public actions. Partisan alternation in power at the national level and assertive actions by federal legislators and judicial authorities in a more effective system of checks and balances have also greatly constrained what was once an all-powerful presidency. Moreover, nongovernmental organizations and other civil society groups with widely divergent goals and partisan loyalties play an important role in what is an increasingly pluralistic public policymaking process.

Nevertheless, Mexico is burdened by multiple legacies of authoritarianism and the rent-seeking coalitions that ruled the country until the end of the twentieth century. For instance, the persistence of public monopolies and private oligopolies in key economic sectors, and the weakness of government regulatory authorities charged with promoting competition and protecting consumer rights, are direct legacies of the concentrated political and economic power that characterized Mexico under the Institutional Revolutionary Party (PRI) and the fact that the privatization of many state-owned firms during the 1980s and early 1990s occurred while that regime still held sway. Similarly, despite important shifts since the 1990s in the balance of political power and the distribution of government spending, the central government retains predominant influence over state and municipal authorities in Mexico's federal system. The existence of both legal and de facto limits on associational autonomy (constraining, for instance, the formation and activities of trade unions) is yet another example of the legacies of long-term authoritarian rule. Even more troubling, weak rule of law and endemic police corruption leave citizens vulnerable to violence and serious human rights violations, including illegal detention and torture.

The consolidation of a competitive electoral democracy swept away some of the country's authoritarian institutions, but thus far it has had more muted effects on other institutional arrangements that emerged during decades of authoritarian rule. These include the judicial and law enforcement, property rights, and taxation systems. Indeed, the fact that they are "systems" rather than "rules" is what makes reforming these institutions so difficult. Changing the way they work requires interlinked reforms across a broad front, and those reforms can only be accomplished at considerable political or fiscal cost.

What It Takes to Establish the Rule of Law

Mexico is now an electoral democracy, but it is not yet governed by the rule of law. Although electoral democracy and the rule of law are linked, achieving the former does not necessarily guarantee the latter. Electoral democracy means that the selection of public officials takes place through competitive elections in which citizens can freely express their preferences for candidates and policies. The rule of law, however, denotes that citizens have effective means of protecting their fundamental rights against attempts by either the government or other citizens to abridge them. Effective rule of law requires that the government protect the rights of citizens universally, regardless of their race, socioeconomic status, gender, or creed. It also means that government officials must themselves obey the law even if they are tempted to violate it to advance their own interests. Therefore, the rule of law further implies that citizens must be able, if need be, to use the government's own legal system against it. Indeed, a simple means of judging whether the rule of law prevails is to gauge to what degree citizens can successfully sue their government in its own courts.

Societies characterized by the rule of law possess institutional arrangements that create veto points in the decision-making process, thereby limiting the discretion of public officials. In some societies, separation of powers and checks and balances among the different branches and levels of government derive from a federal system in which states or provinces limit the powers of the central government. In others, separation of powers and checks and balances exist because multiple branches of the central government (the legislature and the executive, for example) exercise overlapping authority. Some countries have both a strong federal system *and* multiple branches of the central government that check and balance each other. The United States is the quintessential example.

Societies characterized by the rule of law also feature institutions that allow citizens to sanction public officials who exceed their authority. For this to occur, citizens must have recourse to mechanisms that permit them to overcome the substantial disparity in power that exists between themselves and government officials. One of these mechanisms – a free press – reduces the cost of transmitting information about governmental abuse to other citizens, thereby making it easier for individuals to act collectively against the government or its representatives. Similarly, the existence of competitive political parties allows citizens to exercise power in numbers and form alliances that can better hold governmental representatives responsible. Political parties competing for office have a strong incentive to respond to citizens' concerns about governmental abuses: They can gain an electoral advantage by sanctioning public officials from opposing parties who engage in malfeasance.

An effective rule of law may also feature explicit, formal sanctioning mechanisms that can be employed to prosecute public officials for malfeasance or criminal activity. They include impeachment and recall procedures, as well as intervention by an independent judicial branch that is both capable of prosecuting public officials and can be used by citizens to sue the government. Lest unelected judges act with impunity, however, the rule of law further implies the existence of institutions that can review judicial decisions and, if necessary, sanction judges for misconduct. A similar set of institutional arrangements must constrain the police and the bureaucracy. Indeed, if the police and the bureaucracy are not compelled to obey the law, then even the most well-intentioned legislation and judicial decision making in the world will be worthless.

An effective rule of law rests, then, on a broad range of interlinked institutional arrangements. The specific characteristics of those arrangements will, however, vary from one society to another. There is no simple road map for creating them; no two countries follow exactly the same historical path in establishing the rule of law. Moreover, not all of the institutions and procedures necessary for an effective rule of law are legally codified; many are embedded in the attitudes and beliefs that citizens hold about how the legally codified institutions of government *should* work. Thus, societies must find their way, through processes of experimentation and reform, to the creation of that mix of formal and informal institutions necessary to ensure the rule of law. The history of countries that have established rule of law strongly suggests that this is a slow process, one that may require many years (if not generations) to accomplish.

Mexico on the Road to the Rule of Law

Mexico is in the midst of a process of experimentation and reform that may well establish a consolidated, liberal democracy. The Constitution of 1917 delineated a system of separation of powers and checks and balances – separate executive, legislative, and judicial branches of the central government, as well as a federal system in which states and municipalities hold a prominent place. Even though these formal institutional arrangements lost much of their intended significance once an "official" ruling party consolidated its dominance over every branch and level of government, constitutional provisions defining the separation of powers and checks and balances have since sprung to life. The key events in this regard were the PRI's loss of its majority in the federal Chamber of Deputies after the 1997 midterm elections and its defeat in the year 2000 presidential election. Constitutional checks and balances have since been deployed by legislators to constrain the power of the once-dominant Mexican president.

The debate over Mexico's 2005 federal budget provides an apposite example. The budget bill that President Vicente Fox Quesada (2000–2006) submitted to the Chamber of Deputies in September 2004 proposed spending that was slightly higher than that of the previous year in nominal terms, but which was 4.5 percent lower once adjusted for inflation.[1] In an unprecedented act of assertiveness, a broad coalition of legislators from all political parties represented in the Chamber other than Fox's National Action Party (PAN) took advantage of its

---

[1] *La Jornada Virtu@l,* 18 November 2004.

majority status and rewrote those parts of the budget focusing on education and health care.[2] As a result, the authorized 2005 budget allocated some 115 billion pesos (approximately US$10.3 billion) in additional funds to education and social programs.[3]

The Fox administration strenuously contested the opposition legislators' action. Fox first returned the spending bill to the Chamber with his own itemized list of objections, which the opposition coalition immediately rejected. He then sought the Supreme Court's backing for his view that the 1917 Constitution gave the federal executive line-item veto authority. The administration also pledged not to spend any of the contested budgetary allocations until the constitutional controversy was resolved. In the end, Fox prevailed when the Supreme Court ruled that the Chamber of Deputies would need to overrule his specific objections by a two-thirds majority vote in a special legislative session.[4] The broader political significance of the episode, however, lay in what it revealed about a historic shift in executive–legislative bargaining power (especially legislators' willingness to amend executive-sponsored bills and actively propose their own legislative initiatives) and the emergence of an independent judiciary in an increasingly effective constitutional system of checks and balances.[5]

Another example of the incipient emergence of the rule of law involves the key differences between the antipoverty program established by Carlos Salinas de Gortari (1988–1994) and the antipoverty policies adopted by Ernesto Zedillo Ponce de León (1994–2000) and Vicente Fox (2000–2006). These differences reveal how increased scrutiny by the legislature and the press can help check executive discretion. Salinas's National Solidarity Program (PRONASOL) conspicuously embodied a model of centralized and discretionary public

[2] The coalition included the PRI, Party of the Democratic Revolution (PRD), Labor Party (PT), Mexican Ecologist Green Party (PVEM), and Democratic Convergence (CD).

[3] The Chamber of Deputies subsequently claimed public credit for using "two cents of each peso" in the federal government's budget to increase spending on basic and higher education, potable water, and health care. See the paid advertisement in *Proceso*, no. 1466 (5 December 2004), p. 13, bearing the phrase "The Chamber of Deputies comes through for you" ("La Cámara de Diputados te cumple").

[4] Aranda (2005). The Supreme Court declined to rule on the broader issues the case raised concerning executive versus legislative authority over budgetary matters.

[5] The Chamber of Deputies' actions in 2004 built on shifts in executive–legislative relations in the budgetary process that were already evident in the late 1990s. See Weldon (2004a), pp. 146–50.

spending. In contrast, Zedillo's Program for Education, Health, and Nutrition (PROGRESA) and Fox's Opportunities Program (Programa Oportunidades), a continuation of PROGRESA under a different name, emphasized targeted spending under more precise guidelines. To be sure, PROGRESA/Oportunidades was not immune to politicization.[6] By and large, however, the evidence indicates that the public funds used to finance PROGRESA/Oportunidades were subjected to far greater legislative accountability and media scrutiny than PRONASOL. Such accountability was a direct consequence of the political changes, including enhanced citizen access to public information, that Mexico has undergone since the Salinas presidency.[7]

The checks and balances embedded in Mexico's federal system have also taken on new significance as a consequence of democratization.[8] So long as the PRI dominated all levels of government, governors served more as Mexican presidents' regional representatives than the fiduciaries of their states' interests. Increasing political pluralism – embodied in the election of a PAN president in 2000 while the PRI continued to control the majority of state governments – substantially altered relations between federal and state authorities. Not only did governors become much more politically relevant after 2000[9] but they have also emerged as vigorous defenders of state and local interests in negotiations with the federal government over the distribution of tax revenues. Although the federal government still collects 95 percent of all taxes, the proportion of federal tax revenues distributed to state and municipal governments rose from 25 percent in 1993 to 38 percent in 2003.[10] Moreover, governors have, on occasion, successfully pressured their states' representatives in the federal Chamber of Deputies to redirect funds to states and municipalities that would have otherwise

---

[6] For evidence concerning the political uses of PROGRESA/Oportunidades, see Rocha Menocal (2001); Gómez Tagle (2004), pp. 100–1; Mackinlay (2004), pp. 315–16; Bartra (2006), pp. 10–11; Cervantes (2006); Balboa (2007).

[7] The Federal Institute for Access to Public Information (IFAI), created by the 2002 Federal Law on Transparency and Access to Governmental Public Information, contributes significantly to citizens' capacity to scrutinize government spending programs. As of 2006, approximately two-thirds of Mexico's state governments had enacted similar freedom-of-information laws. See de Remes (2006), pp. 194–5.

[8] Díaz-Cayeros (2004); de Remes (2006).

[9] Five of the six candidates representing the PRI, PAN, and PRD in the 2000 and 2006 presidential elections had previously served as governor. The exception was the PAN's Felipe Calderón Hinojosa in 2006.

[10] Díaz-Cayeros (2004), p. 209; de Remes (2006), pp. 190 n13, 192.

supported federal government programs.[11] Through such actions, and with the creation of the National Governors' Conference (CONA-GO) in 2002, and the National Conference of Mexican Municipalities (CONAMM) in 2003, state and local interests have clearly signaled their intent to recalibrate the balance of power between the federal government and the states.[12]

The enhanced autonomy of some federal regulatory agencies has also promoted the rule of law. For example, the Federal Competition Commission (CFC, created in 1994), although still operating with legal limitations on its investigative and sanctioning powers, has challenged oligopolies in several industries.[13] The Federal Institute for Access to Public Information (IFAI) has required elected officials to make public sensitive information concerning the use of government funds.[14] Even more prominently, the Federal Electoral Institute (IFE) has investigated and fined several political parties for violations of campaign finance laws. In 2003, for instance, the IFE levied extremely heavy fines against both the PRI and the PAN for violations of campaign funding laws during the 2000 presidential campaign. It determined that the PRI's candidate had illegally received large transfers of funds from the state-owned Mexican Petroleum Company (PEMEX) via the PRI-allied Mexican Petroleum Workers' Union (STPRM), and the "Friends of Fox" (the nonparty organization that Fox founded to promote his presidential candidacy) had violated federal electoral law by accepting substantial financial contributions from foreign sources.[15]

The growing power and prestige of the Mexican judiciary have especially underpinned gains in public accountability and the rule of law. This development can be traced back to a 1994 constitutional reform that substantially increased the formal authority and institutional autonomy of the Supreme Court. The reform empowered the Supreme Court to review the constitutionality of federal and state laws and establish binding judicial precedents. It also gave the Supreme Court the authority to adjudicate constitutional conflicts between

---

[11] De Remes (2006), pp. 193, 196, 198; *Reforma*, 23 December 2006, p. 6.

[12] De Remes (2006), pp. 187–91.

[13] Ávalos (2006) argues that the Mexican judiciary remains one of the most important obstacles to the effective application of competition policy because offenders can easily secure judicial protection from CFC fines.

[14] Malkin (2004); *Expansión*, 27 December 2006–17 January 2007, p. 94; *La Jornada Virtu@l*, 17 January 2007.

[15] Gómez Tagle (2004), pp. 103–5.

different branches and levels of government. In addition, the 1994 reform introduced selection criteria for justices designed to ensure their professionalism and nonpartisanship, and it altered appointment procedures in ways that increased the judiciary's autonomy vis-à-vis the executive branch of government.[16] In a somewhat similar way to the United States, the Mexican executive branch presents slates of Supreme Court nominees to the Senate, which then makes appointments to staggered 15-year terms on the basis of a two-thirds majority vote.[17]

It was, however, the process of democratization that gave practical importance to the contents of this constitutional reform. When Zedillo appointed an entirely new group of Supreme Court justices in 1995, the PRI's control of the Senate allowed him to do so in a process that did not differ fundamentally from the procedures previous PRI-affiliated presidents had used during the decades when the judiciary was largely subordinated to executive power.[18] In marked contrast, since the year 2000 no single party has controlled two-thirds of the Senate, and so Court appointments must be brokered among rival parties. Even more broadly, the substantial shifts that have taken place in the balance of power between the federal executive and the Congress and between the central government and state and municipal authorities have greatly strengthened the Court's autonomy and political importance by making it an effective constitutional arbiter on an expanding array of public policy and human rights issues.

These developments at the federal level, however, have thus far had less impact on citizens' daily lives than one might suppose because approximately 80 percent of the judicial caseload in Mexico is adjudicated in state courts. Under Mexico's federal system, state courts and other state-level judicial agencies (prosecution, defense, judicial

---

[16] For example, Supreme Court nominees must be law graduates with at least 10 years of professional experience, and they cannot have held a senior political post in the year before their appointment.

[17] The 1994 constitutional reform also reduced the size of the Court from twenty-six to eleven members and established a Judicial Council (Consejo de la Judicatura) to administer the federal judiciary. The Council's responsibilities include the selection of new judges for federal circuit and district courts (as well as judges for special agrarian, labor, military, and tax courts) and oversight of judicial promotions. On judicial reform in Mexico, see Domingo (2000); Giugale, Lafourcade, and Nguyen (2001), pp. 736–7; Magaloni (2003), pp. 280–9; Magaloni and Zepeda (2004), pp. 168–70; Ríos-Figueroa (2007).

[18] González Casanova (1965), pp. 33–7, concluded that the Court did exercise relative autonomy on some issues.

councils, and court clerks) are organized independently of the federal judiciary and operate according to their own procedural and substantive laws. Here, the pace of reform has been much slower. State governors name judges and public prosecutors, who are often subject to a high degree of partisan influence. They and their staffs have a great deal of discretion, carry extremely large caseloads, and are grossly underfunded in comparison to the federal judiciary. Much the same can be said of state prosecutors' offices and especially the police, who continue to be very poorly paid and highly corrupt.[19]

The effectiveness of state-level judicial and law enforcement institutions is particularly important because these institutions constitute citizens' first line of defense against violent crime. Establishing the conditions for citizens' security is a crucial test for new democracies, and since the late 1980s violence and public insecurity have consistently ranked among Mexican citizens' most pressing concerns.[20] Mexican states vary dramatically, however, in terms of their ability to investigate, prosecute, and punish crime. Indeed, in the year 2000 state-level prosecutors failed to conduct effective investigations into 81.5 percent of reported crimes, and a mere 3 percent of criminal suspects were ever brought before a court of law.[21] One important reason for states' poor overall record in combating crime is that most of them fail to devote sufficient resources to this purpose, a point that again underscores the importance of generating substantial additional government revenues in Mexico and distributing a greater proportion of public resources to state and local authorities.

More broadly, Mexico has made only halting progress where government investigations of corruption and human rights violations are concerned. Although not without some foot-dragging, the Fox administration did follow through on its preelection promises to investigate human rights crimes committed during Mexico's "dirty war" of the late 1960s and the 1970s. During this period, actions by the Mexican army and by paramilitary forces against urban and rural guerrilla movements resulted in the killing, forced disappearance, or torture

---

[19] Giugale, Lafourcade, and Nguyen (2001), pp. 137, 735–9; Magaloni and Zepeda (2004), pp. 174–5.

[20] Whitehead (2002), pp. 165–85; Magaloni and Zepeda (2004), p. 176; Middlebrook (2004), p. 27.

[21] Magaloni and Zepeda (2004), pp. 176, 182, 184–6. Even in the most high-profile cases (murders), the best-performing state (Tabasco) only managed a 31.1 percent conviction rate over the 1996–2000 period.

of hundreds of people.[22] Among the most sensational and politically charged cases were the October 1968 Tlatelolco and June 1971 Corpus Christi massacres in which the army and government-trained thugs killed or wounded several hundred student demonstrators. In 2001, therefore, the Fox administration entrusted the investigation of past human rights violations to a Special Prosecutor for Social and Political Movements in the Past (Fiscalía Especial para Movimientos Sociales y Políticos del Pasado). In July 2004 the Special Prosecutor made international headlines by formally indicting former President Luis Echeverría (1970–1976) and ten former civilian and military officials on the charge of genocide in conjunction with the 1971 killings in Mexico City. Among the officials charged were once-untouchable figures, including a former secretary of the interior and presidential candidate, two former directors of the Federal Security Directorate (the internal security agency responsible for the pursuit and interrogation of leftist guerrillas during Mexico's "dirty war"), and retired General Manuel Díaz Escobar, who coordinated the ruthless paramilitary group known as The Hawks (Los Halcones). In February 2005, however, the Supreme Court ruled that the crime of genocide was not applicable in cases originating before 1982, and in 2007 Echeverría obtained a permanent injunction against prosecution.[23] Nevertheless, the formal indictment of a past president on charges of serious human rights violations was an unprecedented development in Mexican political history.

The Enforcement of Property Rights

What holds true for establishing an effective rule of law is also true where the creation of a transparent, enforceable system of property rights is concerned: It cannot be done with the stroke of a pen. In

[22] There is no accurate tally of "dirty war" victims, although human rights activists have documented some 300–600 cases of forced disappearance. There were undoubtedly at least several hundred additional cases of torture. See, for example, Hirales (2004) and Centro de Derechos Humanos Miguel Agustín Pro Juárez (2006), p. 10.

[23] *La Jornada Virtu@l*, 24 February 2005 and 16 June 2005; McKinley, Jr. (2007). Contrary to the initial expectations of democratic reformers seeking to end Mexico's entrenched tradition of official impunity, the Fox administration did not undertake any major effort to reveal and punish former government officials responsible for the many conspicuous cases of corruption that had occurred under PRI rule. Fox administration officials apparently calculated that their political interests would be better served by not opening this Pandora's box because they needed PRI votes in Congress to advance the PAN's programmatic agenda.

point of fact, it is impossible to establish a functioning property-rights system in which claims and contracts can be enforced universally and at low cost without first consolidating the rule of law. Most obviously, if the courts and the police are corrupt, then it is not possible to enforce even the most carefully crafted contract or protect even the most clearly identifiable asset.

If the government's main purpose is to provide privileged constituencies with special rights that raise wealth holders' rates of return on capital or otherwise bestow unequal advantages on a small group, then those who benefit from such arrangements have no incentive to invest in the institutions necessary for universal property-rights enforcement. The members of the rent-seeking coalition can, after all, enforce their claims and contracts through private deals with public officials. Indeed, these groups actually prefer that there be weak property rights for the rest of society because the differential enforcement of property rights establishes barriers to entry that protect their monopolies and oligopolies and simultaneously enhances their ability to prey on others' assets. They are likely, therefore, to oppose reforms seeking to create institutional arrangements that specify and enforce property rights universally – for everyone in society – because such measures would level the playing field.

In a country ruled by an authoritarian rent-seeking coalition, the government also lacks strong incentives to create universal property-rights institutions. Not only are such initiatives likely to face concerted resistance from the coalition members that sustain the government, but reforms such as establishing and maintaining property and commercial registers or providing sufficiently high levels of funding to build honest court systems and police forces also come at considerable fiscal cost. Money spent on property-rights institutions cannot be used to satisfy the demands of the authoritarian coalition's core constituents, and it is not available to be stolen by dishonest government officials.

The institutional arrangements necessary for the universal enforcement of property rights have historically been weak in Mexico. As the country has moved toward electoral democracy and, somewhat fitfully, a more effective rule of law, the incentives to strengthen property-rights institutions have become stronger.[24] We emphasize here that the

---

[24] Elizondo Mayer-Serra (2001), pp. 77, 270, 272, cautions that despite the political constraints established by multiparty electoral competition and partisan alternation in power, the federal executive formally retains broad discretion in the regulation of property rights because the 1936 Law on Expropriation and the 1950 Law on the Federal Executive's Attributions in Economic Matters have not been altered.

wealthiest individuals in a capitalist democracy are not the only ones who value institutional arrangements guaranteeing property rights; these arrangements are at least as important to those with the fewest material assets to protect. For this reason, elected government officials who take meaningful steps to strengthen property rights for all citizens (in such areas as residential housing, for example) can potentially reap substantial electoral rewards for the parties they represent. The PAN is particularly well positioned to do so because it has long been identified programmatically with the defense of private property rights and because, as a conservative party whose traditional core constituencies were middle- and upper-class groups, it has especially strong incentives to broaden its support in a highly competitive electoral environment.[25]

In contemporary Mexico, at least four groups have a strong interest in establishing clearly specified, easily enforced property rights. These groups include: bankers, who seek to enter the market for consumer, housing, and commercial lending but are stymied by the difficulties they face in attaching collateral if borrowers default on their loans; small businesses seeking access to bank credit; housing developers, who seek clear title to the lands that they acquire; and families and individuals aspiring to home ownership.

The effective guarantee of property rights requires, among other steps, the creation of institutions that permit property to be transferred easily. That is, it requires a legal system that allows contracts conveying or assigning property to someone other than the original owner to be enforced at low cost. Take, for example, the case of a loan contract in which a piece of property has been pledged as collateral. In most developed countries, loan contracts represent liens on assets; if the borrower does not repay the loan on the agreed terms, the lending institution can exercise its lien and repossess the asset. Borrowers can slow the repossession process by filing for bankruptcy, but if bankruptcy laws and the judicial system are efficient, the declaration of bankruptcy buys the borrower only a moderate period of time before the bankruptcy court assigns the asset to the creditor. If, however, bankruptcy laws and the courts are inefficient (or corrupt), then filing for bankruptcy can prevent the creditor from repossessing the underlying collateral for years on end.

The protection that such inefficiencies might seemingly provide to small businesses and consumers from big, powerful banks is illusory: If

---

[25] Middlebrook (2001).

creditors know that they cannot repossess the physical assets pledged to secure loans, they are unlikely to lend to small businesses and consumers in the first place. Instead, banks will lend on the basis of reputational collateral (a borrower's past record of repayment or reputation in the business community), a practice that favors large firms and wealthy individuals. The rest of society – farmers, small business owners, and households – will find it much more difficult to access the banking system.

Mexico's inefficient bankruptcy law and judicial system make it difficult to write contracts that convey or assign property. Until 2001, bankruptcy procedures were cumbersome in the extreme. Not only did the country have few bankruptcy judges, but the bankruptcy law also required judges to pass resolutions on each and every objection presented by debtors. Debtors could therefore delay the recovery of property for long periods of time by raising multiple objections, and they could obtain information about how to file these objections from the publications issued by the country's various debtor organizations. Moreover, even when creditors won favorable judgments, they were not always enforced. As a consequence, any attempt to recover collateral through the legal system typically required between 3 and 7 years.[26]

In 2001, the Fox administration pushed through a bankruptcy reform law that permitted some types of loan contracts to be recast to place collateralized assets outside of an individual's or a firm's bankruptcy estate. Those assets are instead assigned to the lender. As a result, courts no longer become involved in repossession efforts because declaring bankruptcy will not protect the collateralized asset. For example, under Mexico's "lease-to-own" automobile finance agreements, a borrower does not actually use bank financing to purchase a car; instead, the bank purchases the car and then leases it to the borrower. The depreciation and interest rates used to calculate the lease payments are structured so that the bank recoups its principal and interest over the period of the lease. When the lease expires, the title passes to the borrower. Until that time, however, the bank holds title to the car and can seize the vehicle whenever the borrower falls behind in lease payments.

A second example of innovation in bankruptcy law involved a 2001 reform of home mortgage contracts that replaced liens on property with bilateral trusts. Under these arrangements, the bank is both the

---

[26] Mackey (1999), p. 101.

trustee and beneficiary of the trust. If the borrower fails to make agreed payments, the bank can evict the debtor and sell the house at auction. Debtors can legally contest the repossession but they are unable to remain in the house during the process. This gives them strong incentives to negotiate an amicable repossession with the bank.[27]

These reforms to bankruptcy law were not, however, a panacea for what are still generally weak property-rights institutions. One remaining problem is the limited effectiveness of the Mexican judicial and law enforcement systems, whose weaknesses are often exacerbated by the clever stratagems that debtors developed in the course of repeated financial crises during the 1980s and 1990s. A mortgage borrower can, for example, use a number of legal and extralegal tactics that raise the costs of repossession relative to the value of her or his house, thereby making it difficult to enforce the terms of bilateral housing trusts. For instance, if a borrower "leases" a house to a family member (even while continuing to live there), the bank can repossess the house if the mortgage holder falls behind in her or his payments. Nevertheless, the bank must do so with the "renter" still living there because, under Mexico's favorable renters' laws, that person cannot be easily evicted. If the bank then decides to sell the house at auction (as the law permits it to do), the price it receives reflects the stream of rent available from the rental contract. Yet the net present value of the stream of rent is likely be far less than the market value of the house if were it unencumbered by a rental agreement (which may in any event be fictitious if the mortgage holder actually occupies the house). Once the bank has taken possession of the house, moreover, the borrower/renter has few incentives to preserve the structure's physical condition or its market value.

A debtor who decides to resist actively the lender's attempt to repossess her or his house can also pay a bribe or organize a public demonstration when the police come to enforce a bank repossession order. The police prefer not to subdue such demonstrations because of the risk that they will escalate into violence. Neighbors often choose to participate in such demonstrations because they know that, should their own mortgage loans go into default, the rest of the neighborhood will reciprocate by demonstrating on their behalf.

For reasons such as these, the mortgage contract reforms enacted in 2001 did not lead to a dramatic increase in commercial bank lending

---

[27] Caloca González (n.d.).

in the residential housing market.[28] Instead, private banks have largely left the mortgage market to nonbank lenders, especially the Limited-Objective Financial Societies (SOFOLES) that fund their mortgage loans by borrowing from a government-backed development bank that also provides insurance in the event of default by the mortgage holder. Yet even these nonbank lenders generally decline to use the police to repossess houses, preferring to pay debtors who are in default to vacate the house.

A second major weakness in Mexico's property-rights institutions concerns the difficulties that individuals often have in establishing clear title to their assets. Mexican property registers are difficult to access and often inaccurate. Almost without exception, they cannot be accessed electronically; instead, the file for each parcel must be examined manually, by consulting the sheaves of paper that comprise the file. Because title searches typically involve handling the original documents (rather than photocopies), portions of the documentation may be inadvertently lost or even tampered with purposely. More-over, because purchasers often seek to avoid the payment of property registration fees, many property sales go unrecorded in the property register. The same is true of liens against titles when bills for prop-erty improvements remain unpaid. Public records often show multiple owners for the same parcel, and parcel boundaries may not be clearly specified.

As if these problems were not serious enough, public property reg-istries in Mexico are not integrated with property tax registries. As a consequence, the municipal governments that collect property taxes have little incentive to ensure that the public registries are up-to-date. Moreover, public property registries do not cover the lands held by *ejidos*.[29] This means that former ejido lands that have been converted to private use (typically ejido lands on the outskirts of urban areas that have been sold to housing developers, who then create parcels that are resold to homeowners) do not have clear title histories.[30]

There is, then, often a high degree of uncertainty as to whether the person who owns a parcel of land, whether it be a farm or an office building, actually has clear title to it.[31] So serious is the problem of uncertain titling that in 2004, across the entire country, commercial

[28] Haber and Musacchio (2006).
[29] Ejido lands are listed in a separate Agrarian Property Registry.
[30] Rajoy (n.d.).
[31] Joint Center for Housing Studies of Harvard University (2004).

banks only made 18,601 loans for the purchase of preexisting housing. Even more shocking, that figure represented a dramatic improvement from previous years, when almost no loans were made for this purpose.[32]

Recognizing the problems that are created by uncertain titles, the Fox administration began a pilot program to modernize property registries, providing US$4 million for the conversion of paper files to an electronic database in three states (Baja California, Colima, and Sonora).[33] Even in these states, however, many of the other difficulties with property registries remain. Thus, resolving the problem of uncertain titling remains a major challenge.

Taxation Revisited

Reforming Mexico's property-rights institutions will be a costly undertaking. A thorough reform would require digitizing paper files, reviewing the documentation on each and every parcel in the country, and then adjudicating any conflicting title claims. Undertaking changes of this magnitude would require substantially increased funding for state-level judiciaries. Of course, making progress in this area also implies providing the financial resources necessary to reform the police departments that, in the end, enforce judicial decisions.

What is true regarding the cost of reforming Mexico's judicial, law enforcement, and property-rights systems also holds for the cost of modernizing Mexico's educational system. As we noted in Chapter Six, the weaknesses of Mexico's educational system place its workers at a significant competitive disadvantage against workers in other countries. Improving the quality of and access to education will necessarily involve raising spending above current levels.

For all these reasons, one of the most serious challenges facing a democratic Mexico is the need to find additional sources of public revenue. As we pointed out in Chapters Two and Three, the Mexican government has collected exceptionally low levels of tax revenue – typically on the order of 10 percent of gross domestic product (GDP). This figure has placed Mexico at the bottom of the distribution

[32] Centro de Investigación y Documentación de la Casa and Sociedad Hipotecaria Federal (2005), p. 21.
[33] Centro de Investigación y Documentación de la Casa and Sociedad Hipotecaria Federal (2005), pp. 73–4.

compared either with other Organisation for Economic Co-operation and Development (OECD) member states or other countries in Latin America. In 2004, for example, Mexican government tax revenues – excluding taxes on the state-owned Mexican Petroleum Company (PEMEX) – were equivalent to 11.4 percent of GDP, compared with an OECD average of 36 percent and a Latin American average of 13.7 percent.[34]

During periods when international petroleum prices have been high, oil export earnings have provided the Mexican government with an important additional source of revenue, typically bumping up the ratio of government revenues to GDP by an additional 4 or 5 percentage points.[35] Even under such favorable circumstances, however, there are strong reasons to doubt whether oil alone can generate the resources necessary to finance the development challenges facing Mexico. First, even including income from oil exports in the calculation, the Mexican government has been poorly funded compared either with other OECD member states or with other large Latin American countries (see Figure 3.13). Second, Mexico has taxed its petroleum sector so heavily that in effect it has discouraged investment in exploration and production, a policy that inevitably must have negative effects on the growth of oil reserves and refining capacity. Most petroleum-producing countries tax the *profits* earned by their state-owned oil companies, whereas until 2006 Mexico taxed the *revenues* earned by PEMEX. It did so, moreover, at the punishing rate of 60.8 percent, making Mexico's taxation rate on its state-owned oil company the highest in the world.[36] As a consequence, between 2001 and 2004 PEMEX's tax payments were greater than its operating income.[37]

Legislation adopted in 2005 created a separate line item in the federal budget to fund PEMEX's exploration projects, and it modified PEMEX's tax regime to permit the company to deduct specified operating expenses before paying tax to the government.[38] In addition, as

---

[34] *The Economist*, 18 November 2006, p. 12.

[35] Oil revenues have consistently funded 30–40 percent of the federal government's total budget and 25–35 percent of government revenues transferred to states and municipalities. See Rodríguez-Padilla (2006), p. 4.

[36] Giugale, Lafourcade, and Nguyen (2001), pp. 183–5. Syria may be the possible exception to this generalization.

[37] *The Economist*, 1 July 2006, p. 25.

[38] The 2005 reform, although allowing PEMEX to claim deductions before taxes, raised the ordinary hydrocarbon tax rate on net revenues to 74.0 percent (declining gradually to 71.5

we pointed out in Chapter Three, the Mexican government has established programs that allow PEMEX to borrow from private investors off budget. Measures such as these, however, do not fully compensate for the fact that PEMEX's tax rate remains so high that many of its operations are only profitable when international petroleum prices are extremely high.[39] Years of underfunding PEMEX's activities have resulted in declining petroleum reserves and stagnating production volumes, and Mexico has been forced to import one-fifth or more of its natural gas and refined petroleum products.[40]

The Mexican government will, therefore, need to find nonoil sources of tax revenue. This will not be an easy task. The government's single largest source of income other than taxes on PEMEX revenues has been the value-added tax (VAT), which was first introduced in 1980. Its contributions are, however, reduced by rampant evasion. Indeed, evasion of the tax (by, for example, paying cash for goods or services) is so common that, although the standard VAT rate is 15 percent, it only produces revenue equal to approximately 3 percent of GDP.

The Fox administration sought to increase VAT-derived revenues by, among other steps, eliminating some of the VAT exemptions often used by firms to hide taxable income.[41] The fiscal reforms the administration proposed in 2001 and again in 2003 would have extended the VAT to food (except for basic staples, such as tortillas), most pharmaceutical products, publications, school tuition, and public transportation. Both initiatives failed to win congressional approval because the VAT, like all consumption taxes, tends to be regressive (that is, its greatest proportional impact is on those individuals whose incomes are lowest), and levying the VAT on food and medicines would have made it more regressive still. From the perspective of the Party of the Democratic Revolution (PRD) and the PRI, the administration's tax reform proposals were a political windfall because they could portray the PAN as a party seeking to tax the poor. Scoring that point was particularly easy because the Fox administration's proposals for

---

percent in 2012). Moreover, although a key goal of the reform was to free up additional resources for PEMEX's exploration and development projects, the Ministry of Finance and Public Credit retains final decision-making authority over PEMEX's annual operating budget. In 2006 and 2007, the Ministry did not permit PEMEX to realize any gain from its reduced tax burden. See Rodríguez-Padilla (2006).

[39] Giugale, Lafourcade, and Nguyen (2001), p. 184.

[40] Malkin (2005), p. 19; *The Economist*, 1 July 2006, p. 25; Malkin (2007), p. 17.

[41] Giugale, Lafourcade, and Nguyen (2001), pp. 183–4.

increasing government revenues, while seeking to extend the VAT to food and medicines and tax blue-collar workers' fringe benefits for the first time, conspicuously omitted any tax on corporate dividends or short-term capital gains on financial investments.[42]

President Felipe Calderón Hinojosa (2006–2012) clearly drew on the political lessons learned in 2001 and 2003 when he submitted his own fiscal reform initiative to the Chamber of Deputies in 2007. The bill did not revive the politically unpalatable idea of a value-added tax on food and medicines; Calderón, who had himself served as a federal deputy (1991–1994, 2000–2003) and coordinator of the PAN's delegation in the Chamber (2000–2003), worked hard to build cross-party support for the package; and treasury officials actively sought compromises with PRI and PRD legislators and with representatives of private-sector organizations.

The legislation that the Chamber of Deputies finally approved in September 2007 sought to increase tax revenues by 2.5–3 percent of GDP and thereby provide funds for substantially expanded public-sector infrastructure investment and social spending.[43] A 16.5 percent levy (rising to 17.5 percent in 2010) on corporate net income – after deductions for long-term investments, physical inputs, salaries, and employee benefits – was a central feature of the legislation. In an attempt to improve tax collection in the informal sector, the measure also established a 2-percent tax on cash bank deposits exceeding a cumulative monthly total of 25,000 pesos (US$2,250 in September 2007). In addition, the reform increased incentives for state and municipal governments to raise their own revenues.

An overhaul of Mexico's property tax system would also raise additional revenues for the government. Municipalities administer the current system. They generally have limited administrative capacity, however, and tend to set tax rates at extremely low levels. Property tax reform is attractive for two reasons. First, it is more difficult to evade taxes on tangible assets than it is on streams of income. Second, an increase in tax rates on real property can be linked to expenditures that enhance the security of property titles, thereby giving taxpayers an incentive to cooperate with tax reform.

---

[42] Musacchio (2003); *La Crónica*, 13 December 2003; *Reforma*, 22 December 2003.

[43] For the legislation comprising Calderón's 2007 fiscal reform package, see *Diario Oficial de la Federación*, 1 October 2007, pp. 3–67. For summaries of its main elements, see *The Economist*, 23 June 2007, pp. 60–1; 15 September 2007, p. 67.

What specific strategies the government adopts to increase public revenues are of course a question of politics. In the past, the country's major political parties have found it difficult to reach agreement on this topic. Unless political leaders from across the partisan spectrum are prepared to reach compromises that provide federal, state, and municipal governments with the necessary financial means, Mexico will find it extremely difficult to address effectively the many development challenges it faces in the twenty-first century.

Bibliography

Aghion, Philippe, Eve Caroli, and Cecilia García-Peñalosa (1999). "Inequality and Economic Growth: The Perspective of New Growth Theories," *Journal of Economic Literature* 37 (4): 1615–60.

Aguayo Quezada, Sergio (1998a). *1968: Los archivos de la violencia.* Mexico City: Grijalbo.

Aguayo Quezada, Sergio (1998b). "Electoral Observation and Democracy in Mexico." In Kevin J. Middlebrook, ed., *Electoral Observation and Democratic Transitions in Latin America.* La Jolla, CA: Center for U.S.-Mexican Studies, University of California, San Diego.

Aguilar Ascencio, Oscar (2000). "La iglesia católica y la democratización en México." In José de Jesús Legorreta Zepeda, ed., *La iglesia católica y la política en México de hoy.* Mexico City: Universidad Iberoamericana.

Alarcón, Diana (2003). "Income Distribution and Poverty Alleviation in Mexico: A Comparative Analysis." In Kevin J. Middlebrook and Eduardo Zepeda, eds., *Confronting Development: Assessing Mexico's Economic and Social Policy Challenges.* Stanford, CA: Stanford University Press/Center for U.S.-Mexican Studies, University of California-San Diego.

Alba, Francisco (1984). *La población de México: evolución y dilemas.* Mexico City: El Colegio de México.

Ames, Barry (1970). "Bases of Support for Mexico's Dominant Party," *American Political Science Review* 64 (1): 153–67.

Arai, Adriana (2006). "In Mexico, Pushing Big Banks to Lend Small," *International Herald Tribune*, 5 June.

Aranda, Jesús (2005). "Decreta la Corte nulas las partidas presupuestales objetadas por Fox," *La Jornada Virtu@l*, 18 May.

Arenas Velázquez, Erika (2004). "Efectos de la apertura comercial en la brecha salarial entre trabajadores calificados y no calificados en México durante el periodo 1987–2000," *Gaceta de Economía* 9 (18): 1–13.

Arriola, Carlos (1988). "La campaña electoral de Manuel J. Clouthier en Sinaloa, México, 1986," *Foro Internacional* 29 (1): 30–48.

Ávalos, Marcos (2006). *Condiciones generales de competencia: el caso de México.* Serie Estudios y Perspectivas. Santiago, Chile: Comisión Económica para América Latina.

Averbug, André (1999). "Brazilian Trade Liberalization and Integration in the1990s." Banco do Nordeste – Programa das Nações Unidas para o Desenvolvimento. Working paper.

Azuara, Oliver (2003). "The Mexican Defined-Contribution Pension System: Perspective of Low-Income Workers." Office of Chief Economist, Background Paper for Regional Study on Social Security Reform. Washington, DC: World Bank.

Balboa, Juan (2007). "Evítense la tentación de intervenir en elecciones: senadores a Zavala Peniche," *La Jornada Virtu@l*, 12 April.

Balinski, Michel, and Victoriano Ramírez González (1996). "A Case Study of Electoral Manipulation: The Mexican Laws of 1989 and 1994," *Electoral Studies* 15 (2): 203–17.

Banco de México (2004). *Indicadores económicos y financieros*. Mexico City: Banco de México.

Banco de México (2005). *Indicadores económicos y financieros*. Mexico City: Banco de México.

Barro, Robert J., and Jong-Wha Lee (2000). "International Data on Educational Attainment: Updates and Implications." Harvard University, Center for International Development Working Paper no. 42.

Bartra, Armando (2006). "El estado de la elección," *Memoria*, No. 208 (June): 9–14.

Basáñez, Miguel (1991). *El pulso de los sexenios: 20 años de crisis en México*. Rev. ed. Mexico City: Siglo Veintiuno Editores.

Bates, Robert (2001). "Institutions and Economic Performance." In Gudrun Kochendorfer and Boris Pleskovic, eds., *The Institutional Foundation of a Market Economy*. Berlin: Deutsche Stiftung für Internationale Entwicklung.

Bazdresch, Carlos, and Santiago Levy (1991). "Populism and Economic Policy in Mexico, 1970–82." In Rudiger Dornbusch and Sebastian Edwards, eds., *The Macroeconomics of Populism in Latin America*. Chicago: University of Chicago Press.

Beatty, Edward (2001). *Institutions and Investment: The Political Basis of Industrialization in Mexico Before 1911*. Stanford, CA: Stanford University Press.

Bensusán, Graciela (2004). "A New Scenario for Mexican Trade Unions: Changes in the Structure of Political and Economic Opportunities." In Kevin J. Middlebrook, ed., *Dilemmas of Political Change in Mexico*. London: Institute of Latin American Studies, University of London/Center for U.S.-Mexican Studies, University of California, San Diego.

Bergoeing, Rafael, Patrick J. Kehoe, Timothy J. Kehoe, and Raimundo Soto (2001). "A Decade Lost and Found: Mexico and Chile in the 1980s." National Bureau of Economic Research Working Paper no. 8520. Cambridge, MA: National Bureau of Economic Research.

Bernstein, Marvin (1964). *The Mexican Mining Industry, 1890–1950: A Study of the Interaction of Politics, Economics, and Technology*. Albany: State University of New York Press.

Bizberg, Ilán (2003). "Transition or Restructuring of Society?" In Joseph S. Tulchin and Andrew D. Selee, eds., *Mexico's Politics and Society in Transition*. Boulder, CO: Lynn Rienner Publishers.

Blum, Roberto E. (1997). "Mexico's New Politics: The Weight of the Past," *Journal of Democracy* 4 (8): 28–42.

Bibliography

Boltvinik, Julio (2003). "Welfare, Inequality, and Poverty in Mexico, 1970–2000." In Kevin J. Middlebrook and Eduardo Zepeda, eds., *Confronting Development: Assessing Mexico's Economic and Social Policy Challenges*. Stanford, CA: Stanford University Press/Center for U.S.-Mexican Studies, University of California, San Diego.

Boltvinik, Julio, and Enrique Hernández Laos (2000). *Pobreza y distribución del ingreso en México*. Mexico City: Siglo Veintiuno Editores.

Bortz, Jeffrey L. (1988). *Los salarios industriales en la Ciudad de México, 1939–1975*. Mexico City: Fondo de Cultura Económica.

Boyer, Christopher R. (2003). *Becoming Campesinos: Politics, Identity, and Agrarian Struggle in Postrevolutionary Michoacán, 1920–1935*. Stanford, CA: Stanford University Press.

Bruhn, Kathleen (1997). "The Seven-Month Itch? Neoliberal Politics, Popular Movements, and the Left in Mexico." In Douglas A. Chalmers, Carlos M. Vilas, Katherine Hite, Scott B. Martin, Kerianne Piester, and Monique Segarra, eds., *The New Politics of Inequality in Latin America: Rethinking Participation and Representation*. New York: Oxford University Press.

Bruhn, Kathleen (2004). *Taking on Goliath: The Emergence of a New Left Party and the Struggle for Democracy in Mexico*. University Park: Pennsylvania State University Press.

Bruhn, Kathleen, and Kenneth F. Greene (2007). "Elite Polarization Meets Mass Moderation in Mexico's 2006 Elections," *PS: Political Science and Politics* 40 (1): 33–8.

Buendía, Jorge (2004). "The Changing Mexican Voter, 1991–2000." In Kevin J. Middlebrook, ed., *Dilemmas of Political Change in Mexico*. London: Institute of Latin American Studies, University of London/Center for U.S.-Mexican Studies, University of California, San Diego.

Bulmer-Thomas, Victor (1994). *The Economic History of Latin America Since Independence*. New York: Cambridge University Press.

Caloca González, Manuel (n.d.). "Mortgage-Backed Securitization: New Legal Development in Mexico." Mimeo.

Camacho Solís, Manuel (2006). *El desacuerdo nacional: orígenes, consecuencias y propuestas de solución*. Mexico City: Aguilar.

Camp, Roderic A. (1980). *Mexico's Leaders: Their Education and Recruitment*. Tucson: University of Arizona Press.

Camp, Roderic A. (1989). *Entrepreneurs and Politics in Twentieth-Century Mexico*. New York: Oxford University Press.

Camp, Roderic A. (1997). *Crossing Swords: Religion and Politics in Mexico*. New York: Oxford University Press.

Cárdenas, Enrique (1996). *La política económica en México, 1950–1994*. Mexico City: El Colegio de México.

Cárdenas, Enrique (2000). "The Process of Accelerated Industrialization in Mexico, 1929–1982." In Enrique Cárdenas, José Antonio Ocampo, and Rosemary Thorp, eds., *Industrialization and the State in Latin America: The Postwar Years*, vol. 3 of *An Economic History of Twentieth-Century Latin America*. London: Palgrave.

Castañeda, Jorge (1999). *La herencia: arquelogía de la sucesión presidencial*. Mexico City: Alfaguara.

Centro de Derechos Humanos Miguel Agustín Pro Juárez, A.C. (2006). "The Sinking of FEMOSPP . . . and the Opportunities to Achieve Justice Before the End of the Fox Administration," *Boletín* 26 (August): 10–12.

Centro de Estudios de las Finanzas Públicas (2005). *Participación del gasto programable del sector público presupuestario en clasificación funcional en el PIB, 1990–2003*. Mimeo.

Centro de Estudios de las Finanzas Públicas (2006). *Evolución del gasto público en educación, 2000–2006*. Mimeo.

Centro de Investigación y Documentación de la Casa and Sociedad Hipotecaria Federal (2005). "Current Housing Situation in Mexico." Mimeo.

Centro Latinoamericano y Caribeño de Demografía (2001). *Boletín Demográfico, edición especial: urbanización y evolución de la población urbana de América Latina, 1950–1990*. Santiago, Chile: Celade.

Cervantes, Jesusa (2006). "El PAN compra el voto rural," *Proceso*, No. 1541 (14 May).

Chand, Vikram K. (2001). *Mexico's Political Awakening*. Notre Dame, IN: University of Notre Dame Press.

Clarkson, Stephen (2002). "NAFTA and the WTO in the Transformation of Mexico's Economic System." In Joseph S. Tulchin and Andrew D. Selee, eds., *Mexico's Politics and Society in Transition*. Boulder, CO: Lynne Rienner Publishers.

Cohen, Daniel, Rocco Macchiavelo, and Marcelo Soto (2001). "Growth and Human Capital in Latin America." Organisation for Economic Co-operation and Development working paper. Paris: OECD.

Comisión Nacional Bancaria y de Valores. *Boletín estadístico de banca múltiple, 1997–2005*.

Condon, Bradly, and Tapen Sinha (2003). *Drawing Lines in Sand and Snow: Border Security and North American Economic Integration*. Armonk, NY: M.E. Sharpe.

Consejo Nacional dePoblación (CONAPO) (2001a). *La población de México en el nuevo siglo*. Mexico City: CONAPO.

CONAPO (2001b) *La situación demográfica de México, 2000*. Mexico City: CONAPO.

CONAPO (2002a). "Sostienen las mujeres 5.6 millones de hogares." Available at www.conapo.gob.mx.

CONAPO (2002b). "Información con motivo del Día de las Madres." Available at www.conapo.gob.mx/prensa/2002/2002may02.htm.

CONAPO (2003a). *La situación demográfica de México, 2002*. Mexico City: CONAPO.

CONAPO (2003b). *Familias y hogares en transición, 2002*. Mexico City: CONAPO.

Cook, Maria Lorena, Kevin J. Middlebrook, and Juan Molinar Horcasitas (1994). "The Politics of Economic Restructuring in Mexico: Actors, Sequencing, and Coalition Change." In Maria Lorena Cook, Kevin J. Middlebrook, and Juan Molinar Horcasitas, eds., *The Politics of Economic Restructuring: State-Society Relations and Regime Change in Mexico*. La Jolla, CA: Center for U.S.-Mexican Studies, University of California, San Diego.

Cortés, Fernando (2000). *La distribución del ingreso en México en épocas de estabilización y reforma económica*. Mexico City: Centro de Investigaciones y Estudios Superiores en Antropología Social.

Craig, Ann L., and Wayne A. Cornelius (1995). "Houses Divided: Parties and Political Reform in Mexico." In Scott Mainwaring and Timothy R. Scully, eds., *Building Democratic Institutions: Party Systems in Latin America*. Stanford, CA: Stanford University Press.

Crespo, José Antonio (2004). "Party Competition in Mexico: Evolution and Prospects." In Kevin J. Middlebrook, ed., *Dilemmas of Political Change in Mexico*. London: Institute of Latin American Studies, University of London/Center for U.S.-Mexican Studies, University of California, San Diego.

Deardorff, Kevin, and Lisa Blumerman (2001). "Evaluating Components of International Migration: Estimates of the Foreign-Born Population by Migrant Status in 2000." Population Division Working Paper Series no. 58. Washington, DC: U.S. Bureau of the Census.

De Grammont, Hubert C. (2003). "The Agricultural Sector and Rural Development in Mexico: Consequences of Economic Globalization." In Kevin J. Middlebrook and Eduardo Zepeda, eds., *Confronting Development: Assessing Mexico's Economic and Social Policy Challenges*. Stanford, CA: Stanford University Press/Center for U.S.-Mexican Studies, University of California, San Diego.

De la Madrid Hurtado, Miguel (2004). *Cambio de rumbo: testimonio de una presidencia, 1982–1988*. Mexico City: Fondo de Cultura Económica.

Del Ángel-Mobarak, Gustavo (2002). "Paradoxes of Financial Development: The Construction of the Mexican Banking System, 1941–1982." Ph.D. diss., Stanford University.

Del Ángel-Mobarak, Gustavo (2005). "La banca mexicana antes de 1982." In Gustavo del Ángel-Mobarak, Carlos Bazdresch, and Francisco Suárez Dávila, eds., *Cuando el estado se hizo banquero: consecuencias de la nacionalización bancaria en México*. Mexico City: Fondo de Cultura Económica.

Del Ángel-Mobarak, Gustavo, Carlos Bazdresch, and Francisco Suárez Dávila, eds. (2005). *Cuando el estado se hizo banquero: consecuencias de la nacionalización bancaria en México*. Mexico City: Fondo de Cultura Económica.

De la Riva Rodríguez, Xavier (1963). "Salubridad y asistencia médico-social." In *México: cincuenta años de revolución*. Mexico City: Fondo de Cultura Económica.

De Remes, Alain (2006). "Democratization and Dispersion of Power: New Scenarios in Mexican Federalism," *Mexican Studies/Estudios Mexicanos* 22 (1): 175–204.

Díaz-Cayeros, Alberto (2004). "Decentralization, Democratization, and Federalism in Mexico." In Kevin J. Middlebrook, ed., *Dilemmas of Political Change in Mexico*. London: Institute of Latin American Studies, University of London/Center for U.S.-Mexican Studies, University of California, San Diego.

Díaz-Cayeros, Alberto (2005). "Endogenous Institutional Change in the Mexican Senate," *Comparative Political Studies* 38 (10): 1196–218.

Díaz-Cayeros, Alberto, and Beatriz Magaloni (2001). "Party Dominance and the Logic of Electoral Design in Mexico's Transition to Democracy," *Journal of Theoretical Politics* 13 (3): 271–93.

Dirección General de Estadística (1962). *VIII Censo General de Población, 1960*. Mexico City: Dirección General de Estadística.

Domingo, Pilar (2000). "Judicial Independence: The Politics of the Supreme Court in Mexico," *Journal of Latin American Studies* 32 (3): 705–35.

Domínguez, Jorge I., and Rafael Fernández de Castro (2001). *The United States and Mexico: Between Partnership and Conflict*. New York: Routledge.

Domínguez, Jorge I., and Chappell Lawson, eds. (2003). *Mexico's Pivotal Democratic Election: Campaigns, Votes, and the 2000 Presidential Race*. Stanford, CA: Stanford

University Press/Center for U.S.–Mexican Studies, University of California, San Diego.

Eckstein, Susan (1982). "Revolution and Redistribution in Latin America." In Cynthia McClintock and Abraham F. Lowenthal, eds., *The Peruvian Experiment Reconsidered*. Princeton, NJ: Princeton University Press.

Economic Commission for Latin America and the Caribbean (2004). *Statistical Yearbook for Latin America and the Caribbean*. Santiago, Chile: Economic Commission for Latin America and the Caribbean.

Eisenstadt, Todd A. (2003). "Thinking Outside the (Ballot) Box: Informal Electoral Institutions and Mexico's Political Opening," *Latin American Politics and Society* 45 (1): 25–54.

Eisenstadt, Todd A. (2004). *Courting Democracy in Mexico: Party Strategies and Electoral Institutions*. Cambridge: Cambridge University Press.

"Ejemplo a seguir, la reactivación del crédito bancario a la vivienda" (2006). *El Economista* 20 (February).

Elizondo Mayer-Serra, Carlos (2001). *La importancia de las reglas: gobierno y empresario después de la nacionalización bancaria*. Mexico City: Fondo de Cultura Económica.

Espinosa-Vega, Marco A., and Tapen Sinha (2000). "A Primer and Assessment of Social Security Reform in Mexico," *Federal Reserve Bank of Atlanta Economic Review* 85 (1): 1–23.

Estrada, Luis, and Alejandro Poiré (2007). "The Mexican Standoff: Taught to Protest, Learning to Lose," *Journal of Democracy* 18 (1): 73–87.

Evans, Peter, and Gary Gereffi (1982). "Foreign Investment and Dependent Development: Comparing Brazil and Mexico." In Sylvia Ann Hewlett and Richard S. Weinert, eds., *Brazil and Mexico: Patterns in Late Development*. Philadelphia: Institute for the Study of Human Issues.

Frenk, J., J. Sepúlveda, O. Gómez-Dantés, and F. Knaul (2003). "Evidence-based Health Policy: Three Generations of Reform in Mexico," *The Lancet* 362 (15 November): 1667–71.

Gilly, Adolfo (1994). *La revolución interrumpida*. Mexico City: Ediciones Era.

Giugale, Marcelo, Olivier Lafourcade, and Vinh Nguyen (2001). *Mexico: A Comprehensive Development Agenda for the New Era*. Washington, DC: World Bank.

Goldsmith, Arthur (1995). "Democracy, Property Rights, and Economic Growth," *The Journal of Development Studies* 32 (2): 157–74.

Gómez Galvarriato, Aurora (1999). "The Impact of Revolution: Business and Labor in the Mexican Textile Industry, 1900–1930." Ph.D. diss., Harvard University.

Gómez Tagle, Silvia (1993). "Electoral Reform and the Party System, 1977–90." In Neil Harvey, ed., *Mexico: Dilemmas of Transition*. London: Institute of Latin American Studies.

Gómez Tagle, Silvia (1997). *La transición inconclusa: treinta años de elecciones en México*. Mexico City: El Colegio de México.

Gómez Tagle, Silvia (2004). "Public Institutions and Electoral Transparency in Mexico." In Kevin J. Middlebrook, ed., *Dilemmas of Political Change in Mexico*. London: Institute of Latin American Studies, University of London/Center for U.S.-Mexican Studies, University of California, San Diego.

González Amador, Roberto (2007). "En 2 años, 10 de 21 Afore elevaron 200% comisiones por saldo de cuenta," *La Jornada Virtu@l*, 21 April.

González Casanova, Pablo (1965). *La democracia en México*. Mexico City: Ediciones Era.

González Casanova, Pablo (1994). "La democracia en México: actualidad y perspectives." In Pablo González Casanova and Marcos Roitman Rosenmann, eds., *La democracia en América Latina: actualidad y perspectives*. Mexico City: La Jornada Ediciones/Centro de Investigaciones Interdisciplinarias en Ciencias y Humanidades, Universidad Nacional Autónoma de México.

Graham, Douglas H. (1982). "Mexican and Brazilian Economic Development: Legacies, Patterns, and Performance." In Sylvia Ann Hewlett and Richard S. Weinert, eds., *Brazil and Mexico: Patterns in Late Development*. Philadelphia: Institute for the Study of Human Issues.

Grandolini, Gloria, and Luis Cerda (1998). "The 1997 Mexican Pension Reform: Genesis and Design Features." Mimeo. Washington, DC: World Bank.

Griffin, Keith, and Amy Ickowitz (2003). "Confronting Human Development in Mexico." In Kevin J. Middlebrook and Eduardo Zepeda, eds., *Confronting Development: Assessing Mexico's Economic and Social Policy Challenges*. Stanford, CA: Stanford University Press/Center for U.S.-Mexican Studies, University of California, San Diego.

Gruben, William C., and Robert McComb (1997). "Liberalization, Privatization, and Crash: Mexico's Banking System in the 1990s," *Federal Reserve Bank of Dallas Economic Review* (First Quarter): 21–30.

Gunther, Jeffrey W., Robert B. Moore, and Genie D. Short (1996). "Mexican Banks and the 1994 Peso Crisis: The Importance of Initial Conditions," *North American Journal of Economics and Finance* 7 (2): 125–33.

Haber, Stephen (1989). *Industry and Underdevelopment: The Industrialization of Mexico, 1890–1940*. Stanford, CA: Stanford University Press.

Haber, Stephen (2005). "Mexico's Experiments with Bank Privatization and Liberalization, 1991–2003," *Journal of Banking and Finance* 29 (August-September): 2325–53.

Haber, Stephen (2006). "Authoritarian Government." In Barry R. Weingast and Donald Wittman, eds., *The Oxford Handbook of Political Economy*. New York: Oxford University Press.

Haber, Stephen, and Aldo Musacchio (2006). "Foreign Entry and the Performance of the Mexican Banking Industry." Mimeo. Stanford University.

Haber, Stephen, Armando Razo, and Noel Maurer (2003). *The Politics of Property Rights: Political Instability, Credible Commitments, and Economic Growth in Mexico, 1876–1929*. Cambridge: Cambridge University Press.

Hagerstrom, Mark (2006). *Decentralized Service Delivery for the Poor*. Washington, DC: World Bank.

Handa, Sudhanshu, and Benjamin Davis (2006). "The Experience of Conditional Cash Transfers in Latin America and the Caribbean," *Development Policy Review* 24 (5): 513–36.

Handa, Sudhanshu, Mari-Carmen Huerta, Raúl Pérez, and Beatriz Straffon (2000). *Poverty, Inequality, and "Spillover" in Mexico's Education, Health, and Nutrition Program*. Washington, DC: International Food Policy Research Institute.

Hanson, Gordon (1996). "Localization Economies, Vertical Organization, and Trade," *American Economic Review* 86 (5): 1266–78.

Hanson, Gordon (2003). "What Has Happened to Wages in Mexico Since 1990? Implications for Hemispheric Free Trade." National Bureau of Economic Research Working Paper no. 9563. Cambridge, MA: National Bureau of Economic Research.

Hart, John Mason (1987). *Revolutionary Mexico: The Coming and Process of the Mexican Revolution*. Berkeley: University of California Press.

Harvey, Neil (1998). *The Chiapas Rebellion: The Struggle for Land and Democracy*. Durham, NC: Duke University Press.

Henisz, Witold (2000). "The Institutional Environment for Economic Growth," *Economics and Politics* 12 (1): 1–31.

Hernández Laos, Enrique (1985). *La productividad y el desarrollo industrial de México*. Mexico City: Fondo de Cultura Económica.

Hernández Laos, Enrique (2000). "Crecimiento económico, distribución del ingreso y pobreza en México," *Comercio Exterior* 50 (10): 863–73.

Hernández Laos, Enrique, and Jorge Velázquez Roa (2000). *Globalización, desigualdad y pobreza: lecciones de la experiencia mexicana*. Mexico City: Universidad Autónoma Metropolitana/Plaza y Valdés.

Hernández Rodríguez, Rogelio (1988). *Empresarios, banca y estado: el conflicto durante el gobierno de José López Portillo, 1976–1982*. Mexico City: Facultad Latinoamericana de Ciencias Sociales/Grupo Editorial Miguel Ángel Porrúa.

Hernández Rodríguez, Rogelio (2003). "Ernesto Zedillo: la presidencia contenida," *Foro Internacional* (January-March): 39–70.

Heston, Alan, Robert Summers, and Bettina Aten (2002). *Penn World Table Version 6.1*. Center for International Comparisons at the University of Pennsylvania.

Hirales, Gustavo (2004). "Los avatares de una justicia pospuesta," *Nexos* 319 (July): 22–8.

Hoddinott, John, and Emmanuel Skofias (2004). "The Impact of PROGRESA on Food Consumption," *Economic Development and Cultural Change* 53: 37–61.

Hughes, Sallie (2003). "From the Inside Out: How 'Institutional Entrepreneurs' Transformed the Mexican Press." Paper presented at the International Congress of the Latin American Studies Association, Dallas, Texas.

Instituto Federal Electoral (IFE) (2006). *Elecciones federales 2006: encuestas y resultados electorales*. Mexico City: IFE.

Instituto Nacional de Estadística, Geográfia e Informática (INEGI) (1994). *Estadísticas históricas de México*. 2nd ed. Aguascalientes, Mexico: INEGI.

INEGI (1999). *La familia mexicana*. 2nd ed. Aguascalientes, Mexico: INEGI.

INEGI (2000). *Estadísticas históricas de México*. 3rd ed. Aguascalientes, Mexico: INEGI.

INEGI (2001a). *Indicadores sociodemográficos de México, 1930–2000*. Aguascalientes, Mexico: INEGI.

INEGI (2001b). *XII Censo General de Población y Vivienda, 2000*. Aguascalientes, Mexico: INEGI.

INEGI (2002a). *Sistema de Cuentas Nacionales*. Mexico City: INEGI.

INEGI (2002b). *México en el mundo: edición 2002*. Aguascalientes, Mexico: INEGI.

INEGI (2005). *La producción, salarios, empleo y productividad de la industria maquiladora de exportación: total nacional, 1999–2004*. Mexico City: INEGI.

International Labour Office (ILO) Bureau of Statistics (1995). *Yearbook of Labor Statistics*. Geneva: ILO.

ILO Bureau of Statistics (1997). *Yearbook of Labor Statistics*. Geneva: ILO.

ILO Bureau of Statistics (2002). *Yearbook of Labor Statistics*. Geneva: ILO.

ILO Bureau of Statistics (2005). *Yearbook of Labor Statistics*. Geneva: ILO.

International Monetary Fund (IMF). *International Financial Statistics, 1950–2006*. Washington, DC: IMF.

IMF (2006). *International Financial Statistics Database*. Washington, DC: IMF.

Izquierdo, Rafael (1995). *La política hacendaría del desarrollo estabilizador, 1958–1970*. Mexico City: Fondo de Cultura Económica.

Jackson, Richard (2005). *Building Human Capital in an Aging Mexico: A Report of the U.S.-Mexico Binational Council*. Washington, DC: Center for Strategic and International Studies.

Joint Center for Housing Studies of Harvard University (2004). "The State of Mexico's Housing, 2004." Joint Center for Housing Studies, Harvard University.

Katz, Friedrich (1981). *The Secret War in Mexico: Europe, the United States, and the Mexican Revolution*. Chicago: University of Chicago Press.

Katz, Friedrich (1998). *The Life and Times of Pancho Villa*. Stanford, CA: Stanford University Press.

Keefer, Philip (2003). "All Democracies Are Not the Same: Identifying the Institutions that Matter for Growth and Convergence." Paper presented at conference on "Successes and Failures in Real Convergence," October. Bank of Poland.

Keefer, Philip, and Stephen Knack (2002). "Social Polarization, Political Institutions, and Country Creditworthiness." In Jac C. Heckelman and Dennis Coates, eds., *Collective Choice: Essays in Honor of Mancur Olson*. New York: Springer-Verlag.

Kent, Rollin (2004). "Private Sector Expansion and Emerging Policy Responses in Mexican Higher Education." Working paper. Alliance for International Higher Education Policy Studies and the Universidad Autónoma de Puebla.

Klesner, Joseph L. (1993). "Modernization, Economic Crisis, and Electoral Alignment in Mexico," *Mexican Studies/Estudios Mexicanos* 9 (2): 187–223.

Klesner, Joseph L. (1997). "Democratic Transition? The 1997 Mexican Elections," *PS: Political Science and Politics* 30 (4): 703–11.

Klesner, Joseph L. (2001). "Divided Government in Mexico's Presidentialist Regime: The 1997–2000 Experience." In Robert Elgie, ed., *Divided Government in Comparative Perspective*. Oxford: Oxford University Press.

Klesner, Joseph L. (2003). "The Structure of the Mexican Electorate: Social, Attitudinal, and Partisan Bases of Vicente Fox's Victory." In Jorge I. Domínguez and Chappell Lawson, eds., *Mexico's Pivotal Democratic Election: Campaigns, Votes, and the 2000 Presidential Race*. Stanford, CA: Stanford University Press.

Klesner, Joseph L. (2007). "The 2006 Mexican Elections: Manifestation of a Divided Society?" *PS: Political Science and Politics* 50 (1): 27–32.

Knight, Alan (1986). *The Mexican Revolution*. 2 vols. Cambridge: Cambridge University Press.

Knight, Alan (1991). "The Rise and Fall of Cardenismo." In Leslie Bethell, ed., *Mexico Since Independence*. Cambridge: Cambridge University Press.

Krueger, Anne O., and Aaron Tornell (1999). "The Role of Bank Restructuring in Recovering from Crises: Mexico, 1995–1998." National Bureau of Economic

Research Working Paper no. 7042. Cambridge, MA: National Bureau of Economic Research.

Lake, David A., and Matthew A. Baum (2001). "The Invisible Hand of Democracy: Political Control and the Provision of Public Services," *Comparative Political Studies* 34 (6): 587–621.

Lamas, Marta (2003). "The Role of Women in the New Mexico." In Joseph S. Tulchin and Andrew D. Selee, eds., *Mexico's Politics and Society in Transition*. Boulder, CO: Lynne Rienner Publishers.

Langston, Joy (2007). "The PRI's 2006 Electoral Debacle," *PS: Political Science and Politics* 50 (1): 21–5.

La Porta, Rafael, Florencio López-de-Silanes, and Guillermo Zamarripa (2003). "Related Lending," *Quarterly Journal of Economics* 118 (1): 231–68.

Laurell, Asa Cristina (2003). "The Transformation of Social Policy in Mexico." In Kevin J. Middlebrook and Eduardo Zepeda, eds., *Confronting Development: Assessing Mexico's Economic and Social Policy Challenges*. Stanford, CA: Stanford University Press/Center for U.S.-Mexican Studies, University of California, San Diego.

Lawson, Chappell H. (2000). "Memorandum on Mexican Voting Behavior, 1988–2000." Mimeo. Department of Political Science, Massachusetts Institute of Technology.

Lawson, Chappell H. (2002). *Building the Fourth Estate: Democratization and the Rise of a Free Press in Mexico*. Berkeley: University of California Press.

Lawson, Chappell H. (2007). "How Did We Get Here? Mexican Democracy after the 2006 Elections," *PS: Political Science and Politics* 50 (1): 45–8.

Leblang, David A. (1996). "Property Rights, Democracy, and Economic Growth," *Political Research Quarterly* 49 (3): 5–26.

Levy, Santiago (2006). "Notes on Mexico's Oportunidades (Progresa) Program," found at www.gov.mu/portal/goc/mof/files/speechlevy.pdf.

Lieuwin, Edwin (1968). *Mexican Militarism: The Political Rise and Fall of the Revolutionary Army*. Albuquerque: University of New Mexico Press.

Lindemann, David, David Robalina, and Michal Rutkowski (2006). "NDC Pension Schemes in Middle- and Low-Income Countries." In Robert Holzmann and Edward Palmer, eds., *Pension Reform: Issues and Prospects for Non-Financial Defined Contribution (NDC) Schemes*. Washington, DC: World Bank.

Lindert, Peter (2004). *Growing Public: Social Spending and Economic Growth Since the Eighteenth Century*. Cambridge: Cambridge University Press.

Loaeza, Soledad (1999). *El Partido Acción Nacional: la larga marcha, 1939–1984; oposición leal y partido de protesta*. Mexico City: Fondo de Cultura Económica.

Loaeza, Soledad (2006). "Vicente Fox's Presidential Style and the New Mexican Presidency," *Mexican Studies/Estudios Mexicanos* 22 (1): 3–32.

López-Acevedo, Gladys (2000). "Earnings Inequality after Mexico's Economic and Education Reforms." Latin American and Caribbean Economic Association. Mimeo.

López-Acevedo, Gladys (2006). "Mexico: Two Decades of the Evolution of Education and Income Inequality." World Bank Working Paper no. 3919. Washington, DC: World Bank.

Lujambio, Alonso (2001). "Democratization through Federalism? The National Action Party Strategy, 1939–2000." In Kevin J. Middlebrook, ed., *Party Politics and the Struggle for Democracy in Mexico: National and State-Level Analyses of the Partido Acción Nacional.* La Jolla, CA: Center for U.S.-Mexican Studies, University of California, San Diego.

Luna, Matilde (2004). "Business and Politics in Mexico." In Kevin J. Middlebrook, ed., *Dilemmas of Political Change in Mexico.* London: Institute of Latin American Studies, University of London/Center for U.S.-Mexican Studies, University of California, San Diego.

Mackey, Michael W. (1999). "Report of Michael W. Mackey on the Comprehensive Evaluation of the Operations and Function of the Fund for the Protection of Bank Savings (FOBAPROA) and the Quality of Supervision of the FOBAPROA Program, 1995–1998."

Mackinlay, Horacio (1991). "La política de reparto agrario en México (1917–1990) y las reformas al artículo 27 constitucional." In Alejandra Massolo et al., eds., *Procesos rurales y urbanos en el México actual.* Mexico City: Universidad Autónoma Metropolitana-Iztapalapa.

Mackinlay, Horacio (2004). "Rural Producers' Organizations and the State in Mexico: The Political Consequences of Economic Restructuring." In Kevin J. Middlebrook, ed., *Dilemmas of Political Change in Mexico.* London: Institute of Latin American Studies, University of London/Center for U.S.-Mexican Studies, University of California, San Diego.

Mackinlay, Horacio, and Juan de la Fuente (1996). "Las reformas a la legislación y a la política crediticia relativas al medio rural." In vol. 3 of Hubert C. de Grammont and Héctor Tejera Gaona, eds., *La sociedad rural mexicana frente al nuevo milenio.* Mexico City: Plaza y Valdés.

Magaloni, Beatriz (2003). "Authoritarianism, Democracy, and the Supreme Court: Horizontal Exchange and the Rule of Law in Mexico." In Scott Mainwaring and Christopher Welna, eds., *Democratic Accountability in Latin America.* New York: Oxford University Press.

Magaloni, Beatriz (2006). *Voting for Autocracy: The Politics of Party Hegemony and Its Demise in Mexico.* New York: Cambridge University Press.

Magaloni, Beatriz, Alberto Díaz-Cayeros, and Federico Estévez (2006). "Clientelism and Portfolio Diversification: A Model of Electoral Investment with Applications to Mexico." In Herbert Kitschelt and Steven I. Wilkinson, eds., *Patrons, Clients, and Policies: Patterns of Democratic Accountability and Political Competition.* Durham, NC: Duke University Press.

Magaloni, Beatriz, and Guillermo Zepeda (2004). "Democratization, Crime, and Judicial Reform in Mexico." In Kevin J. Middlebrook ed., *Dilemmas of Political Change in Mexico.* London: Institute of Latin American Studies, University of London/Center for U.S.-Mexican Studies, University of California, San Diego.

Magar, Eric, and Vidal Romero (2007). "El *impasse* mexicano en perspectiva," *Foreign Affairs en Español* 7 (1): 117–31.

Mainwaring, Scott (1993). "Presidentialism, Multipartism, Democracy: The Difficult Combination," *Comparative Political Studies* 26 (2): 198–228.

Malkin, Elisabeth (2004). "Unmuzzling Mexico's Watchdog," *International Herald Tribune,* 12 November.

Malkin, Elisabeth (2005). "In Oil Boom, Mexico's Pemex Struggles," *International Herald Tribune,* 21 September.

Malkin, Elisabeth (2007). "Mexico's Oil Monopoly in Trouble," *International Herald Tribune*, 10–11 March.

Manne, Alan (1966). "Key Sectors of the Mexican Economy, 1962–72." In Irma Adelman and Erik Thorbecke, eds., *The Theory and Design of Economic Development.* Baltimore, MD: Johns Hopkins University Press.

Markiewicz, Dana (1993). *The Mexican Revolution and the Limits of Agrarian Reform, 1915–1946.* Boulder, CO: Lynne Rienner Publishers.

Márquez Colin, Graciela (2002). "The Political Economy of Mexican Protectionism, 1868–1911." Ph.D. diss., Harvard University.

Martínez Peria, María Soledad, and Sergio L. Schmukler (2001). "Do Depositors Punish Banks for Bad Behavior? Market Discipline, Deposit Insurance, and Banking Crisis," *Journal of Finance* 56 (June): 1029–51.

Massad, Carlos (1986). "External Financing in Latin America: Developments, Problems, and Options." In Kevin J. Middlebrook and Carlos Rico, eds., *The United States and Latin America in the 1980s: Contending Perspectives on a Decade of Crisis.* Pittsburgh, PA: University of Pittsburgh Press.

Mattli, Walter (1999). *The Logic of Regional Integration: Europe and Beyond.* Cambridge: Cambridge University Press.

Maurer, Noel (2002). *The Power and the Money: The Mexican Financial System, 1876–1932.* Stanford, CA: Stanford University Press.

Maurer, Noel, and Stephen Haber (2007). "Related Lending and Economic Performance: Evidence from Mexico," *The Journal of Economic History* 67 (3).

Maxfield, Sylvia (1989). "International Economic Opening and Government-Business Relations." In Wayne A. Cornelius, Judith Gentleman, and Peter H. Smith, eds., *Mexico's Alternative Political Futures.* La Jolla, CA: Center for U.S. Mexican Studies.

McKinley, James C., Jr. (2007). "Federal Judge Overturns Ruling Against Mexico's Former President in 1968 Student Killings," *New York Times* (on-line edition), 13 July.

McQuerry, Elizabeth (1999). "The Banking Sector Rescue in Mexico," *Federal Reserve Bank of Atlanta Economic Review* 84 (3): 14–29.

Meyer, Lorenzo, and Isidro Morales (1990). *Petróleo y nación, 1900–1987: la política petrolera en México.* Mexico City: Fondo de Cultura Económica.

Middlebrook, Kevin J. (1986). "Political Liberalization in an Authoritarian Regime: The Case of Mexico." In Guillermo O'Donnell, Philippe C. Schmitter, and Laurence Whitehead, eds., *Latin America.* Pt. 2, *Transitions from Authoritarian Rule: Prospects for Democracy.* Baltimore, MD: Johns Hopkins University Press.

Middlebrook, Kevin J. (1995). *The Paradox of Revolution: Labor, the State, and Authoritarianism in Mexico.* Baltimore, MD: Johns Hopkins University Press.

Middlebrook, Kevin J. (1997). "Movimiento obrero y democratización en regímenes posrevolucionarios: las políticas de transición en Nicaragua, Rusia y México," *Foro Internacional* 149 (July-September): 365–407.

Middlebrook, Kevin J. (2001). "Party Politics and Democratization in Mexico: The Partido Acción Nacional in Comparative Perspective." In Kevin J. Middlebrook, ed., *Party Politics and the Struggle for Democracy in Mexico: National and State-Level Analyses of the Partido Acción Nacional.* La Jolla, CA: Center for U.S. Mexican Studies, University of California, San Diego.

Middlebrook, Kevin J. (2004). "Mexico's Democratic Transitions: Dynamics and Prospects." In Kevin J. Middlebrook, ed., *Dilemmas of Political Change in Mexico*. London: Institute of Latin American Studies, University of London/Center for U.S.-Mexican Studies, University of California, San Diego.

Middlebrook, Kevin J. (2007). "World Affairs: Mexico." In *2007 Britannica Book of the Year*. Chicago: Encyclopaedia Britannica.

Middlebrook, Kevin J., and Eduardo Zepeda (2003). "On the Political Economy of Mexican Development Policy." In Kevin J. Middlebrook and Eduardo Zepeda, eds., *Confronting Development: Assessing Mexico's Economic and Social Policy Challenges*. Stanford, CA: Stanford University Press/Center for U.S.-Mexican Studies, University of California, San Diego.

Mishkin, Frederic (1996). "Understanding Financial Crises: A Developing Country Perspective." National Bureau of Economic Research Working Paper no. 5600. Cambridge, MA: National Bureau of Economic Research.

Mitchell, Olivia (1999). "Evaluating Administrative Costs in Mexico's Afores Pension System." Pension Research Council Working Paper no. 99–1. Philadelphia: The Wharton School of the University of Pennsylvania.

Mizrahi, Yemile (1995). "Entrepreneurs in the Opposition: Modes of Political Participation in Chihuahua." In Victoria E. Rodríguez and Peter M. Ward, eds., *Opposition Government in Mexico*. Albuquerque: University of New Mexico Press.

Molinar Horcasitas, Juan, and Jeffrey A. Weldon (1994). "Electoral Determinants and Consequences of National Solidarity." In Wayne A. Cornelius, Ann L. Craig, and Jonathan Fox, eds., *Transforming State-Society Relations in Mexico: The National Solidarity Strategy*. La Jolla, CA: Center for U.S.-Mexican Studies, University of California, San Diego.

Molinar Horcasitas, Juan, and Jeffrey A. Weldon (2001). "Reforming Electoral Systems in Mexico." In Matthew Soberg Shugart and Martin P. Wattenberg, eds., *Mixed-Member Electoral Systems: The Best of Both Worlds?* New York: Oxford University Press.

Molyneux, Maxine (2006). "Poverty Relief and the New Social Policy in Latin America: Mothers at the Service of the State?" Mimeo. Institute for the Study of the Americas, University of London.

Moreno, Alejandro (2003). *El votante mexicano: democracia, actitudes políticas y conducta electoral*. Mexico City: Fondo de Cultura Económica.

Moreno, Alejandro (2007). "The 2006 Mexican Presidential Election: The Economy, Oil Revenues, and Ideology," *PS: Political Science and Politics* 50 (1): 15–19.

Moreno-Jaimes, Carlos (2007). "Do Competitive Elections Produce Better-quality Governments? Evidence from Mexican Municipalities, 1990–2000," *Latin American Research Review* 42 (2): 136–53.

Morgan Guaranty Trust Company, *World Financial Markets*, various years.

Morris, Stephen D. (1999). "Corruption and the Mexican Political System: Continuity and Change," *Third World Quarterly* 20 (3): 623–43.

Moss, David, Anna Dias, and Bertrand Stephann (1999). "The French Pension System: On the Verge of Retirement?" Harvard Business School Case no. 9–799–143. Cambridge, MA: Harvard Business School.

Muñoz, Alma E. (2007). "En vigor, la Ley del ISSSTE," *La Jornada Virtu@l*, 3 April.

Murillo, José Antonio (2005). "La banca después de la privatización: auge, crisis y reordenamiento." In Gustavo del Ángel-Mobarak, Carlos Bazdresch, and Francisco Suárez Dávila, eds., *Cuando el estado se hizo banquero: consecuencias de la nacionalización bancaria en México*. Mexico City: Fondo de Cultura Económica.

Musacchio, Humberto (2003). "Entre gitanos," *El Norte*, 24 December.

Navarro, Juan Carlos (2005). "The Education Policymaking Process in Latin America." Mimeo. Inter-American Development Bank.

Negrin, José Luis (2000). "Mecanismos para compartir información crediticia: evidencia internacional y la experiencia mexicana." Dirección General de Investigación Económica, Banco de México, Working Paper no. 2000–05. Mexico City: Banco de México.

North, Douglass C. (1981). *Structure and Change in Economic History*. New York: W.W. Norton and Company.

North, Douglass C. (1990). *Institutions, Institutional Change, and Economic Performance*. Cambridge: Cambridge University Press.

North, Douglass C., William R. Summerhill, and Barry R. Weingast (2000). "Order, Disorder, and Economic Change: Latin America vs. North America." In Bruce Bueno de Mesquita and Hilton L. Root, eds., *Governing for Prosperity*. New Haven, CT: Yale University Press.

North, Douglass C., and Barry R. Weingast (1989). "Constitutions and Commitment: The Evolution of Institutions Governing Public Choice in Seventeenth-Century England," *The Journal of Economic History* 49 (December): 803–32.

Notimex (2007). "Se compromete Sedesol a no desviar programas con fines partidistas," *La Jornada Virtu@l*, 17 April.

Olvera, Alberto J. (2004). "Civil Society in Mexico at Century's End." In Kevin J. Middlebrook, ed., *Dilemmas of Political Change in Mexico*. London: Institute of Latin American Studies, University of London/Center for U.S.-Mexican Studies, University of California, San Diego.

Organisation for Economic Co-operation and Development (OECD) (2002). *Economic Survey of Mexico*. Paris: OECD.

OECD (2003). "Health at a Glance – Country Notes (Mexico)." Paris: OECD.

OECD (2004a). *Direct Investment Statistics Yearbook, 1992–2003*. Paris: OECD.

OECD (2004b). *Education at a Glance, 2003*. Paris: OECD.

OECD (2005). *OECD Review of Health Care Systems, 2005*. Paris: OECD.

OECD (2006). *Education at a Glance, 2005*. Paris: OECD.

Orme, William A., Jr. (1996). *Understanding NAFTA: Mexico, Free Trade, and the New North America*. Austin: University of Texas Press.

Oxford Latin American Economic History Database. Available at http://oxlad.qeh.ox.ac.uk/.

Parker, Susan W., and Carla Pederzini (2001). "Gender Differences in Education in Mexico." In Elizabeth G. Katz and Maria C. Correia, eds., *The Economics of Gender in Mexico*. Washington, DC: World Bank.

Partida Bush, Virgilio (1999). "Situación actual y perspectivas demográficas." In Rodolfo Tuirán, ed., *La población de México: situación actual y desafíos futuros*. Mexico City: Consejo Nacional de Población.

Passel, Jeffrey (2005). *Unauthorized Migrants: Numbers and Characteristics*. Pew Hispanic Center Background Briefing. Washington, DC: Pew Hispanic Center.

Pastor, Manuel, Jr., and Carol Wise (1998). "Mexican-Style Neoliberalism: State Policy and Distributional Stress." In Carol Wise, ed., *The Post-NAFTA Political Economy: Mexico and the Western Hemisphere.* University Park: Pennsylvania State University Press.

Pastor, Manuel, Jr., and Carol Wise (2002). "A Long View of Mexico's Political Economy: What's Changed? What Are the Challenges?" In Joseph S. Tulchin and Andrew D. Selee, eds., *Mexico's Politics and Society in Transition.* Boulder, CO: Lynne Rienner Publishers.

Pension Research Council (2006). "Lessons from Pension Reform in the Americas." Pension Research Council Working Paper no. 2006–8. Philadelphia: The Wharton School of the University of Pennsylvania.

Pérez Astorga, Javier (1988). "Mortalidad por causas en México, 1950–1980." In Mario Bronfman and José Gómez de León, eds., *La mortalidad en México: niveles, tendencias y determinantes.* Mexico City: El Colegio de México.

Persson, Torsten, Gérard Roland, and Guido Tabellini (1997). "Separation of Powers and Political Accountability: Towards a Formal Approach to Comparative Politics," *Quarterly Journal of Economics* 112 (4): 1163–202.

Pescador Osuna, José Ángel (1988). "El esfuerzo alfabetizador en México (1910–1985): un ensayo crítico." In Martha Curiel et. al., eds., *México: setenta y cinco años de revolución.* Mexico City: Fondo de Cultura Económica.

Petróleos Mexicanos (PEMEX) (1985). *Anuario estadístico 1985: exploración y producción.* Mexico City: PEMEX.

Pichardo Pagaza, Ignacio (2001). *Triunfos y traiciones: crónica personal, 1994.* Mexico City: Editorial Oceano.

Pill, Huw (2002). "Mexico: Reform and Crisis, 1987–95." Harvard Business School Case no. 9–797–050. Cambridge, MA: Harvard Business School.

Prawda, Juan (1988). "Desarrollo del sistema educativo mexicano, pasado, presente y futuro." In Martha Curiel et al., eds., *México: setenta y cinco años de revolución.* Mexico City: Fondo de Cultura Económica.

Preston, Julia, and Samuel Dillon (2004). *Opening Mexico: The Making of a Democracy.* New York: Farrar, Straus and Giroux.

Purnell, Jennie (1999). *Popular Movements and State Formation in Revolutionary Mexico: The Agraristas and Cristeros of Michoacán.* Durham, NC: Duke University Press.

Qian, Yingyi, and Barry R. Weingast (1997). "Federalism as a Commitment to Preserving Market Incentives," *Journal of Economic Perspectives* 11 (4): 83–92.

Rachide, Mary, Isabelle Niño, Luis Calzada, Alberto Gómez, and Stephen Smith (2003). "Mexican Road Re-privatization: A New Attempt to Attract Private Investment to the Road Network." Mimeo. Durham, NC: Fuqua School of Business.

Ragir, Alexander, and James Attwood (2007). "Around the Markets: Stability in Latin America," *International Herald Tribune,* 22 August.

Rajoy, Enrique (n.d). "El registro de la propiedad en México: principios y reformas." Mimeo.

Randall, Laura (1996). *Reforming Mexico's Agrarian Reform.* Armonk, NY: M.E. Sharpe.

Ravelo, Ricardo (2004). "Ahora falta la verdad . . . ," *Proceso* 1447 (25 July): 32–4.

236   **Bibliography**

Razo, Armando (2003). "Social Networks and Credible Commitments in Dictatorships: Political Organization and Economic Growth in Porfirian Mexico, 1876–1991." Ph.D. diss., Stanford University.

Reiter, Daniel, and Allan C. Stam (2002). *Democracies at War*. Princeton, NJ: Princeton University Press.

Reuters (2004). "Diabetes Now Mexico's Leading Cause of Death," 2 November.

Revista Salud Pública de México (2004).

Reynolds, Clark W. (1970). *The Mexican Economy: Twentieth-Century Structure and Growth*. New Haven, CT: Yale University Press.

Reynolds, Clark W. (1997). "Porqué el desarrollo estabilizador de México fue en realidad desestabilizador," *El Trimestre Económico* 176 (4): 997–1023.

Ríos-Figueroa, Julio (2007). "Fragmentation of Power and the Emergence of an Effective Judiciary in Mexico, 1994–2002," *Latin American Politics and Society* 49 (1): 31–57.

Roberts, Sam (2004). *Who We Are Now*. New York: Henry Holt.

Rocha Menocal, Alina (2001). "Do Old Habits Die Hard? A Statistical Exploration of the Politicisation of Progresa, Mexico's Latest Federal Poverty-Alleviation Program, under the Zedillo Administration," *Journal of Latin American Studies* 33 (3): 513–38.

Rodríguez, Ruth (2006). "En 2010, la mitad de los mexicanos tendrá Seguro Popular," *El Universal*, 16 August.

Rodríguez-Padilla, Víctor (2008). "La saga del nuevo régimen fiscal de Pemex, pilar de la modernización de la industria petrolera de México." In Francisco Colmenares, ed., *Situación actual y futuro de Petróleos Mexicanos*. Mexico City: Instituto de Investigaciones Económicas, Universidad Nacional Autónoma de México.

Salas, Carlos, and Eduardo Zepeda (2003). "Employment and Wages: Enduring the Costs of Liberalization and Economic Reform." In Kevin J. Middlebrook and Eduardo Zepeda, eds., *Confronting Development: Assessing Mexico's Economic and Social Policy Challenges*. Stanford, CA: Stanford University Press/Center for U.S.-Mexican Studies, University of California, San Diego.

Salas, Fernando, and Tridib Sharma (2004). "Management Fees in Mexican Afores." Paper presented at the Stanford Center for International Development. Stanford University.

Sales-Sarrapy, Carlos, Fernando Solís-Soberón, and Alejandro Villagómez-Amezcua (1996). "Pension System Reform: The Mexican Case." National Bureau of Economic Research Working Paper no. 5780. Cambridge, MA: National Bureau of Economic Research.

Salinas de Gortari, Carlos (2002). *México: un paso difícil a la modernidad*. Barcelona: Plaza y Janés.

Santibáñez, Lucrecia, Georges Vernez, and Paula Razquin (2005). *Education in Mexico*. Santa Monica, CA: The Rand Corporation.

Schedler, Andreas (2007). "The Mexican Standoff: The Mobilization of Distrust," *Journal of Democracy* 18 (1): 88–102.

Schelling, Thomas C. (1956). "An Essay on Bargaining," *American Economic Review* 46 (3): 281–306.

Schelling, Thomas C. (1960). *The Strategy of Conflict*. Cambridge, MA: Harvard University Press.

Schmidley, Dianne, and J. Gregory Robinson (2003). "Measuring the Foreign-born Population in the United States with the Current Population Survey, 1994–2002." Population Division Working Paper Series no. 73. Washington, DC: U.S. Bureau of the Census.

Schultz, Kenneth A, and Barry R. Weingast (2003). "The Democratic Advantage: The Institutional Foundations of Financial Power in International Competition," *International Organization* 57 (1): 3–42.

Secretaría de Educación Pública (SEP) (2005). *Estadística histórica del sistema educativo nacional.* Mimeo. Unidad de Planeación y Evaluación de Políticas Educativas, Dirección General de Planeación y Programación. Mexico City: SEP.

Secretaría de Economía, Dirección General de Inversión Extranjera. Available at www.inegi.gob.mx.

Serrano, Carlos (1999). "Social Security Reform – How Much It Will Cost and Who Will Pay for It: The Mexican Case." Mimeo. Washington, DC: World Bank.

Shepsle, Kenneth A. (1991). "Discretion, Institutions, and the Problem of Government Commitment." In Pierre Bourdieu and James S. Coleman, eds., *Social Theory for a Changing Society.* Boulder, CO: Westview Press.

Shugart, Matthew Soberg, and Martin P. Wattenberg (2001). "Conclusion: Are Mixed-Member Systems the Best of Both Worlds?" In Matthew Soberg Shugart and Martin P. Wattenberg, eds., *Mixed-Member Electoral Systems: The Best of Both Worlds?* New York: Oxford University Press.

Sinha, Tapen (2001). "Analyzing Management Fees of Pension Funds: A Case Study of Mexico," *Journal of Actuarial Practice* 9 (1–2).

Sinha, Tapen, and Alejandro Renteria (2005). "The Cost of the Minimum Pension Guarantee." Mimeo. Departamento Académico de Actuaría y Seguros, Instituto Tecnológico Autónomo de México.

Sinha, Tapen, and María de los Ángeles Yañez Acosta (2006a). "A Decade of Government-Mandated Privately-Run Pensions in Mexico: What Have We Learned?" Mimeo. Departamento Académico de Actuaría y Seguros, Instituto Tecnológico Autónomo de México.

Sinha, Tapen, and María de los Ángeles Yañez Acosta (2006b). "Una década del nuevo sistema de pensiones en México." Mimeo. Departamento Académico de Actuaría y Seguros, Instituto Tecnológico Autónomo de México.

Skoufias, Emmanuel, and Susan W. Parker (2001). "Conditional Cash Transfers and their Impact on Child Work and School Enrolment: Evidence from the PROGRESA Program in Mexico," *Economía* 2 (1): 45–96.

Smith, Peter H. (1991). "Mexico Since 1946: Dynamics of an Authoritarian Regime." In Leslie Bethell, ed., *Mexico Since Independence.* Cambridge: Cambridge University Press.

Soares, Sergei, Rafael Guerreiro Osório, Fábio Veras Soares, Marcelo Medeiros, and Eduardo Zepeda (2007). *Conditional Cash Transfers in Brazil, Chile, and Mexico: Impacts upon Inequality.* International Poverty Centre Working Paper no. 35. Brasilia: International Poverty Centre, United Nations Development Programme.

Sonin, Constantine (2003). "Why the Rich May Favor Poor Protection of Property Rights," *Journal of Development Economics* 31: 715–31.

Spalding, Rose J. (1980). "Welfare Policymaking: Theoretical Implications of a Mexican Case Study," *Comparative Politics* 12 (4): 419–38.

Stallings, Barbara, and Wilson Peres (2000). *Growth, Employment, and Equity: The Impact of the Economic Reforms in Latin America and the Caribbean*. Washington, DC: Brookings Institution Press.

Stasavage, David (2003). *Public Debt and the Birth of the Democratic State: France and Great Britain, 1688–1789*. Cambridge: Cambridge University Press.

Story, Dale (1986). *The Mexican Ruling Party: Stability and Authority*. New York: Praeger.

Székely, Miguel (1998). *The Economics of Poverty, Inequality, and Wealth Accumulation in Mexico*. New York: St. Martin's Press.

Tamez Guerra, Reyes S., Leonel Zúñiga Molina, and Rafael Freyre Martínez (2005). *Sistema educativo de los Estados Unidos Mexicanos: principales cifras*. Mexico City: Secretaría de Educación Pública.

Tavera Fenollosa, Ligia (1988). "Social Movements and Civil Society: The Mexico City 1985 Earthquake Victims' Movement in Mexico City." Ph.D. diss., Yale University.

Taylor, Alan M. (1998). "On the Costs of Inward-Looking Development: Price Distortions, Growth, and Divergence in Latin America," *Journal of Economic History* 58 (March): 1–28.

Tello Díaz, Carlos (1995). *Chiapas: la rebelión de las cañadas*. Madrid: Acento Editorial.

Ten Kate, Adriaan, Robert Bruce Wallace, Antoine Waarts, and María Delfina Ramírez deWallace (1979). *La política de protección en el desarrollo económico de México*. Mexico City: Fondo de Cultura Económica.

"The Afores Story: Ten Years On" (2007). *Latin America Monitor: Mexico* 24 (3): 1, 3.

The Economist (2002). "Floundering in a Tariff-free Landscape," 28 November.

The Economist (2004a). "Housing in Mexico: An Overlooked Revolution," 28 August.

The Economist (2004b). "Sins of the Fleshy," 18 December.

The Economist (2006a). "Six Years of Refried Beans, and Little Confidence of Better to Come," 1 July.

The Economist (2006b). "Time to Wake Up: A Survey of Mexico," 18 November.

Thorp, Rosemary (1998). *Progress, Poverty, and Exclusion: An Economic History of Latin America in the Twentieth Century*. Washington, DC: Inter-American Development Bank.

Tornell, Aaron, and Gerardo Esquivel (1995). "The Political Economy of Mexico's Entry into NAFTA." National Bureau of Economic Research Working Paper no. 5322. Cambridge, MA: National Bureau of Economic Research.

Tornell, Aaron, Frank Westermann, and Lorenza Martínez (2004). "NAFTA and Mexico's Less than Stellar Performance." National Bureau of Economic Research Working Paper no. 10289. Cambridge, MA: National Bureau of Economic Research.

Tuirán, Rodolfo, Virgilio Partida, Octavio Mojarro, and Elena Zúñiga (n.d.). "Fertility in Mexico: Trends and Forecast." Mimeo.

Unal, Haluk, and Miguel Navarro (1999). "The Technical Process of Bank Privatization in Mexico," *Journal of Financial Services Research* 16 (September): 61–83.

United Nations. *World Marriage Patterns*. Available at www.un.org/esa/population/publications/worldmarriage/worldmarriage.htm.

United Nations Conference on Trade and Development (UNCTAD) (1992). *World Investment Report, 1992*. New York: United Nations.

UNCTAD (1997). *World Investment Report, 1997*. New York: United Nations.

UNCTAD (2002). *World Investment Report, 2002*. New York: United Nations.

UNCTAD (2005). *World Investment Report, 2005*. New York: United Nations.

United Nations Development Programme (UNDP) (2005). *Human Development Report, 2005*. New York: UNDP.

United States Bureau of Labor Statistics (2002). *Occupational Employment and Wages, 1981–2000*. Washington, DC: U.S. Bureau of Labor Statistics.

United States Bureau of the Census (2000). *United States Census 2000*. Washington, DC: U.S. Government Printing Office.

United States Bureau of the Census (2003). *Statistical Abstract of the United States: 2002*. Washington, DC: U.S. Government Printing Office.

United States Department of Commerce, Bureau of Economic Analysis. *Survey of Current Business*, various years.

Urquidi, Víctor L. (2003). "Mexico's Development Challenges." In Kevin J. Middlebrook and Eduardo Zepeda, eds., *Confronting Development: Assessing Mexico's Economic and Social Policy Challenges*. Stanford, CA: Stanford University Press/Center for U.S.-Mexican Studies, University of California, San Diego.

Valdés Ugalde, Francisco (1994). "From Bank Nationalization to State Reform: Business and the New Mexican Order." In Maria Lorena Cook, Kevin J. Middlebrook, and Juan Molinar Horcasitas, eds., *The Politics of Economic Restructuring: State-Society Relations and Regime Change in Mexico*. La Jolla, CA: Center for U.S.-Mexican Studies, University of California, San Diego.

Vega, Gustavo, and Luz María de la Mora (2003). "Mexico's Trade Policy: Financial Crisis and Economic Recovery." In Kevin J. Middlebrook and Eduardo Zepeda, eds., *Confronting Development: Assessing Mexico's Economic and Social Policy Challenges*. Stanford, CA: Stanford University Press/Center for U.S.-Mexican Studies, University of California, San Diego.

Vegas, Emiliana, and Ilana Umansky (2005). *Improving Teaching and Learning through Effective Incentives: What Can We Learn from Education Reforms in Latin America?* Mimeo. Washington, DC: World Bank.

Vélez Bustillo, Eduardo (2001). "Education Sector Strategy." In Marcelo Giugale, Olivier Lafourcade, and Vinh Nguyen, eds., *Mexico: A Comprehensive Development Strategy for the New Era*. Washington, DC: World Bank.

Verduzco, Gustavo (2003). "La migración mexicana a los Estados Unidos: estructuración de una selectividad histórica." In Rodolfo Tuirán, ed., *Migración México-Estados Unidos: opciones de política*. Mexico City: Consejo Nacional de Población.

Vernon, Raymond (1963). *The Dilemma of Mexico's Development: The Roles of the Private and Public Sectors*. Cambridge, MA: Harvard University Press.

Villa Lever, Lorenza, and Roberto Rodríguez Gómez (2003). "Education and Development in Mexico: Middle and Higher Education Policies in the 1990s." In Kevin J. Middlebrook and Eduardo Zepeda, eds., *Confronting Development: Assessing Mexico's Economic and Social Policy Challenges*. Stanford, CA: Stanford University Press/Center for U.S.-Mexican Studies, University of California, San Diego.

Wacziarg, Roman, and Karen Horn Welch (2003). *Trade Liberalization and Growth: New Evidence*. National Bureau of Economic Research Working Paper no. 10152. Cambridge, MA: National Bureau of Economic Research.

Warman, Arturo (2001). *El campo mexicano en el siglo XX*. Mexico City: Fondo de Cultura Económica.

Weingast, Barry R. (1995). "The Economic Role of Political Institutions: Market-Preserving Federalism and Economic Development," *Journal of Law, Economics, and Organizations* 11: 1–31.

Weingast, Barry R. (1997). "The Political Foundations of Democracy and the Rule of Law," *American Political Science Review* 91 (2): 245–63.

Weldon, Jeffrey A. (2001). "The Consequences of Mexico's Mixed-Member Electoral System, 1988–1997." In Matthew Soberg Shugart and Martin P. Wattenberg, eds., *Mixed-Member Electoral Systems: The Best of Both Worlds?* New York: Oxford University Press.

Weldon, Jeffrey A. (2004a). "Changing Patterns of Executive-Legislative Relations in Mexico." In Kevin J. Middlebrook, ed., *Dilemmas of Political Change in Mexico*. London: Institute of Latin American Studies, University of London/Center for U.S.-Mexican Studies, University of California, San Diego.

Weldon, Jeffrey A. (2004b). *Mexican Congressional Report Series: The Fall 2003 Term of the Mexican Congress*. Washington, DC: Center for Strategic and International Studies.

Weldon, Jeffrey A. (2006). *Mexican Congressional Report Series: The Fall 2005 Term of the Mexican Congress*. Washington, DC: Center for Strategic and International Studies.

Whitehead, Laurence (2002). *Democratization: Theory and Experience*. Oxford: Oxford University Press.

Whitehouse, Edward (2000). "Administrative Charges for Funded Pensions: An International Comparison and Assessment." World Bank Social Protection Working Paper no. 16. Washington, DC: World Bank.

Whiting, Van R., Jr. (1992). *The Political Economy of Foreign Direct Investment in Mexico: Nationalism, Liberalism, and Constraints on Choice*. Baltimore, MD: Johns Hopkins University Press.

Womack, John, Jr. (1970). *Zapata and the Mexican Revolution*. New York: Vintage Books.

World Bank (2003). *Poverty in Mexico: An Assessment of Conditions, Trends, and Government Strategy*. Washington, DC: World Bank.

World Bank (2005). *Mexico: Infrastructure Public Expenditure Review*. Washington, DC: World Bank.

Wright, Gavin, and Jesse Czelusta (2003). "The Myth of the Resource Curse," *Challenge* 47 (2): 6–38.

Yacamán, Jesús Marcos (2005). "Reflexiones respecto al desarrollo de la intermediación bancaria y el efecto de la nacionalización en el sistema financiero." In Gustavo Del Ángel-Mobarak, Carlos Bazdresch, and Francisco Suárez Dávila, eds., *Cuando el estado se hizo banquero: consecuencias de la nacionalización bancaria en México*. Mexico City: Fondo de Cultura Económica.

Yates, Paul Lamartine (1981). *Mexico's Agricultural Dilemma*. Tucson: University of Arizona Press.

Zahniser, Stephen, and William Coyle (2004). "U.S.-Mexico Corn Trade During the NAFTA Era." United States Department of Agriculture Economic Research Service. Washington, DC: U.S. Department of Agriculture.

Index